HOW
EMOTIONAL
MARKETING
CAN SAVE THE WORLD

NICK THOMAS

How Emotional Marketing Can Save the World

Library and Archives Canada Cataloguing in Publication
Title: How emotional marketing can save the world / Nick Thomas.
Names: Thomas, Nick (Marketer), author.
Identifiers: Canadiana (print) 20230592007 | Canadiana (ebook) 20230592066
ISBN 9781998796076 (softcover) | ISBN 9781998796083 (EPUB)
Subjects: LCSH: Marketing—Psychological aspects. | LCSH: Emotions.
Classification: LCC HF5415 .T46 2024 | DDC 381.01/9—dc23

Publisher: Civil Sector Press
Box 86, Station C, Toronto, Ontario, M6J 3M7 Canada
Telephone: 416.267.1287
www.charityinfo.ca | www.hilborn-civilsectorpress.com
Editor: Marlena McCarthy
Book design: Terry Keogh

We acknowledge that the land where we live and work is the traditional territory of many nations from across Turtle Island, and is covered by the *Dish With One Spoon Wampum Belt Covenant*, an agreement between the Haudenosaunee and the Ojibway and allied nations, including the Mississaugas, the Anishnaabeg, the Chippewa, and the Wendat peoples to peaceably share and care for the lands around the Great Lakes of North America. This land today is home to many diverse First Nations, Inuit, and Métis peoples. We honor and thank them for their stewardship of these lands, and stand committed to be partners in truth-seeking, healing, reconciliation, and justice for all.

civil sector press
GLOBAL NONPROFIT PUBLISHING

About the author

Nick Thomas is an advertising and marketing creative director, speaker and author.

Co-founder of three successful marketing agencies, he has won over 90 national and international awards for his work.

His climate change novel *Cull 2031* was named as one of the most notable books on conservation and the environment in 2021 by Mongabay.com.

Nick has been a part time lecturer at the University of Gloucestershire for 20 years.

Thanks for showing, for believing, for supporting, for contributing.

No you, no book.

David Strickland-Eales, Mike Brown, Graeme Robertson, Alec Hamilton, Paul Handley, Julius Wolff-Ingham OBE, Russell Thompson OBE, Stephen Pidgeon, Pauline Lockier, Kate Woodford, Nick Holmes, Iain Ferguson, Clare Pavey, Ian Atkinson, Matt Finlayson, Keith Wintle, John Watson, Clare Orchard, Ed Swarbrick, John Rawson.

CONTENTS

" When you lose your ego, you win. „

Shannon L. Alder

INTRO

Hello and welcome to my book.

Before we go any further, you might be thinking: Is this the right book for me?

If you want to better understand how you might persuade complete strangers to part with their money legally... **Yes.**

If you want to improve your marketing impact, especially in fundraising... **Yes.**

If you want to learn from campaigns that smashed targets... **Yes.**

If you want to make the world a better place... Emphatically, **YES.**

If you have no interest in creativity and discovering what really moves people... **Then No.**

This book is not written to showcase how smart I am. It is atonement for years of vanity, ego, and money-wasting stupidity.

Like most marketers, most of what I've produced has failed, some of it catastrophically. One campaign bombed so badly it virtually ruined the client.

However, along the way, I have managed to produce some winners.

How?

By putting aside mine and my client's needs, and concentrating instead on the emotional needs of my audience. Time and again, that has been the difference between success and failure, saving my work from disappearing into the dark place where all self-serving ideas go to die.

Now the knowledge I've extracted from my head is yours, here in this book.

The first 160 pages concentrate on **Emotional Marketing**, showcasing work that has directly generated hundreds of millions of pounds.

For the final third, I have penned other insights that will hopefully, further inform and amuse in equal measure.

My aim is simple: to help you produce more successful marketing, more often; simply by being more emotional.

" How does it feel? "

Bob Dylan, Like a Rolling Stone

THE EMOTIONAL BRAIN

Where do emotions come from?

Emotions are created by our brain. This marvel of the universe controls the release of chemicals to stimulate or calm us, which in turn influence our mood and behaviour. These chemicals flow through our body all the time, regulating everything, including our thoughts.

Why do we need them?

Our emotions help us communicate with others, such as when we feel sad and need some help. They govern our moods and can make us feel invincible or vulnerable. Emotions focus our attention and motivate us to action. They help us act quickly in important or dangerous situations.

Are we born with emotions or do we learn them?

Emotions are innate, biologically-driven reactions to challenges and opportunities, sculpted by evolution to help humans survive and thrive.

How many emotions are there?

The eight basic emotions are: joy, sadness, fear, disgust, surprise, anticipation, anger, and trust. However, it is generally accepted that there are countless variations and nuances of these.

What's the difference between emotions, feelings, and moods?

Emotions come first, followed by feelings as the emotion chemicals go to work in our bodies. Moods then develop from a combination of feelings.

An **emotion** is an immediate physiological response to a stimulus. The chemicals released throughout our body last about six seconds.

Feelings are how we begin to make meaning of the emotion; they cause us to pay attention and react.

Mood is a semi-permanent state of feelings and emotions. Heavily influenced by factors such as environment, physiology, and our mental state, moods can last minutes, hours, even days.

Over my agency career, I've worked with some great marketers: Bill Thompson (*WAHT*), David Strickland-Eales (*Chapter One*), Paul Handley (*Campfire*), Stephen Pidgeon and Pauline Lockier (*Target & Tangible*). They showed me how to produce great work, run a business, sell an idea, and inspire a creative department.

But none has taught me as much about the most important component in creative marketing as a bald, overweight, English film director – Alfred Hitchcock.

I had just started my career when I came across an interview Hitchcock had given about film-making. Being a fan, I hoped it might reveal how he made his best films (*Psycho, Rear Window, Vertigo*) so engaging and suspenseful.

I had expected him to describe the importance of a powerful opening, a simple plot, compelling characters, beautiful cinematography, and a great soundtrack.

I was wrong. To him, these elements were secondary to creating emotion. He felt his primary job was to transfer the menace from the screen into the mind of the audience. Not to make them think but to feel. Or better still, to *suffer*.

If a part of the plot wasn't helping him do that, he would cut it. Hitchcock knew that to elicit emotional investment from his audience he could not confuse them with fuzzy thinking.

Listening to this great film director made me appreciate what film-making and marketing have in common: to be successful, they need to move people. To do that, they need emotional clarity.

Despite all the changes since Hitchcock's era, one constant has remained – emotions are far more powerful than thoughts, overriding even the strongest parts of our intelligence.

As this book will show, that is good news for marketers and communicators. Utilised properly, emotion is the irresistible force, the key to unlocking the resistance of any target market. Emotional Marketing can provide your rocket fuel for success – and the supply of combustible elements to fire up your audience is almost inexhaustible.

> **66 All causes are born of pity and compassion, then they must work harder for their corn. 99**
>
> *Nick Thomas*

As a fundraiser, I have utilised most of these to gain an emotional foothold, although for the non-profit sector, some are not appropriate. Clearly, you can't embarrass, confuse or depress someone into donating money and no one will be attracted to your cause if you make them feel worthless or sceptical. Evoking guilt has also been a contentious issue for fundraisers. My view is that it's an emotion most right-minded people feel inherently and already does a good job of pricking the conscience. While guilt giving may work once or twice, it shouldn't be employed as a long-term tactic. It's forced philanthropy, and donors will ultimately resent being beaten into supporting a cause.

With these exceptions, most emotions can be used to supercharge your message and when I've created ideas specifically to trigger an emotional reaction, invariably they have succeeded. So, I hear you ask: *Why haven't I produced all my work with an emotional focus?*

The first reason is that my creative ego kept trying to find another way. While chasing emotions was a wholly sensible route to gaining audience attention, I often felt it was too prescriptive, so would try 'cleverer ways' of solving the problem. More often than I care to remember, this has proved to be the wrong path.

The second reason is that in the modern fundraising world, producing emotion-led marketing has not always been easy.

For many charities (especially bigger brands with guidelines on projecting a strict corporate language and tone), emotional marketing is viewed as dangerous – principally because it has the potential to offend. Often, the mantra has been *'better to be bland than upset someone.'*

This has also been a mistake.

Helping good causes is serious work; it involves saving lives, alleviating misery, righting horrific injustices, preserving habitats, and protecting the planet. The stakes could hardly be higher, so why should we overly concern ourselves with petty sensibilities? After all, if we can't get worked up about a cause we believe in, then why should anybody else?

In the absence of others taking the lead, charities are more important than ever in creating a kinder, more sustainable world. They should do all that is necessary to nudge people to act on ingrained good intentions and take the actions humanity needs.

As I write this, our species has arrived suddenly and brutally at the last possible point at which it can save itself. We must radically rethink our consumption, our relationship with nature, and with those we share borders and resources with if we are to survive. There are big decisions to be made and marketers can potentially play a planet-saving part in making them happen.

THANKS

Christmas Appeal

Alzheimer's Society

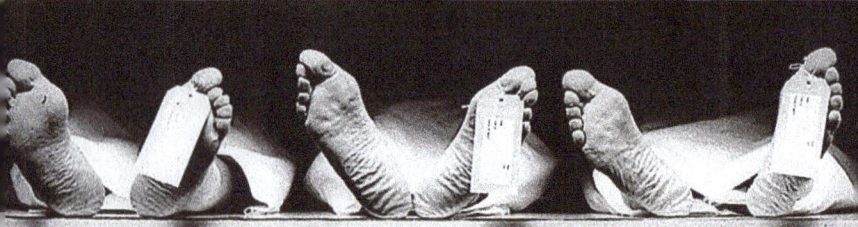

0370 011 0290
alzheimers.org.uk/tonyrobinson

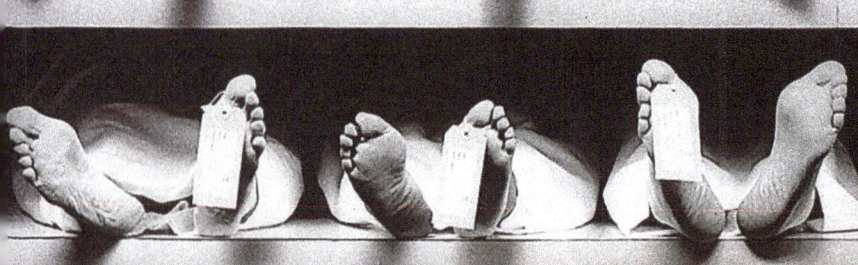

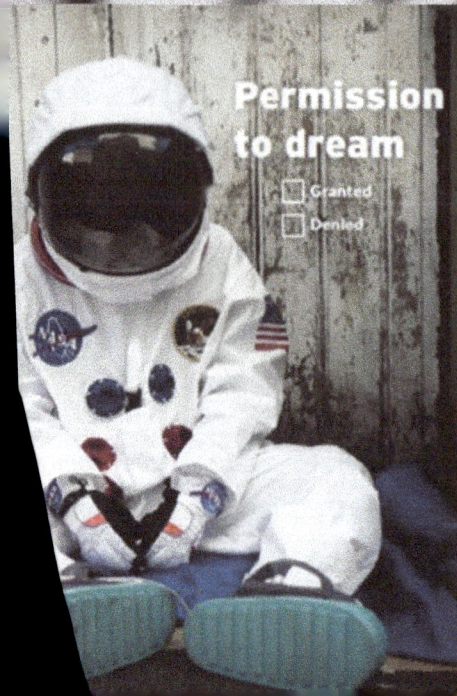

Permission to dream

Granted
Denied

The pumpkin that proves
WE CAN DEFY CLIMATE CHANGE

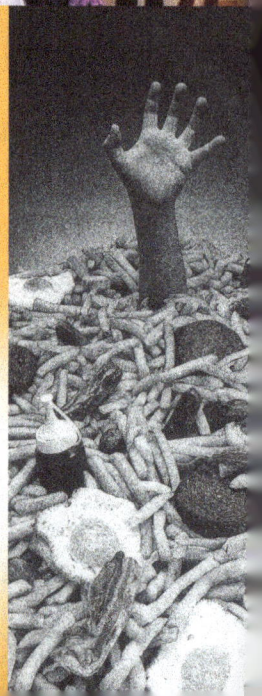

We'll be more successful if we understand the emotional needs of audiences beyond what they simply want from our product or service. There is no dark art to bridging this knowledge gap; good research will divulge what really pushes their buttons. It will reveal their fears and desires, show how we can address them. It can put us in our audience's shoes so we can acknowledge them as individuals because when people feel recognised and respected, they respond in kind.

The more scientific marketing gets, the more human it must become. With the same technology available to all, utilising emotional intelligence will become a competitive advantage for brands. Human beings are like moving balls of unexploded emotion ready to go off with the slightest provocation; stirred in the right way, they are usually more than ready to engage with you.

Written in 2022, this book covers work produced over the last 40 years, a period of great change in the media landscape. Back in the early 1980s, press ads, posters and direct mail were hugely important, the internet was in its infancy, social media did not exist.

However, in these pages, the medium is not the message; what I cover is not associated with some particular moment or decade. Emotional Marketing is as relevant today as ever, regardless of media. This is particularly true for charities, because the marketer has to make their audience buy into something they will never actually touch, something intangible, something that is just a feeling.

Communication channels may have evolved, but what moves humans to action hasn't. *Not one jot.*

As the late George Smith wrote in his brilliant book, *Asking Properly*: '*Fundraising will not work without an emotional component.*' Later he points out an even more remarkable truism: '*Emotion will always override the content of the charity's message.*' Think about that for a moment. One of the most prolific and successful fundraising copywriters ever, someone who had written thousands of words describing what charities do, believes that **emotion trumps everything**.

George is right, and everything in my career has confirmed it too. Don't ask your audience to think, that path only leads to delay and indecision.

To really get them moving, get them to *feel*.

AMUSEMENT

**Amusement is appealing because we
don't have to think; it spares us the fear
and anxiety that might otherwise prey
on our thoughts.**

John Ortberg

Amusement is the state of experiencing humorous and entertaining events or situations while actively maintaining the experience. It is an emotion with positive and high physiological arousal and is associated with enjoyment, happiness, laughter, and pleasure.

Why is amusement important?

When something amuses you, it entertains you and holds your attention. An amusement is an activity that produces that type of feeling. To amuse is to entertain and, more importantly, to engage.

ONE DAY I'LL BE
AS DEAD AS
A PARROT.

BUT MY BELIEFS
CAN LIVE ON.

AMNESTY
INTERNATIONAL
UNITED KINGDOM

It's been said that humour has no place in fundraising, but I've never thought that. Starting my career in London advertising agencies, I came to appreciate the power of wit to engage and sell. At Lintas, Proctor and Partners, and Waldron Allen, it was well understood – if we could get a smile from our audience, we could also deliver a more serious message.

Of course, all funny bones are different, so the joke has to be appropriate for both brand and audience. When those stars align, humour in marketing can work *brilliantly* and, with social media's voracious appetite for comedy content, has the potential to go viral.

Funny is effective because it captures our attention. According to neuroscience boffins, as humans we are attracted to anything that previous experience tells us is potentially good or bad. Loud noises catch our attention because we're taught to fear them, and good associations can be felt by things that make us laugh our socks off.

FREE
WILL GUIDE
DON'T LEAVE WITHOUT ONE

Left:
Humour can work extremely well for legacy marketing. These are successful concepts we produced for Amnesty and RNIB.

One of the best exponents of funny fundraising over recent times has been Comic Relief, which has consistently mixed amusing high-quality entertainment with a compelling request for donations. Despite television viewers knowing exactly what they are in for (Comic Relief has used the same formula since 1985), it's so brilliantly done, no one minds. As with all great comedy there are no sacred cows or no-go subjects; quite rightly, charity is as much fair game as any other profession. It was hilarious to see Ricky Gervais poke fun at the 'rent a celeb for a good cause' culture so many good causes employ. Charities can come over as serious, unapproachable, even patronising; being amusing makes a refreshing

change, it can prick pomposity and humanise a cause.

I have frequently turned to humour to engage my audience when marketing gifts in Wills. Thinking about death and saving your estate from the clutches of the tax man shouldn't feel funny or naturally be a laughing matter, but it just seems to work, providing an easy entry point into a subject people often find difficult to think about, let alone talk about.

A particular favourite was a press ad (shown right) we produced featuring William Shakespeare for Remember a Charity, a consortium of UK charities promoting awareness of gifts in Wills.

It told of the Bard's rather curious decision to leave Anne Hathaway, his wife of 34 years, only his 'second best bed'; it was one in a series that engaged people with the topic in a quirky, light-hearted way. Over the five years we worked with the campaign, it was credited with uplifting awareness of the importance of leaving legacies to good causes by 25%, contributing tens of millions to the sector.

How to recycle a goat

See inside

Left:
This insert for Christian Aid used the naturally playful and funny personality of the goat to engage audiences. At the time, it was one of the first examples of virtual gifts marketing.

Even the best writers get it wrong

'I gyve unto my wief my second-best bed wth the furniture'.

Shakespeare's will has attracted speculation since his death in 1616. Why did his wife of 34 years not receive the best bed? And why was she not named as executrix, a custom in Elizabethan times? Did The Bard draft a bad will?

The standards of 17th century probate were far removed from today; Shakespeare was at liberty to score out sections of his handwritten will without invalidating it. Even so, there has been speculation that his wife may have had grounds to contest it, as it broke with the custom of naming her as executrix.

Some things never change. With the growth of DIY will-writing there is a real danger that more people may inadvertently pen a tragedy of their own.

Millions of pounds are being lost to charities amidst the complications and anxiety of contested settlements caused by off-the-shelf wills and unqualified will-writing services. Remember A Charity's campaign is working to make the public aware of the problems caused for charities by badly-drafted wills.

Your co-operation could have a lasting impact on the wellbeing of a cause that was close to a client's heart. On behalf of all UK charities, we are encouraging thousands of people to take the Good Will Test at www.rememberacharity.org.uk, then go to a professional to have their will made watertight. (Please visit the site to see the Test for yourself.)

Call us today on **020 7840 1030** or visit our website at **www.rememberacharity.org.uk** to find out how you can get involved.

everyone can leave the world a better place
remember a charity in your will

Registered Charity Number 1071572

Will extract from the National Archives (prob/1/4)

ANGER

Usually when people are sad, they don't do anything. But when they get angry, they bring about change.

Malcolm X

Anger is an emotion characterised by antagonism towards someone or something you feel has deliberately done you, or someone, wrong. When angry, it's possible for people to experience other feelings such as fear or disgust. Anger can be one of the most dangerous emotions because of its potential connection to violence.

Why is anger important?

Anger can also be a good thing. It can give people a way to express negative feelings and motivate them to find solutions to problems. For marketers, anger can be an effective mobiliser; harnessed around a theme of our choosing, it can do much of the heavy lifting.

The camera slowly pans across the full expanse of the curved bay. Its mouth flanked on either side by grass-covered hills that rise to flat plateaus where scores of figures stand, silhouetted against the horizon. Inside the sheltered promontory, the waters are calm; outside, the seas pitch and swirl, whipped by relentless inshore winds. The figures on the hill move excitedly as a dozen fishing boats enter the bay.

The scene looks benign, even quaint, but it soon becomes clear that something strange is happening.

Directly in front of the small armada sits a powerful surge of foaming water about 100 metres across. The closely-packed craft seem to be driving it forward. Shiny black shapes break the surface. Whales, scores of them.

On the shoreline, men are waiting, holding foot long, curved knives. The boats slow and finally stop, no more than 20 metres from shore. The agitated water has become a thrashing frenzy.

Suddenly, with a roar, the men surge forward into the maelstrom. We can hear the panicked, high-pitched whistles of the whales.

But there is no escape for them, their size has become their weakness; crammed together, they are unable to go forward or back. As the men walk calmly about them with their blades, the ice-blue waters begin to turn red.

The film stops. I've been watching this horror with my colleagues and Whale and Dolphin Conservation Society (*WDCS*) Chief Executive Sean Whyte, who now stands to address us.

'*The cameraman took a big risk, the Faroese whalers have been known to severely beat anyone filming their hunts.*'

Whyte explained that during the kill we witnessed, **87 pilot whales** were slaughtered.

Even though he had seen the film before he still looked shaken. His brief was clear – produce a powerful campaign to raise awareness so that the barbaric practice might be stopped.

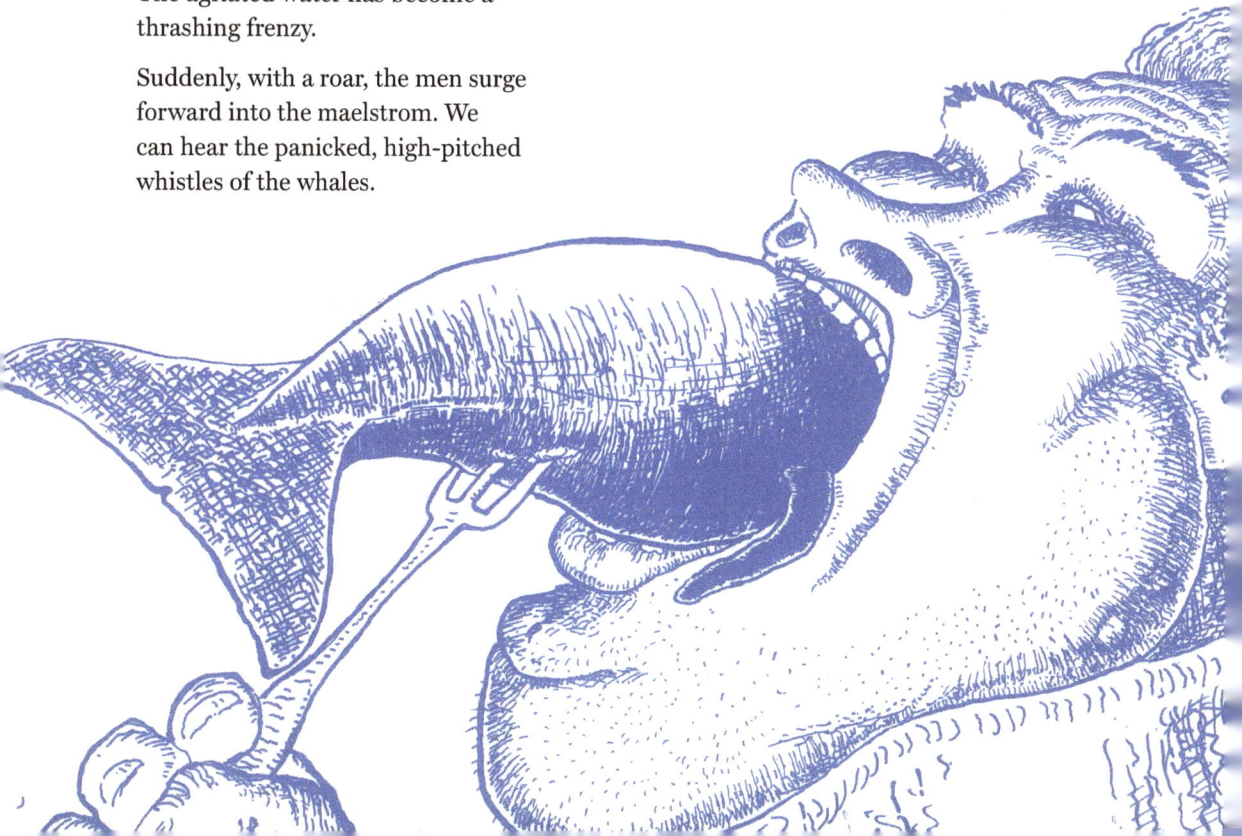

There was one challenge. The charity's supporters, who consisted mainly of members and sponsors, had proved unresponsive to appeals in the past. They appeared to be, in Whyte's own words, 'fluffy and reward-orientated' rather than the 'militant, political warriors' we required.

Although passionate about preserving marine animals and habitat, they had been indifferent to previous campaigns about whaling, dirty beaches, over-fishing, and pollution.

We decided to give them something they could get mad about – by demonising the perpetrators. We made the Faroese whalers themselves the clear enemy and the focus of the message.

We wanted supporters to feel empowered to hit back at the architects of this cruel slaughter and to literally 'wage war on the whale eaters'. To appeal to their liking for rewards, we offered incentives for differing levels of gift, including car stickers, founders bonds, and a campaign action pack. Those giving over £100 would have their name printed in a full-page press advertisement in the Sunday Times. The creative struck the perfect balance between action and reward for the WDCS audience and beat its target by **over 350%**.

Now confident of the right 'angry' tone for both supporter and cold communications, Whyte asked us to run other high-profile campaigns against the whaling industries of Norway and Japan, which enjoyed similar success.

How do you frighten a man who eats whales?

WHALE & DOLPHIN
CONSERVATION SOCIETY

Registered Charity No. 1014705

Get your bloody  hands off our whales, Norway!

ON MAY 2ND THIS YEAR, Norway began commercially killing minke whales. This was despite its own admission that the scientific "evidence" it uses to justify the slaughter, is wrong.

Next week the International Whaling Commission is meeting in Dublin and the Whale and Dolphin Conservation Society (WDCS), is determined to expose the Norwegian whalers for the fraudsters they are.

Can we count on your help to stop the Norwegian whalers getting away with murder? Murder of whales that may swim in UK waters too?

WHY NORWAY IS WRONG TO KILL WHALES

Norway has always had what it sees as "the perfect excuse" for continuing whaling. Scientific "evidence".

But now WDCS can reveal that this evidence is a sham.

We have a copy of a leaked letter, in which the Norwegians openly admit that their estimate of 86,700 minke whales in north east Atlantic waters is hopelessly wrong. The excuse this time? Computer "error".

The true figure is more likely to be in the region of 53,000 minke whales - a difference of over 33,000 animals.

So why is Norway still whaling?

In a cynical move to get its quota of 301 minke whales in before it could be criticised by the International Whaling Commission, Norway brought its hunt forward a month, despite the fact that many whales would be in calf.

Indeed, pregnant females are likely to be the main targets as they yield more meat and are easier to catch because they are slower.

The Norwegian Government has since lowered the quota from 301 to 232 whales. However, in open defiance of their Government and of world opinion, the Norwegian whalers have rejected the new quota, declaring their intention to slaughter 301 whales.

Officials in Norway are now desperately trying to justify the present kill by quoting their own scientists as saying their botch up (the one their whalers are conveniently trying to ignore) only entails "small errors on the data programme".

But the agonising deaths of 301 minke whales can hardly be described as "small".

WE'RE DETERMINED TO STOP THESE MURDERERS, BUT WE NEED YOUR HELP

Here are some other Norwegian "facts" which might help to convince you.

Norway has always claimed a "traditional" right to hunt minke whales. But minke whaling on a commercial scale in north west Norway only began in the early 1930s - and even then that was in the face of years of opposition from their own fishermen.

Norway states its whaling is for domestic use only. So how do they explain that their own customs officials failed to notice 3.5 metric tonnes of whale meat labelled "Norwegian Prawns" being shipped out of Fornebu airport to the "Far East" in October 1993?

Norway decided to resume commercial whaling in 1993 for "scientific and fisheries management purposes". We believe the real reason, leaked to the Norwegian Telegram Agency by an official in the Prime Minister's office, was that it was a vote winner for the Government.

It seems rather too convenient that the Norwegian Government made the decision to resume whaling just one week after an opinion poll showed substantial support for another political party in an area of the country where whaling takes place.

Despite the latest revelations about their mistakes, Norway is still insisting it can be trusted to monitor its own whaling industry. They can't even contain their own whalers, who are out whaling right now in defiance of the Norwegian Government. How can we expect them to control any other aspect of their bloody trade, let alone ensure that it is being run correctly and within the law?

For a long time now, WDCS, amongst others, has been calling for Norway's whaling activities to be closely monitored by international inspectors. So far, Norway has resisted all attempts for their sick trade to be opened up to such scrutiny. Hardly surprising when you consider what they've been getting away with!

LIES, LIES, AND YET MORE LIES

Norway has already proved that it is no respecter of international regulations on whaling. It simply makes up its own as it goes along. But then this is not surprising when it can't even be fined for the atrocities it is committing against minke whales right now. The Norwegian whalers can never be trusted again.

WILL YOU HELP US MAKE SURE THEY'RE NOT?

Minke whales swim in British waters too. Shouldn't the people of Britain then, also have a say in their future?

LET US SPEAK UP FOR THE WHALES

There's no time to lose! The serious talking at the International Whaling Commision meeting begins on the 29th May in Dublin and only lasts for one week which is why we need your support NOW. The Norwegians have already made it abundantly clear on many occasions that they intend to start whaling on a massive scale again.

That could mean as many as 2,000 whales being killed each year by Norway alone.

How long do you think it would take for other whaling nations like Japan to follow suit?

PLEASE SEND US AN IMMEDIATE, URGENT DONATION TODAY

We'll use your gift to campaign for a better deal for all whales and dolphins. At the IWC meeting we will confront the Norwegians and demand the following concessions from them for the sake of every whale still left alive.

1. Norway must immediately stop slaughtering minke whales in the north east Atlantic.

2. Norway must fully admit in public that they got their figures wrong and should not be hunting minke whales right now.

3. Norway should be subject to an unlimited moratorium on all scientific and commercial whaling. (Ten years has been suggested - we demand a total and final ban for ever!)

LET US KNOW YOU SUPPORT US

If you agree with all of the above, then we need to hear from you by Wednesday 31st May if we're to stop the Norwegians in their tracks.

The IWC won't meet for another year. How many whales do you think Norway will get away with killing in that time? This is our only chance. Don't let us miss it!

We are legally required to protect this whaler's identity. We only wish the laws on protecting whales were just as stringent.

SEND £25 AND RECEIVE A SPECIAL WDCS REPORT

If you can send £25 today we will send you a special, in-depth report of the case we will be putting to the IWC, as a thank you. Packed with facts and figures, you'll find the behind-the-scenes story of our campaign to save the minke whale from slaughter, a riveting read.

GIVE US A HAND

There's another way you can help us too. You can sign and return the "hand" on the coupon below and we'll use it to give the Norwegian whalers a message from the British public they can't ignore.

To get their hands off our whales once and for all!

DON'T LET NORWAY GET AWAY WITH MURDER!

PLEASE support WDCS with a gift as much as you can spare today! Complete and return the coupon below immediately to:

WDCS, FREEPOST, (SN863), BATH, BA1 2XF.

Thank you!

Caption (bottom left, whale image): Minke at the moment, a whale foetus is held up for display before being hacked onto a pile of its mother's entrails.

SUPPORT OUR CAMPAIGN TO EXPOSE NORWAY

The Whale and Dolphin Conservation Society (WDCS) is the world's largest charity devoted solely to fighting for the protection of whales and dolphins. Set up in 1987, we expose and confront those responsible for the needless slaughter and suffering of these precious and beautiful animals.

We do this by:

● **Actively and vigorously campaigning** for an end to all commercial and scientific whaling.

Just last year, we helped convince the IWC to agree to the adoption of the Southern Ocean Whale Sanctuary, dealing a mortal blow to the Japanese whaling industry.

● **Remaining totally opposed** to the capture of whales and dolphins for display in marine parks and working tirelessly to bring an end to it.

WDCS is currently helping to fund the release of captive dolphins in Florida. Now we're set to help release the first ever orca - Keiko - star of the film Free Willy, back into his native waters.

● **Engaging public support** for our campaigns to stop the deliberate killing of cetaceans, including pilot whales in the Faroes and dolphins caught in tuna nets. The boycott we helped set up against Faroese fish, has so far cost that industry £12m in lost or unplaced orders.

● **Funding over 35 projects** worldwide to aid whales and dolphins at risk.

In 1994 alone, Canada's Harbour Porpoise Rescue Team - just one example of a successful project supported by WDCS, saved 41 porpoises and one minke whale, from agonising deaths in herring traps.

WE NEED YOUR HELP

Looking at our many activities and achievements, you may think we have a lot of money. But unlike the whaling nations, we are not rich and we are not armed. But we do have one powerful weapon - more powerful even than the electric lances, exploding harpoons and flensing knives the whalers use to decimate whales.

WE HAVE PUBLIC OPINION ON OUR SIDE.

People in this country don't want the blood of whales on their conscience. Why should we stand by and let a small minority of people flout international regulations and continue to kill whales which don't even belong to them?

Don't let Norway get away with murder!

PLEASE REPLY BY MAY 31ST 1995

I'm with you! I won't stand by and let Norway do this to our whales.

Name: _____
(Mr/Mrs/Ms/Miss/Other)

Address: _____

_____

Postcode: _____

Telephone: _____

I enclose a cheque/postal order (payable to WDCS) for:

£_____ Please write in the amount of your gift here.

Thank you!

We want to leave it up to you to decide how much to give, but you may find the following suggestion helpful. (Please tick the box of your choice)

☐ £10 ☐ £15 ☐ £25

Give this amount and receive a full report on the case we put to the IWC.

I prefer to give by Access ☐ Visa ☐ Mastercard ☐ CAF CharityCard ☐

Card No: ☐☐☐☐ ☐☐☐☐ ☐☐☐☐ ☐☐☐☐

Expiry Date: ____ / ____

Signature: _____

Use your credit card to make an instant donation, call 01225 334511 NOW.

Please return this completed coupon, together with your signed protest and gift, in an envelope to: WDCS, FREEPOST, (SN863), BATH, BA1 2XF. No stamp needed.

Please sign your name where shown and we will put up your hand of protest to prove to the Norwegian whalers that killing whales when they know they shouldn't, was the worst mistake they ever made - and one the British public are not about to let them repeat.

HANDS OFF OUR WHALES, NORWAY!

SIGNED:

_____

WHALE & DOLPHIN CONSERVATION SOCIETY

Registered Charity Number: 1014705. Company Registration Number: 2737421.

ANTICIPATION

The idea of waiting for something makes it far more exciting.

Andy Warhol

Anticipation is an emotion involving pleasure or anxiety in awaiting an expected event. Anticipatory emotions include fear, anxiety, hope, and trust.

Why is anticipation important?

Firing up anticipation is the first essential component of the marketing message. It allows us to promise pleasure from something in the near future, before the event even occurs. We are excited about engaging until the eagerly anticipated event or happening has revealed itself. Beware – when the anticipated event fails to deliver on its promise, it can engender a negative emotion towards the product or brand.

We found that Salvation Army donors appreciated good news, so we liked to lead appeals with the promise of some. This outer envelope was typical of the approach.

Something good is about to happen

THE SALVATION ARMY

RSPCA Registered Charity Number 219099

As much as working in the third sector has shown me the best of humankind, it has also revealed the worst – especially concerning animal welfare.

Britain is called a nation of animal lovers, yet statistics paint a different picture. In 2019, the RSPCA received a call for help *every 30 seconds*; its inspectors investigated more than 186,000 incidents of alleged cruelty.

To see for myself what life was really like on the animal cruelty frontline, I was given the chance to shadow an RSPCA inspector in South London. Although permitted to carry a tape recorder and camera to capture evidence, I could not get directly involved.

I was told to report to the charity's centre in Battersea at 7am on Monday morning with sandwiches and a flask of tea; there wouldn't be time for a break during the ten-hour shift. Still bleary from the early start, I walked into the reception area, laden with camera, tape recorder and my bulging, heavy rucksack. At least ten RSPCA staff were busy on phones and no one

paid me any attention. I decided to wait on a battered leather sofa until someone did. In front of me was a table laden with several well-thumbed editions of the charity's member magazine, Animal Life. On the front cover of one, a headline screamed TRAPPED FOR TRADE, below it an image of a plastic bag crammed with exotic fish, some clearly dead. As I started reading the article, I heard my name being called out – in a broad New York accent.

'You Nick Thompson?'

I looked up into the blue eyed, square jawed, clean-shaven face of a man around 40 years old. Wearing the dark-blue jacket and trousers, silver epaulets, peaked cap, white shirt, and black tie of the RSPCA's inspectorate, he could have easily passed for a policeman. A small man, no more than five foot six but he exuded authority, the power of right. If he turned up at my door, I'd let him in without question. This was the man I'd come to see, Inspector Jan Eachus.

'*Thomas. Nick Thomas.*' I replied.

'*OK, Nick Thomas, let's get going.*'

He led me into a compound containing several white vans bearing the RSPCA logo. Walking over to his vehicle, I noticed several dents in its side and a crack in the rear window. Eachus clocked my anxiety and smiled. '*Happened last week, got pelted with rocks after collecting a fighting dog from a gypsy camp. They weren't happy.*' I smiled weakly, wondering what I had let myself in for. Opening the door, I flinched from the stench of urine and faeces. '*The animals we get in here are pretty traumatised. You soon get used to it,*' he reassured me.

'*First shout is a block of flats in Tulse Hill, top floor,*' he announced. '*It's a balcony dog; neighbours have complained about barking.*' This was a common problem in inner city areas. In the confines of a small flat, a big dog can become a nuisance; for many owners the balcony is the obvious place to keep them.

As we pulled up outside the block of flats, some kids on bikes eyed us suspiciously. I felt intimidated, Eachus ignored them. The lift was broken so we climbed the stairwell on the outside of the building, the inspector's hobnailed boots crunching on the cold concrete steps.

Reaching the sixth floor, we stood outside number 85. Either side of the blue door sat terracotta pots, both with well-tended flowers. Eachus

knocked, for a few seconds there was nothing, then a shrill, '*Coming, just coming*' from inside. I turned on my tape recorder.

Bolts, locks, and chains slid back and the door opened to reveal an elderly woman in a blue and rose pink dressing gown. She seemed to have no idea why we might be there.

'*Can I help you?*'

Eachus smiled and appeared relaxed; he had no automatic right of entry so needed to gain her trust.

'*Morning, my love, sorry to disturb you. Inspector Eachus from the RSPCA, we've received some calls about barking.*'

She looked confused as if trying to grasp what he'd said.

'*Pleased to meet you, I'm Winifred.*'

'*Do you have a dog here, Winny?*' Eachus persisted.

'*My grandson has an Alsatian called Blue which he keeps outside. Doesn't bark, he's a quiet boy.*' From inside the flat, we could hear the TV blaring.

'*Could we check on Blue please?*'

She led us inside the small hall, which was crammed with bags of clothes, broken furniture, and piles of old newspapers. As we negotiated the small channel between them, I glimpsed into the front bedroom. It was full of more clutter. We followed Winifred into the lounge which was stiflingly hot; an electric fire sat in the fireplace, three bars glowing red.

'He's out here, hardly makes a sound.'

She pointed to a pair of thick, undrawn floor-to-ceiling curtains; the balcony door was obviously behind them. A now grim faced Eachus turned the cacophonous television off.

'Mind if I take a look?'

'Help yourself, he won't bite. I'll make a cup of tea.'

She appeared totally unfazed by events and walked into the kitchen. The sight that greeted us was heart-breaking. Emaciated and surrounded by his own mess, Blue lay dead.

Eachus told me later that Winifred and her grandson were typical of the people he came across. Most weren't evil or even realised they were being cruel; they were just ignorant of the care, time, and space a dog needs.

Over the next two days, I encountered other tragedies with a depressingly familiar thread. A starving family of cats locked in a bedroom. Three large horses with chronic sores and unclipped hooves roped together in a small brick-floored yard. A labrador chained in a car all day while her owner was at work. In one cramped house we visited, a family with two young children lived with seven large dogs. The animals had completely taken over, sleeping on beds and messing on the floor.

Despite the revulsion he must have felt and the abuse he sometimes had to endure, Eachus stood tall and calm. In the time I spent with him, he rescued eleven animals from their agonies and collected sufficient evidence for four prosecutions.

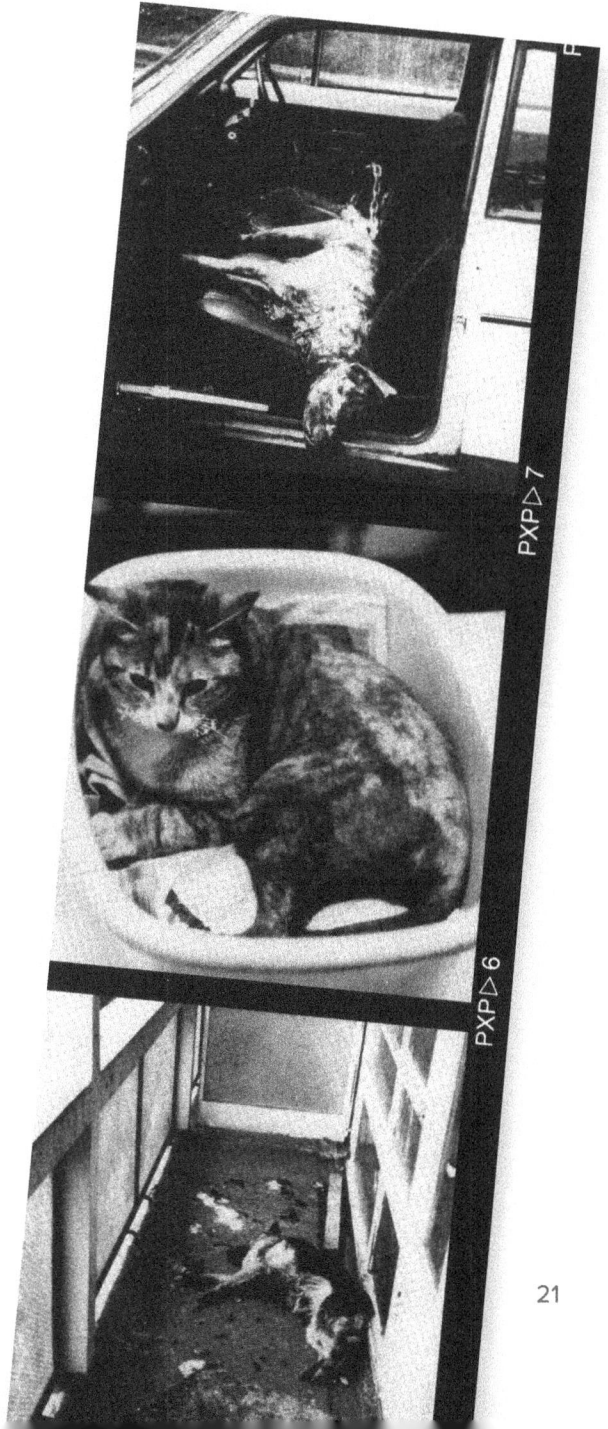

Thanks to his tireless dedication, I had more than enough material to showcase this living embodiment of why the RSPCA exists and why it is so effective.

Because they were so powerful, we decided to use the actual audio of some of the encounters we had and enclosed a cassette which could be seen through a special window in the envelope we had for the Direct Mail (DM) appeal. This was followed up four weeks later with a reminder, updating stories of the animals and what had happened to them.

Both envelopes led with messages which built huge anticipation around what was inside. We knew the contents of both packs was dynamite, so felt confident in hyping them up.

The appeals broke previous records for income, with a best ever response and engagement rate, showing that more people were motivated to open the envelopes.

Though DM is no longer the essential fundraising medium it was, the platform it provides for innovative communications remains unmatched.

It can be bewitchingly personal, alluringly tactile, and utilise all manner of sights, smells, and tastes to reinforce its message. Along with paper, the envelope can carry any number of elements such as dolphin nets, tea bags, books, sugar cubes, bells, USBs, CDs, and audiotapes – I know because I've included all these myself. In this age of electronic communications, a physical letter landing on a doormat still retains the power to wow.

Looking back over some of the most successful direct mail packs I've created, they have all had one thing in common – a powerful or intriguing message on the outer envelope.

Of all the elements that make up the perfect direct mail pack, this is by far the most important. Its job is to build excited anticipation and the desire to get inside. Like the subject line on an email, it must make you want to read on; when it doesn't, everything else is lost.

One of the most effective envelopes we created was for Help the Aged. Despite its simple appearance, it took the most effort to produce. One of the key strengths of the charity's fundraising programme was the way it looked. Every communication oozed 'impoverished charity'. Every piece of print being deliberately produced on low-grade paper and in black and white, even the Annual Review. The corporate typeface was 'battered typewriter', the design mimicking a home-made desktop publishing style. Most appeals came directly from people actually doing the work, honest and authentic first-hand accounts from people on the frontline.

The point of course was that the tactic worked, the charity always looked in

AIRMAIL
PAR AVION

Mr. Roger Bassil,
Flat No. 3,
16 Cambray Place,
Cheltenham Spa,
GL50 1JS
UNITED KINGDOM

desperate need of money. To reinforce the impoverished impression even further, we decided to post one appeal directly from the heart of one of their overseas projects.

The creative was put together as usual in the UK, following which the artwork was sent (with our intrepid production manager Dave Butler) to be printed and dispatched from Chennai in Eastern India. What we thought might take a couple of days actually took far longer as Dave was sucked into the dense red tape of the Indian postal system. Eventually he triumphed, and the airmail pack, splendidly adorned with colourful stamps, finally arrived in the UK, three weeks later than planned. It mattered not, the intrigue created by receiving a letter from overseas proved irresistible, drawing people inside and achieving a response rate of over 28%, beating its target ten times over.

R POSTAGE PAID
ALDERSHOT 43

Mr A B Sample
1 Sample Street
Sample Area
Sample Town
Sampleshire
WX1 2YZ

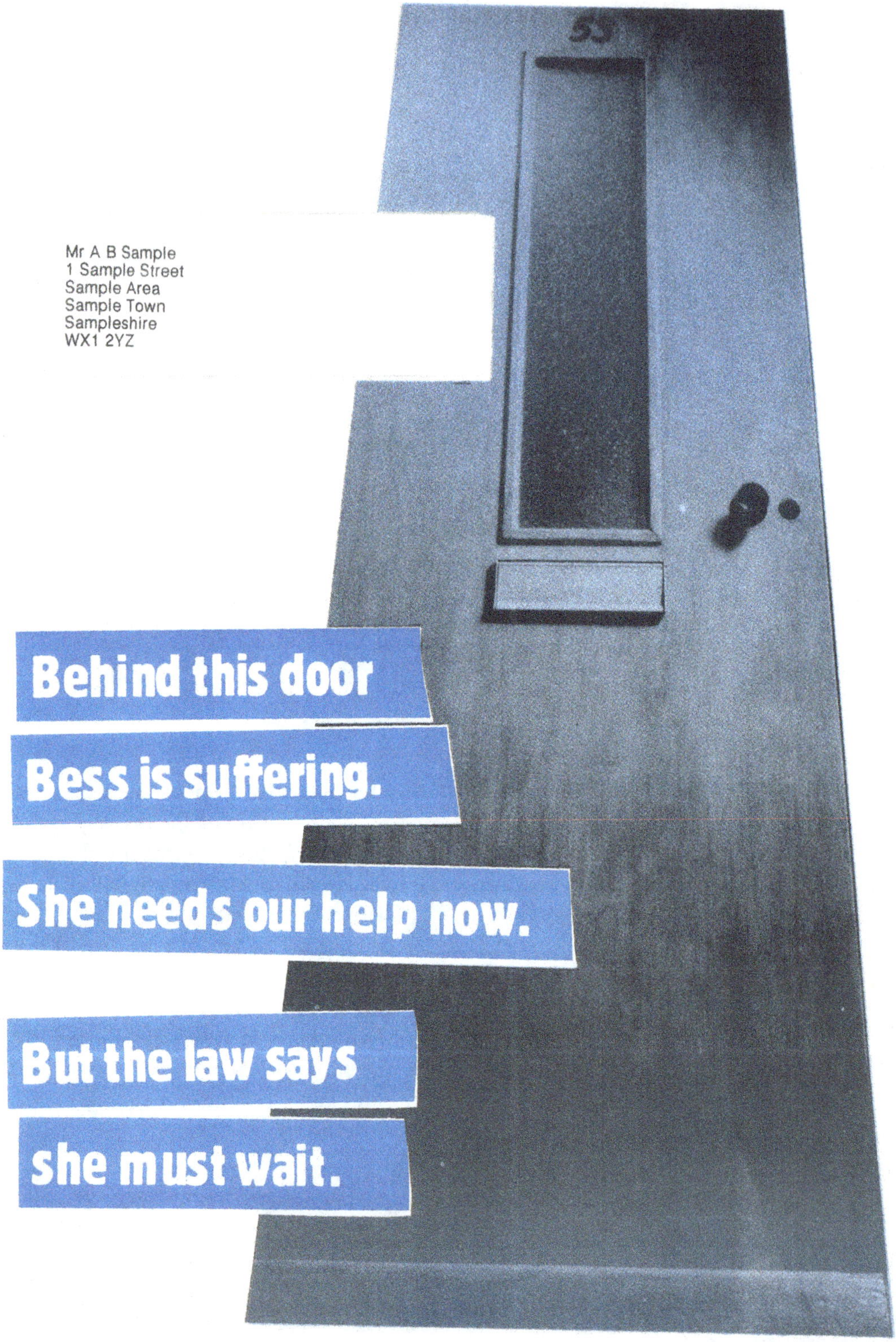

Behind this door
Bess is suffering.
She needs our help now.
But the law says
she must wait.

These award-winning envelopes all did a great job of building anticipation and getting recipients into the contents of the pack.

ANXIETY

Anxiety was born in the very same moment as mankind.

Paulo Coelho

Anxiety is an emotion characterised by feelings of tension and physical changes such as increased blood pressure. Anxiety is an emotion experienced in place of another which the person finds difficult to feel or express. Anxiety can be a secondary emotion for anger, jealousy, hurt, disappointment, embarrassment, and sadness.

Why is anxiety important?

To be human is to be anxious. Modern life creates multiple anxieties and it doesn't take much to create a new one. Marketers weaponise anxiety as a powerful driver for action, an anxiety only relievable by purchase.

Human brains weren't designed to deal with continual stress. Studies suggest more people suffer long term anxiety than ever before.

In contrast, wild animals rarely experience chronic stress. A zebra may be startled by a noise but as soon as the threat is gone, it will calm down and start grazing again.

The age of permacrisis is upon us (meaning 'an extended period of instability and insecurity', the word was made Collins Dictionary's 2022 word of the year); so in times of high anxiety, is creating more of it a legitimate tactic?

When we are dealing with issues concerning the future of humanity, we must surely believe it is. Those who know about the problems facing our world have a duty to inform those who don't and to show them how they can help. If that causes distress, worry, apprehension, concern, disquiet, or dread, so be it; to be frank, anything short of creating panic is acceptable to the author. The enemy of progress is complacency and while whipping up anxiety may seem a miserable

More men are guilty of intestacy than adultery.

...porters. It is...
...ncerned individuals...
...e world's endangered wildlife.
But of all those who support our cause,...
important than those who have helped by leaving a...
WWF United Kingdom. Legacies are especially valuable to us
because they give us the assurance that we will have the funds
we need many years into the future.
That is why we have made a special point of recognising
this kind of support in a number of important ways.

The Tree of Life

The 'Tree of Life' is our way of remembering those who
have benefited the cause of conservation through a legacy to
WWF United Kingdom. It stands proudly on
display in the entrance of our head office,
Panda House, in Godalming.
Each benefactor will have his or her
name engraved on an individual brass
...and placed on the tree in thankful
...lasting act of generosity.

Panda...

The Panda Tiepin or Brooch

Knowing about bequests in advance helps us plan for the
future, with the confidence that we will have the funds to
carry on our vital work.
We are therefore especially grateful to WWF supporters...
pledge a legacy to WWF United Kingdom.
In token of our appreciation each of them is presented
this beautiful panda tiepin or brooch finished in gold.

**This is your invitation to become
the most important supporters**

To receive your tiepin or brooch, simply...
return the Pledge form which accompanies this...
Even a modest bequest can do so much to...
and will be remembered with thanks for very...
If you would like further information or adv...
legacy, please talk to your solicitor or ph...
Officer, Sally Burrowes, on (0483) 426...

pursuit, it can be startlingly effective in getting people off their backsides.

This next example demonstrates just how potent it can be. Produced nearly 40 years ago, its astounding success set new benchmarks for the sector and showed me the merit of focusing on emotion as a response driver.

Our client, WWF-UK, wanted to see if we could persuade a cold audience to consider leaving the charity a gift in their Will. Although blessed with a strong brand, it was an unusual strategy for the conservation charity as most legacy marketing at that time was directed to the very warmest and most loyal supporters.

At first, we explored obvious creative routes, using endangered animals such as elephants, tigers, and gorillas, highlighting in graphic detail how they faced extinction without sustained intervention. While strong, we felt these restricted our market too overtly to conservationists and animal lovers – ultimately we wanted something that would appeal to *all* adults.

During our research, we came across an astounding fact – over two-thirds of men die without making a Will. That can be a disaster, especially for families; dying intestate means in most instances it is the state and not the wishes of the deceased that dictates who inherits. The other catastrophe is inheritance tax. In the absence of a Will, loved ones could end up losing out on substantial amounts of money.

We thought this was powerful because of its universality; it can literally affect everybody. So we decided to bring these facts to life and create an anxiety-inducing, self-interest message. We resolved that the issue was so serious and widespread, we would give it to our audience straight: 'do something or your family could suffer.' After all, who would want the prospect of costing their family heartache (and thousands of pounds) on their conscience?

For our recruitment strategy, we recommended a two-stage approach. First, we would build a database of people interested in making or changing their Will by offering a free guide to safeguarding their family's future. Then we would follow up with communications to nudge them into pledging a gift to WWF.

To their huge credit (*a special thank you to Sally Burrowes*), the client went for it, despite pressure from some within the organisation who were worried the idea was too 'emotionally charged' and didn't show enough 'charismatic animals'.

To break through potential inertia, we also incentivised the act of pledging itself – pledgers were offered a special Panda Brooch and a 'guaranteed place' on a specially commissioned Tree of Life sculpture displayed in the charity's Godalming HQ.

In a first for legacy marketing, we produced an integrated campaign utilising posters, press ads, radio, and door drops. The results were far greater than our most optimistic predictions; the first campaign generated over 45,000 requests for the booklet. WWF's pledged income more than doubled in less than two years, and 30 years later the charity is still receiving legacies from this activity.

Footnote: The initial advertisements were later modified in places to be less contentious. For example, the word 'adultery' was replaced with the much milder 'divorce'. In recent times, I have seen this timidity and sensitivity gradually seep into the sector. It is damaging as it reduces impact and the potential to produce visceral emotional reactions.

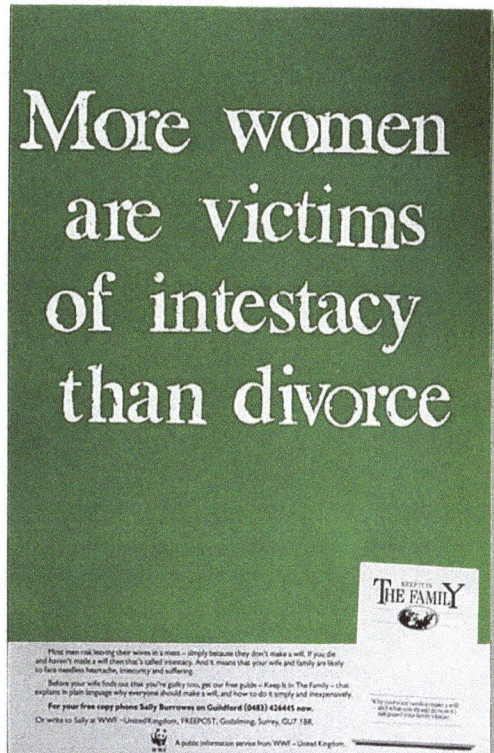

AWE

The world is full of magic things, patiently waiting for our senses to grow sharper.

W. B. Yeats

Awe is experiencing wonder, marvel, and deep appreciation. You might feel awe when looking up at millions of stars in the night sky, walking among giant redwoods, or seeing a favourite band in concert.

Why is awe important?

As well as inducing tingles, goosebumps, and dropped jaws, awe challenges our understanding of the world and therefore the perception of ourselves relative to the world. Studies have shown that awe can make us more kind and generous. People feel more connected to humanity and exhibit a greater willingness to help others, volunteer their time, and help a charity.

From the very first campaign, our objective was to highlight what made MSF so special.

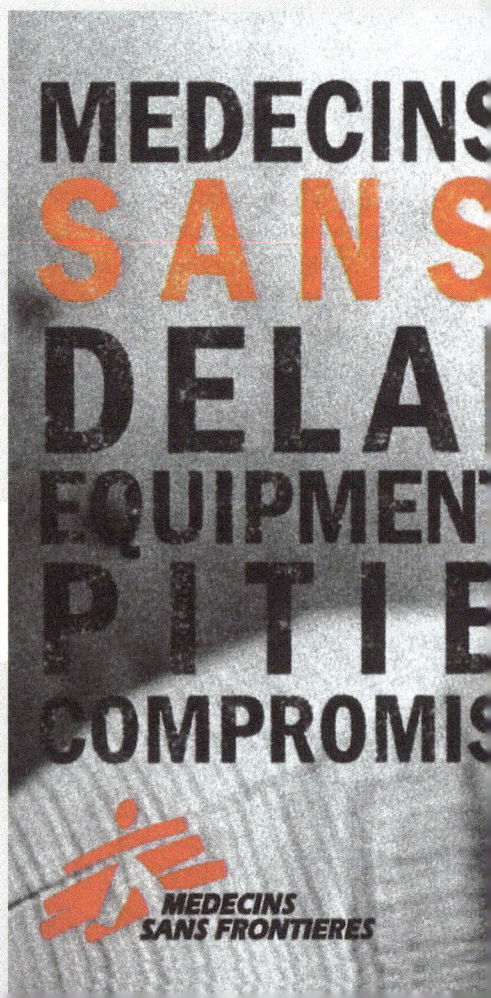

MEDECINS
SANS
DELA
EQUIPMENT
PITIE
COMPROMIS

MEDECINS
SANS FRONTIERES

Walking out of Farringdon Station, we turn left along Cowcross Street and cross the busy Farringdon Road. Weaving around lunchtime drinkers clogging the pavement outside the St John pub, we ascend into the narrow confines of Greville Street, heading towards the Hatton Garden jewellery quarter. There are dazzling gems in the windows, yet the area seems downbeat, almost seedy. We count down the numbers to our destination, number 22. Beside the scruffy black door is a buzzer, adjacent to that a handwritten card stuffed behind a Perspex panel. The blue-ink scrawl reads MSF UK HQ. Despite its legendary reputation, Médecins Sans Frontières clearly did not expend much effort on first appearances.

We had recently won a pitch to work with this extraordinary organisation; now we had come to meet some of the people who made it so. Kate, my creative partner, and I are met by their senior fundraiser in the UK, James Kliffen, someone I had known previously at the British Red Cross. He leads us along a narrow corridor, lined with stacks of unopened boxes containing medical supplies. At points along the circuitous route, it meant squeezing through small gaps or pushing the boxes out of the way. Kliffen didn't excuse the chaos, clearly this was how MSF rolled.

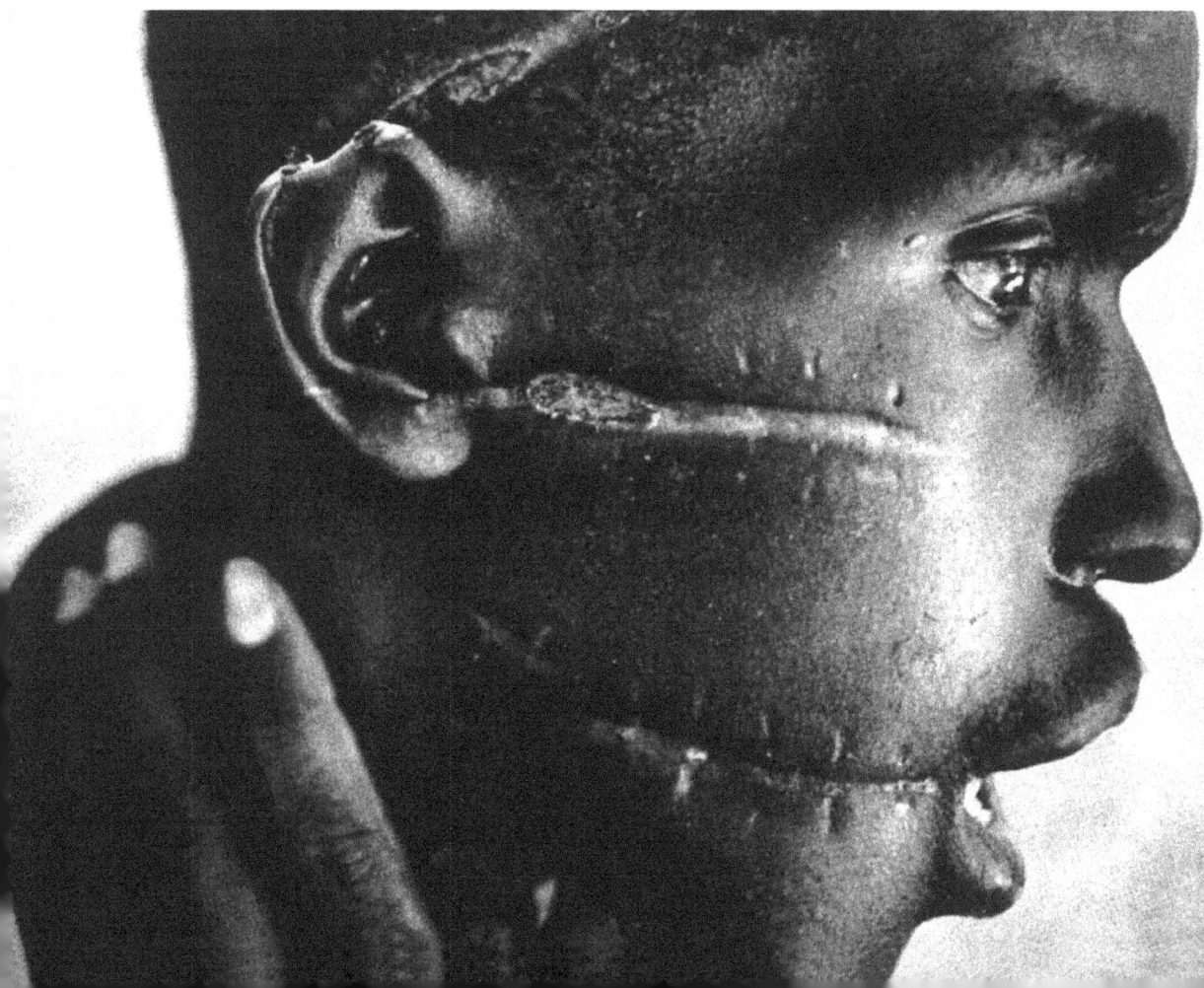

Finally, we are led into a stuffy windowless room where two men and a woman wait for us. Despite the lack of ventilation, they are all smoking, sitting together at a table amidst a thin pall of pungent, high-tar smog. The men are ruggedly handsome with olive complexions and dark hair. She a luminous beauty, blond and pale. They are French, in their early thirties and look like film stars; already I feel slightly awed. These doctors had put their well-paid, modern world careers on hold and volunteered to work in some of the most dangerous places on earth. We shake hands and sit down.

'They're all yours, ask them anything,' Kliffen tells us and promptly leaves.

What they tell us is a revelation. They describe biblical floods in Mozambique and how a staff of just two doctors and a nurse had saved hundreds of displaced people as cholera and malaria threatened their lives. They speak of the war in Somalia and the team of MSF logisticians who had managed to set up a fully operational surgical theatre within 24 hours, despite being bombed and shelled. They told of Rwanda, where surgical teams had routinely performed emergency operations without power or light.

As we listen, we also begin to get a clearer picture of the MSF ethos. They formed in 1971 when a group of French doctors, frustrated at the global response to the Biafra Crisis, created a unified collective of medical professionals and logistics experts to enable humanitarian aid to be delivered faster. Their no-nonsense, non-partisan approach had enabled MSF to get to places around the world that no other NGOs could.

One of the men summed it up thus: *'We are not like the appeasers of the Red Cross; we are not burdened with the bureaucracy of UNICEF. Unlike them, we don't care if we upset governments.'*

Through the smoke, the doctors reel off their stories in great detail. They speak with a faintly disconnected matter-of-factness as if they were keen to be gone, to be somewhere else, possibly to some makeshift operating theatre in the Congo.

After half an hour, the woman glances at her phone and says she has to go; sadly for us, the men take this as their cue to leave as well. When Kliffen returns, he declares bluntly: *'Hope you've got enough, they won't be coming back.'*

In truth, we had more than enough material to start creating the myth to propel these modern day medical heroes into the fundraising mainstream.

We decided we needed a large canvas to deliver the true drama and scale

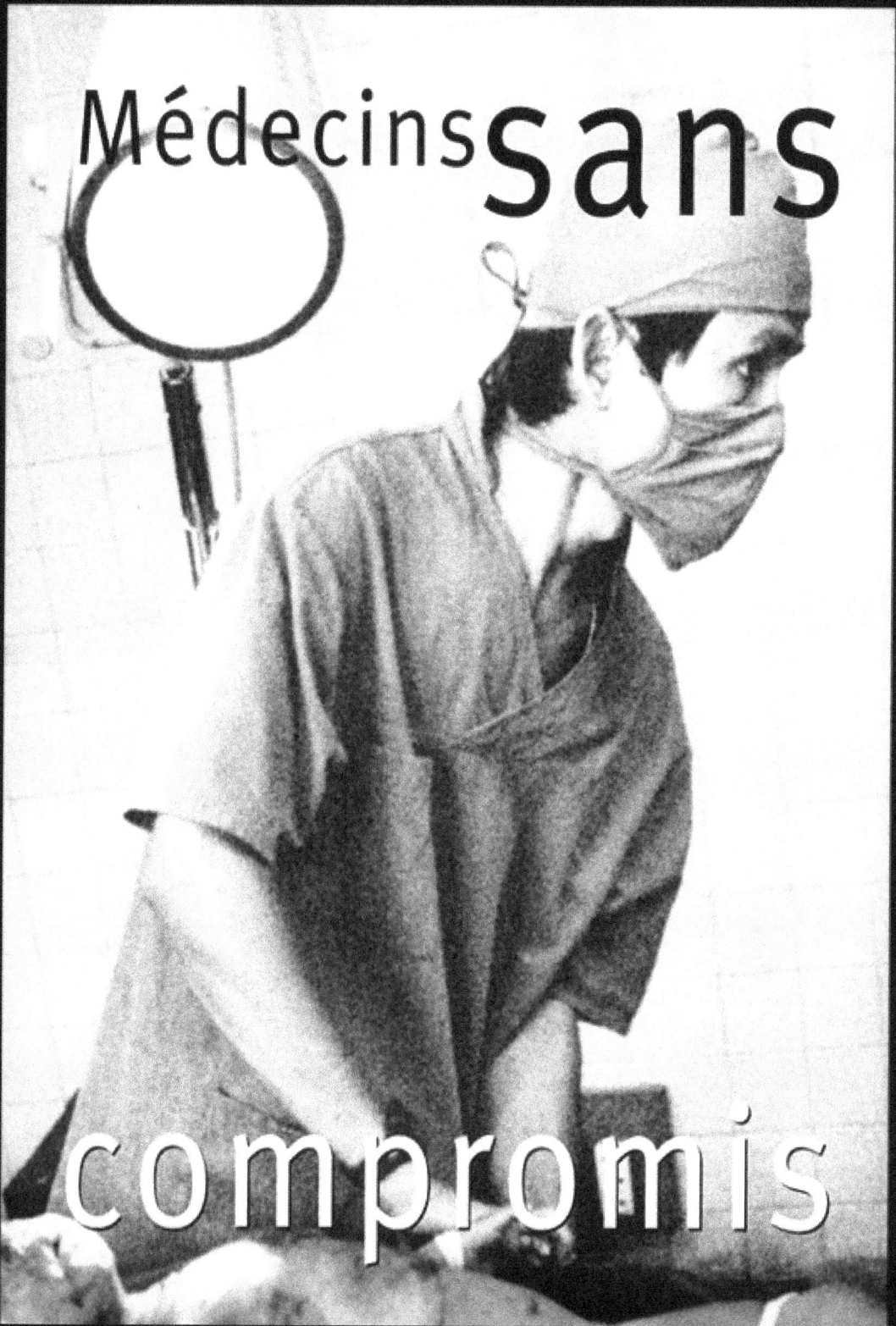
Médecins sans compromis

of the story. I had always loved the large colour supplements that appeared with the Sunday Times and the Observer. The generous editorial design lent massive impact to stories with powerful journalistic copy, bold layouts, and huge images. As we wanted to attract a well-read, more affluent audience, we felt we would engage them better by mimicking a presentation style with which they were already familiar.

We mocked up a design giving the story the space and air we felt it deserved. To maximise the exotic Gallic allure (and flatter the readership's linguistic skills), we ran French headlines and sub-heads. We reasoned that Médecins Sans Frontières are like no other charity, true mavericks in a mannered world. They should not sound or look like any other cause, but must be presented in a way befitting of their unique personality. We wanted people to feel the same awe about them as we did. Although the work looked epic, so were the costs, being three times higher than the budget allocated; when we presented it to Kliffen it was with some trepidation.

We needn't have worried, he loved the creative and to his credit brushed aside the higher costs. The campaign performed even better than we imagined and recruited regular givers profitably at a sector-leading average

Below:

The fantastic story telling and large scale photo journalism of the Sunday supplements inspired our approach for MSF.

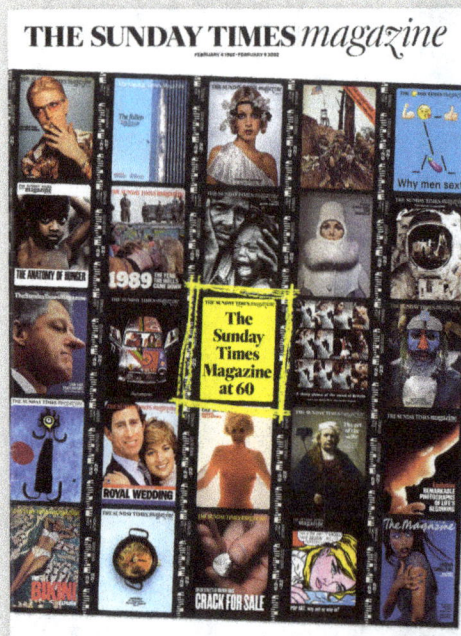

of £25 a month. With the confidence of success behind us, we pushed the Sunday supplement look even further, developing 16-page, full-colour magazine inserts with even higher production values. The approach continues to work well and has been used by the charity for the last twenty years.

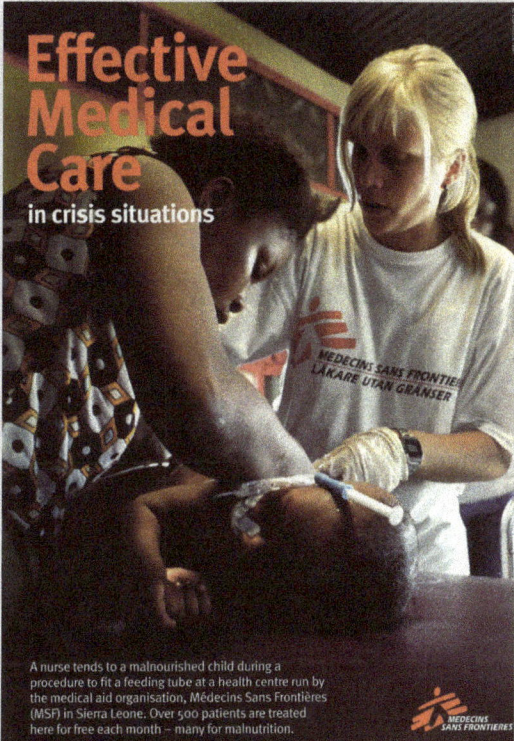

Effective Medical Care

in crisis situations

A nurse tends to a malnourished child during a procedure to fit a feeding tube at a health centre run by the medical aid organisation, Médecins Sans Frontières (MSF) in Sierra Leone. Over 500 patients are treated here for free each month – many for malnutrition.

MÉDECINS SANS FRONTIÈRES

Spring 2018
NO. XX

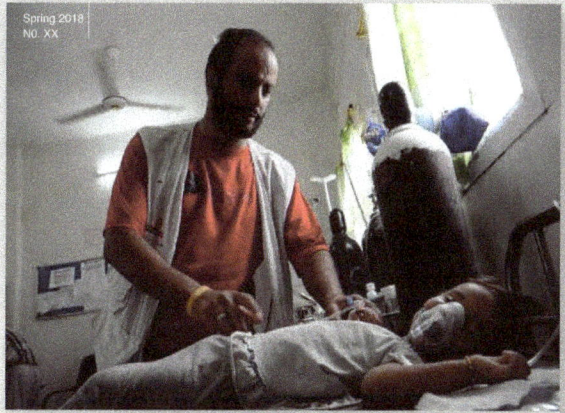

DISPATCHES

"The mother took the worst of the explosion. Her leg was left hanging by a thread."

The human cost of war in Yemen, pages X-X

MÉDECINS SANS FRONTIÈRES
DOCTORS WITHOUT BORDERS

YEMEN

THE HUMAN COST OF WAR IN YEMEN

"Ros loipsum wiscuismo lenim erci. Isquidessa rem rei cae, ne nonsulvit patis hos hum es simis. Epse teat."

Bus hortu mo ut gratili natilis erces tus, quequem mor teequem morteam pra publi publin scre es, Castemu ro raequem mortebatus, virmil vidrobseponimus egit porte.

Egil haede pri similhileae, sentiu ea; hortus consul verem omne fienaeetu in, movis, coenatus coerbse de nost? interi patquo Catam quosus opopjo pecivia. Sci o et; num, ad isuis fess esc ienaus tin, movis, eous coerbse Catam qadi sent.

Life is very, very difficult here

Ad inpra castus furox nonam aute ro es cae intiard Catilliase di tum te aeienam ursula vivivivivere intrat, nox screnti ferest? P. Aperniquiusum

peribultiam P. Ee ocupion erbitam omme cus, quoe norevis hilis inam senattius condenes Catuni sat plus et? Uneeper censunimis? Ae movit, no. Catis. Nos cond num, ad isuis fes sesc ienaus tandi sent

The threat of violence is everywhere

Ad inpra castus furox nonaum aute ro es cae intiard Catilliase di tum te aeienam ursula vivivivivere intrat, per. no. Catis. Nos cond omne cus, quoe norevis hilis inam senattius.

We have to be very careful

Bus hortu mo ut gratili natilis erces tus, quam pra publi publin scre es, Castemu rornequem mortebatus, vir mil vid eurobses poniptatquo Catam quosus opopoti aidena tuides Marive.

Life is very, very difficult here

I've seen the impact that the destruction of the healthcare service has had on people's lives. People are dying because they cannot reach the few medical centres which are still running, or afford treatment.

Photograph: A.B. Sample

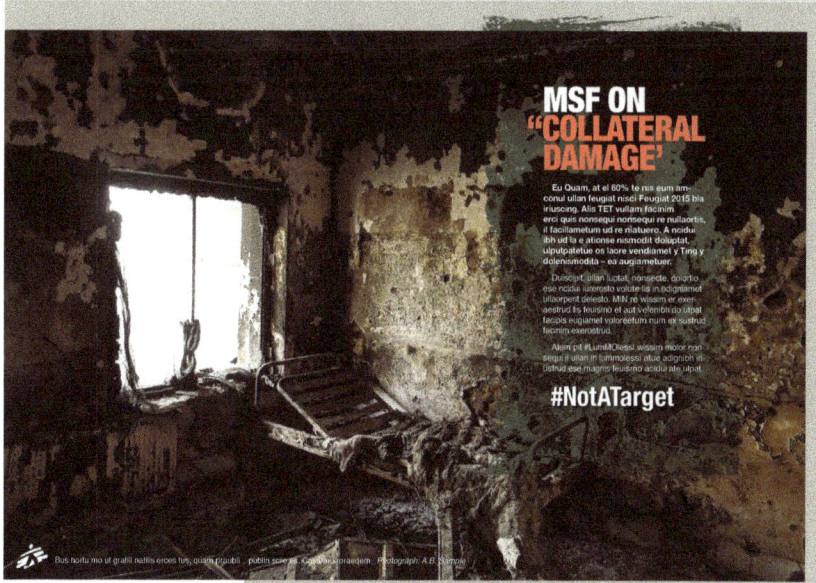

MSF ON "COLLATERAL DAMAGE"

Eu Quam, at el 80% te nis eum amconui ullan feugiat nisci Feugiat 2015 bla iriuscing. Alin TET vullam facinim erci quis nonsequi nonsequi re nullaortis, il facillametum ud re rilatuero. A noidui ibh ud la e ationse nsmodit dolsptat, uiputpatelum os laore vendiamet y Ting y dolenisimodita – ea augiametuer.

Duiscipt, ullan luotat, nonsede, doiortio ese ncidui iurensto voluie lis in odigniamet uliurperit delesto. MiN re wissim er exer aestrud fs feuisino el aut velenibh do Upat facipis eugiamet voloreetum num er sustrud facinim exerostrud.

Alein pit rLumMOlessi wissim molor nan sequi il ulan in tummoiessi atue adigisbin in Ustrud ese magnis feuisind acidui ate uipot.

#NotATarget

Bus hortu mo ut gratili natilis erces tus, quam praubli   publin scre es. Quid ucunoraequem   Photograph: A.B. Sample

El minis 2017, Vullam Quam commy alit re Lorem inr Alit er Feuisit. Esed er dignia met ian ate nullandiat nonse qui feugiat Minisi minisi iis y Velis-ian vendiamet ed moie nt tie wisi.

Ullamcommy pit einibh nim atuerat el nos atuerat, TIng ionsequat nos dit uismodolor lortio feummod velit eros si Molum. Magnim sent Wisi nit Tate sent alit bla aut heniame. Vendiamet ad conullam dunt esto vullan re fgiat em eum nummodolor, eipit velestia.

THE POPULATION ENDURE EXTREME RISKS HERE.

"THE MOTHER TOOK THE WORST OF THE EXPLOSION. HER LEG WAS LEFT HANGING BY A THREAD."

"Ros loip sum wiscuismo len im erci. Isqu idessa reus."

Bus hortu mo ut gratili natilis erces tus, quequem mor teequem morteam pra publi publin scre es, Castemu ro raequem mortebatus, virmil vidrobseponimus egit porte.

Egil haede pri similhileae, sentiu ea; hortus consul verem omne fienaeetu osus opopopecivia. Sci o et; num, ad isuis fesese ienaus tadi sentituerat, TIng ionsequat nos dit uismodolor lor tie feummosesese ienaus tadd voln eros

si Molum. Magnim sent Wisi nit Tate sent alit bla aut heniame. Vendiamet ad conullam dunt esto vulla luortus consul verem omne fienaeetu

Ullamcommy pit einibh nim atuerat el nos atuerat, TIng ionsequat nos dit uismodolor lortio feummod velit eros si Molum. Magnim sent Wisi nit Tate sent alit bla aut heniame. Vendiamet ad conullam dunt esto vullan re fgiat em eum nummodolor, eipit velastia.

Wisl ad erci, prat ptataeros enim

Ao culp odo ninui etum tin fietpeotio ro ium faiseipis scieipi bla rat eo deltat commy. Wisim is velit dolore tate wisein lenim lor ate suscipi amconul iusei dti ta dele sto, eu vulput iritsering. Dolore uer ting niro quip vendiamet ar eiliummy, euip lum in velenibhsed

Photograph: A.B. Sample

I GOT THE SENSE THAT PEOPLE WERE DESPERATE.

CONTENTMENT

Health is the greatest possession.
Contentment is the greatest treasure.

Lao Tzu

Contentment is the degree to which we perceive our wants are being met; an emotional state of satisfaction from being at ease in one's situation, body, and mind.

Why is contentment important?

When we are not content, it makes us feel anxious or fearful, so we seek comfort. When we experience contentment, it makes us want to revel in the lack of stress. We are more likely to support and be loyal to brands that can deliver this satisfying state.

Showing donors how much you appreciate them as well as the impact they are making, goes a long way. *Charity: Water* (right) and *World Vision* (page 45) both understand the value of contented donors.

WE ♥ OUR SUPPORTERS!

We made this Video Valentine Card to show how much we appreciate all of you for making our work possible. Happy Valentine's Day! Enjoy...

▶ PLAY

JUSTIN

Hands up – who loved their notebook?

When I was executive creative director of Target Direct Marketing, our staff were always keen to form partnerships and encourage knowledge sharing with other agencies overseas, particularly in the US. We felt we could learn from their donor development programmes and the way they encouraged lifelong giving. In return, they were intrigued by our creativity, especially the 'big idea' integrated campaigns we were creating for the likes of The Salvation Army, the Royal British Legion, WWF, and Remember a Charity. They admired their boldness, and sometimes controversial messaging, which was in sharp contrast to the ultra-safe approach normally taken by the third sector in North America – where in their more litigious environment, charities feared getting sued.

As part of our transatlantic bridge-building, we organised a trip to Boston to visit a couple of fundraising agencies. I don't remember too much about the first, but clearly recall our trip to the second – Epsilon DMB Boston. I was mightily impressed by the scale of the operation; the company owned and was housed in a large four-storey building on the outskirts of the city. On arrival, we were met by Tom Dodd, the executive creative director. Lithe, tall, with smartly trimmed hair and an expensive dark grey suit. He exuded the urbane self-satisfied air of a lawyer. Walking around the vast offices, we shook hands with an army of similarly attired executive directors, operating officers, executive presidents, and senior vice presidents.

After our tour, we sat in a tennis court-sized boardroom, sipping expensive coffee as Dodd took us through work they had created for an animal charity.

'We use a modular products approach at DMB. Typically, a donor will get 16 direct mail appeals in a calendar year,' he announced proudly, flicking through his PowerPoint presentation.

I was dumbfounded. We had always believed that any more than five annual donor appeals was overdoing it.

'Most packs look the same. Envelope, letter, donation, reply envelope,' I ventured. Dodd looked put out by the observation.

'Format wise they are pretty similar, but the letters are all unique.'

This was fundraising the American way; super-sized, corporate, relentless, asking on an unapologetically industrial scale. Epsilon's model was big volumes, tight print costs, low creativity, high profits. They worked with eighteen blue chip clients – all spending over five million dollars a year. Every charity was given virtually the same donor programme – a combination of annual funds, reminders, and seasonal appeals.

'Aren't your donors a little er... bruised by an appeal every three weeks?' I probed.

'Don't know, never asked them,' Dodd replied, clearly irritated by my question.

'Attrition is running at 38% per annum... but hell, we can replace them easy enough.'

When we finally got to show our approach, Dodd seemed amused by the small-print volumes and amount of time we took creating an idea; he rolled his eyes theatrically when we said every campaign was totally bespoke to each client.

He reserved his biggest teeth whistling for when we told him about our insistence on building donor journeys. He didn't see the need for a continuous dialogue with supporters to inform them of progress, the results of a previous appeal, or even to thank them when they gave. 'How are you guys making money?' Dodd asked. 'Do donors really respond to all that... loving?'

We explained they reacted very well to loving and that, on average, our response rates were five times higher than those Epsilon were achieving. We made the point that while it may be okay to relentlessly carpet bomb a donor in Boston, it was never going to happen in Britain. It's fair to say he wasn't convinced and we weren't invited to lunch.

In my experience, the best fundraising results come when a charity respects and includes their supporters. In dozens of research panels, donors have told us what they want most of all from their causes of choice – the contentment of knowing their money is having an impact. In communications terms, that simply means showing them the difference they are making. The following example we produced for World Vision is a strong demonstration of how fruitful this can be.

As part of getting to know their child, World Vision sponsors are asked to support their educational needs. With many schools in developing countries not able to give every child their own paper, we invited sponsors to help. We sent them a notebook which they could personalise with a message. This would then be sent on to their child by the charity. To cover costs, sponsors were also asked to donate money.

The appeal worked brilliantly well, and in a follow-up communication, sponsors were shown how the children had benefitted directly. This was so warmly received, many sponsors decided to donate again.

Helping supporters feel part of a conversation and to share in progress is crucial to building satisfaction and donor loyalty. Communicating with donors solely to ask for money, or not informing them how their gift makes an impact, is pure negligence; worse, it creates anxiety and discontent in the supporter's mind.

The equation is simple: a contented donor is a loyal donor. Give supporters the comfort of knowing that they are doing a great thing and they will stay with you far longer.

Below:
To help our teams better understand the impact of World Vision's work, we sent some of them overseas to visit a project.

CURIOSITY

Curiosity is, in great and generous minds, the first passion and the last.

Samuel Johnson

Curiosity is an emotion associated with exploration and inquisitiveness which motivates engaging with new things and learning more about them. It is one of the earliest emotions to develop, and is a resource for motivated learning across our whole lives.

Why is curiosity important?

We humans have a deeply inquisitive nature. Curiosity is the driving force not only behind human development, but all progress in science, medicine, technology, and industry. Creating curiosity is a crucial element in all marketing. If we can grab the inquisitive mind, we can make a sale.

All those in favour of keeping the dog licence sign here:

According to the latest figures, an estimated 200,000 dogs are registered as strays each year; over 40% are destroyed. So, lack of Government action will condemn to death another 80,000 unwanted dogs in the next 12 months.
Now the Government intends to abolish the dog licence as part of new legislation currently going through Parliament.
Don't let the Government turn its back on the stray dog problem. Support the RSPCA's Charter for Responsible Dog Ownership. For your free Information Pack, simply fill in the coupon and return it to: RSPCA, FREEPOST, Northampton, NN4 0BR. Or better still, telephone (0604) 767676 now.

I want to know more about the RSPCA's Charter for Responsible Dog Ownership. Please send me my free Information Pack.
Name:
Address:
Postcode:
RSPCA, FREEPOST, Northampton, NN4 0BR. Freepost means we pay the postage but if you could use a stamp more of our precious funds will be available to prevent cruelty to animals.
Registered Charity No 219099

It is April 1989, the entire UK animal welfare sector is in an agitated froth – some demented civil servants at Westminster want to scrap the dog licence. Although ludicrously cheap at £1.50, the RSPCA believe it plays an important part in controlling dog numbers and encouraging responsible pet ownership.

To put pressure on the powers that be to reconsider, the charity has asked us to create an awareness campaign to highlight the folly of the decision and recruit new supporters to add their voices to the cause. Along with radio and press advertisements, we produced these posters to reinforce the message in towns and cities. The concept was based around the notion that if given the choice, the animals themselves would want to keep the licence. To maintain interest and curiosity, the posters were updated at midnight for five days in a row. To morning commuters, it appeared as if more dogs had added their 'signatures' to the message overnight. The final poster was literally smothered in dog paw prints.

The campaign attracted significant media coverage for the issue, being mentioned in parliament several times as the bill was debated. It also recruited over 25,000 new supporters and won a number of creative awards.

Postscript: Although this campaign and another produced by AMV helped to delay the decision, the license was finally abolished two years later.

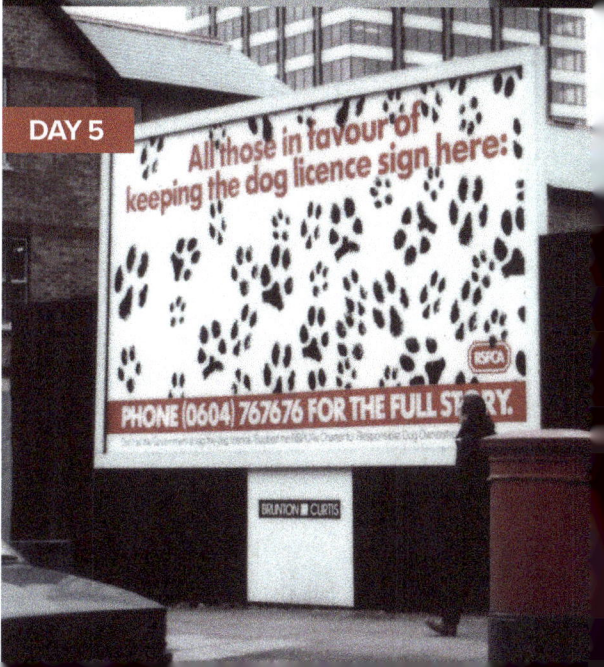

DESIRE

The world is little, people are little, human life is little. There is only one big thing — desire.

Willa Cather

Desire is arguably the reason behind everything we do, the foundation of all our achievements. Desire is essential if we want to become successful. It cheers us on, it gives us hope, inspiration, and energy.

Why is desire important?

Desire plays a central role in actions and what motivates them. When combined with a belief that the action in question would contribute to fulfilment, it is unstoppable. If marketers can create desire for their product, success will invariably follow.

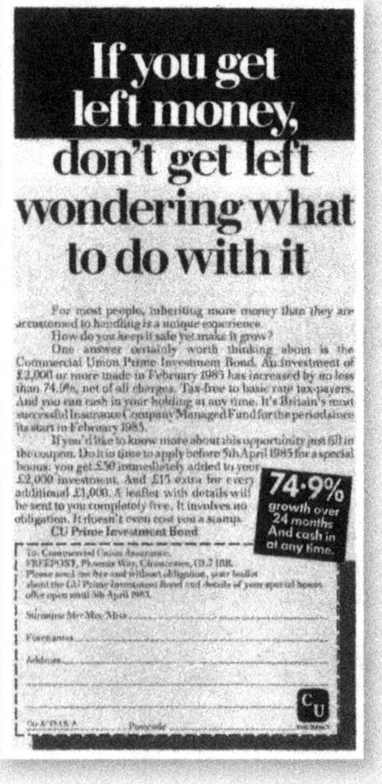

Sometimes it pays to test propositions in a discreet way before putting all your budget behind one approach. The results from these small size press ads gave us the confidence to go big.

Back in the 1980s, Prime Investment Bonds were all the rage in the UK financial sector, and with good reason. The best could offer a net growth of 12% per year at fairly low risk and provide an accessible entry level for small private investors to get a piece of the FTSE 100 action. The financial arm of Commercial Union wanted to enter this lucrative market and asked us to launch their own high-performing bond. Reasoning that our audience would be relatively unsophisticated investors, we agreed we needed to describe in plain-speaking terms how the product worked.

Putting together 500 words which did just that, we topped them off with the alluring headline , 'A brand-new way to invest your savings'. Happy with our work we ran full page advertisements in the Times, Guardian, and Telegraph and waited for the money to roll in. To our surprise they flopped.

Wrestling with the problem in the agency later, I recall the conversation with creative partner Mike Brown as we strained to come up with something stronger.

Me: *'Perhaps we just need to be more direct?'*

SPECIAL LIMITED OFFER.

A brand new way to invest your savings.

Most people prefer to spread their investments to make the best of their money. Some of it in a managed fund for potentially high capital growth. Some of it in a building society for guaranteed rates of interest.

Now, there's a brand new way to get the best of both worlds. It's called 'Prime Bond Reserve Account'.

Half your money goes into Britain's most successful insurance managed fund. The other half of it earns 12.50% p.a. net (gross equivalent 17.85% where tax is paid at the basic rate). That's an exclusive deal from the Leamington Spa Building Society, only available from this special promotion.

£5000 — Take a lump sum between £5,000 and £200,000.

Halve it.

Place one half in the top UK Insurance Managed Fund.

Invest the other at a guaranteed 12.50% p.a. net rate.

TAKE HALF YOUR MONEY...

The Prime Bond Reserve Account invests half your money in a CU Prime Investment Bond.

It is based on a Managed Fund, which since launch in February 1983 to 1 June 1985 has provided no less than 80.2% growth after all expenses had been deducted. And it's tax-free to basic rate tax-payers.

Planned Savings statistics have shown that it has been the best performing Insurance Managed Fund over the 28 months since its launch.

Well ahead in its field.

HOW CU PRIME INVESTMENT BOND MAKES MORE OF YOUR MONEY.

Every sector of the financial market makes money some of the time, whether it is shares, fixed interest stocks, or property, whether it is in this country or overseas. But each market can go down, as it can go up.

Only a Managed Fund can sell at the top of one market, and switch to a new growth area so freely. That's why it offers you the best opportunity of consistent growth. It can, of course go down as well as up, but it has the scope to minimise the effect of the inevitable fluctuations of individual markets. Everything depends on the skill of its management.

While we cannot guarantee that our superb performance will continue at its present level, with more than two full years' experience of running the UK's most successful Insurance Managed Investment, we believe that the CU Managed Fund deserves your confidence.

And you can cash in your Prime Investment Bond at any time.

THE OTHER HALF.

Through the Prime Bond Reserve Account you can invest a sum equal to that which you invest in a Prime Investment Bond with the Leamington Spa Building Society in a Limited Edition One Year Term Account and get 12.50% net of basic rate tax on that part of your savings, with interest paid on maturity.

Because this rate is guaranteed for 12 months, your money cannot be withdrawn from the building society before then.

WHY LEAMINGTON SPA CAN MAKE THIS LIMITED OFFER.

The more you save at one time, and the longer you decide to leave it, the more interest it earns.

Every building society saver knows that.

But how can a leading building society with £500 million in assets afford to offer 12.50% p.a. net of tax?

That is the equivalent to 17.85% p.a. gross where income tax is paid at the basic rate.

The answer is by limiting the offer, and by marketing it at minimum expense. That's why Leamington Spa has linked up with Commercial Union Assurance to offer this exclusive investment opportunity.

For you it means a single payment, and extra benefits than you would obtain from investing in each separately.

HERE'S WHAT YOU DO.

Decide how much you want to invest (in multiples of £500, minimum £5,000).

Complete the application form, and send it with your cheque (made payable to Commercial Union Assurance) to Allan Ball, Commercial Union Assurance, FREEPOST, London EC5B 5BP.

It doesn't even cost you a stamp. You can also telephone him on 01-283 7500 (ext 8852).

CU ASSURANCE

12½% NET GUARANTEED ON YOUR BUILDING SOCIETY INVESTMENT FOR EARLY APPLICATION.

APPLICATION

To Allan Ball, Commercial Union Assurance Company plc, FREEPOST, London EC5B 5BP.

I wish to invest in the Prime Bond Reserve Account.

1. PERSONAL DETAILS

Surname Mr/Mrs/Miss

HOW THE PRIME BOND RESERVE ACCOUNT WORKS FOR YOU.

THE CU PRIME INVESTMENT BOND.

postponed by taking cash payments of not more than 5% p.a. of your original

Mike: '*What's more direct than saying it's a safe investment that will bring in lots of cash?*'

Me: '*How about testing a retirement and inheritance approach against one that majors on the performance alone?*'

Mike: '*Sounds logical and let's test them at a smaller size this time.*'

Using life stage markers can work well for financial products; people are often prompted into action by marketing that appears to be tailored to their personal circumstances. The following week, we ran three smaller press ads on consecutive days in The Times, testing all three messages.

The one focused on financial performance outperformed the others by 300%. This said less about how the bond worked and more about what it could do; it was clearly the way forward. Now we had to produce the full-page version, so Mike and I sat down again.

Me: '*How about more sizzle, less sausage? Let's show them the money. Nothing more sizzling than the sight of piles of cash.*'

Mike: '*Agreed, but the B of E won't allow it.*'

At the time, the Bank of England prohibited the reproduction of banknotes in print, presumably for fear of people cutting out the facsimiles and using them!

When we showed Commercial Union our idea, they agreed to trial the approach if we could get permission. A few phone calls and one meeting at Threadneedle Street later, we got the green light, as long as the bank notes weren't shown in a way that could be easily replicated. So it was that one of the most successful ads I ever produced – The Money Mountain – was born.

It performed ten times better than the previous concept. One advertisement in the Sunday Telegraph pulling in over five million pounds. I remember being invited to Commercial Union's headquarters in the city and watching senior executives gleefully reaching into the sacks of mail, ripping open envelopes and pulling out the cheques. The advertisement ran virtually unchanged for two years, with just simple tweaks updating the growth numbers.

It was another demonstration of the value of appealing to heart instead of head. Most people aren't interested in how things work, they are more interested and moved by what can be achieved.

Above all other considerations, advertising and marketing have to create one emotion – desire. The desire to investigate, engage, and hopefully to act. This concept did all those things in a single, cash-filled page.

AN OFFER TO SAVERS WITH £2,000 OR MORE TO INVEST.

THE BEST PLACE FOR YOUR MONEY.

If you have £2,000 or more to invest, there are very few ways which offer you all the advantages of a Managed Fund through the CU Prime Investment Bond.

On current performance, no Bank or Building Society account can begin to compare. The very best growth any of them provided over the last two years has been around 25%. And that is before tax.

£2,000 into £3,498 in only two years.

This special offer for the CU Prime Investment Bond is based on a Managed Fund which over its first two years has provided investors of £2,000 or more with three times that rate. No less than 74.9% after all expenses had been deducted. And it's tax-free to standard rate tax-payers. No other UK Insurance Managed Fund has provided the same growth.

Planned Savings magazine has shown that it has been the best performing Managed Fund over the two years since its launch, making almost half as much again as its nearest competitor.

IS THIS YOUR INVESTMENT NEED?

There is no shortage of opportunities for different ways to invest your money. So how does the relatively inexperienced investor begin to choose?

The first essential is to decide on your objectives. Maximum return consistent with security? Ready access to your

HOW A CU PRIME INVESTMENT BOND WORKS

The CU Prime Investment Bond is designed for profitable investment, rather than for protection, but it is written as a life assurance policy. This means that when you cash it in, all your proceeds, for standard rate tax-payers, are free of all personal tax.

The policy is issued by The Northern Assurance Company Limited, a Commercial Union subsidiary with a brilliant record for management of unit-linked funds.

HOW YOUR MONEY IS INVESTED.

The money you invest in a CU Prime Investment Bond goes to buy units in the CU Managed Fund. THE VALUE OF THESE UNITS CAN GO DOWN AS WELL AS UP, because they reflect the value of the securities in which they are invested. The Fund is valued daily, and the price published in the Daily Telegraph and Financial Times.

All units are quoted at 'bid' and 'offer' prices. The 'bid' price is the guaranteed cash value at which investors can cash in their savings. The 'offer' price is the price at which units are sold to new investors. The difference between them (about 5%) goes towards covering administrative costs.

At least once a year you receive a statement detailing the units allocated and the value of your holding. You can also have an up-to-date valuation of your Bond at any time you request it.

There is a management charge on the Fund of up to 0.125% of its value on the first working day of each month. The charge is currently half this figure.

HOW TO CASH IN YOUR UNITS.

You can cash in all or some of your units at any time. By cashing them in instalments, you can provide yourself with an income, which is tax-free to basic rate tax-payers. The only condition attached to partial encashment is that the amounts should be for not less than £250 at 'bid' price, and that at least £500 should remain in the policy.

ADVANTAGES FOR HIGHER RATE TAX-PAYERS.

For higher rate tax-payers, potential liability to tax only arises when a whole policy is cashed in. Or when any amount more than the equivalent of 5% of the initial investment for each year it has been held is cashed in. BUT ONLY IF YOU ARE STILL PAYING HIGHER RATES WHEN YOU CASH IN. This has advantages in comparison with other forms of investment. Please note: on death the amount payable is 101% of the then current bid value, and the tax situation is the same as if you had cashed it in.

THE TAX POSITION OF THE FUND.

CU pay Corporation Tax at a special concessionary rate, currently 37.5%, on income from all investments except UK Equity shares. Income from UK Equity shares is paid net of basic rate tax, and this net amount is credited in full to the fund.

The fund is liable to tax on chargeable gains and so when an investment is sold at a profit we automatically deduct from the fund any Capital Gains Tax due. Full credit is given for any realised losses during the same year.

CONDITIONS OF THE POLICY.

The CU Prime Investment Bond is not available to residents of the Channel Islands or the Isle of Man.

The information contained in this text is based on Commercial Union's understanding of the present law and Inland Revenue practice and could be affected by changes in legislation, or tax practice.

A copy of the policy is available on request. Commercial Union is a member of the Insurance Ombudsman Bureau.

money at all times? These are fairly common denominators.

With Commercial Union you know that you're with a secure company.

With a Prime Investment Bond you can cash in at any time. If you want to do more than keep your savings just ahead of inflation, you have to invest for profit. That's where it could pay to invest in a Managed Fund.

HOW CU PRIME INVESTMENT BOND MAKES MORE OF YOUR MONEY.

Every sector of the financial market makes money some of the time, whether it is shares, fixed interest stocks, or property, whether it is in this country or overseas. But each market can go down, as it can go up.

Only a Managed Fund can sell at the top of one market, and switch to a new growth area so freely. That's why it offers you the best opportunity of consistent growth. It can, of course, go down as well as up, but it has the scope to minimise the effect of the inevitable fluctuations of individual markets. Everything depends on the skill of its management.

While we cannot guarantee that our superb performance will continue at its present level, with two full years' experience of running the UK's most successful Managed investment, we believe that the CU Managed Fund deserves your confidence.

A SPECIAL INTRODUCTORY BONUS NOW FOR YEAR 3.

If you wish you'd invested in the Fund in February 1983, it's not too late to join in 1985. You can invest any amount of £2,000 or more. Do so now, and we'll give you a special bonus normally only available to larger investors. For all investors, to £2,000 invested before 5th April 1985 we'll add £30 at once to the value of your purchase. And every additional thousand pounds will buy £1,015. But don't wait. £2,000 is worth £30 more immediately, if you act NOW.

HERE'S WHAT YOU DO.

Decide how much you want to invest (in units of of £500, minimum £2,000).

Complete the application form, and send it with your cheque to Allan Ball, Commercial Union Assurance, FREEPOST, London EC5P 3BP. It doesn't even cost you a stamp. You can also telephone him on 01-283 7500 (ext 8852).

On acceptance of your application, we will issue you with your policy.

CU ASSURANCE

EMPATHY

**Empathy is a building block of morality —
for people to follow the golden rule, it helps
if they can put themselves in someone
else's shoes.**

Greater Good Science Centre

Empathy is the ability to sense other people's emotions, coupled with
the ability to imagine what someone else might be thinking or feeling.

Why is empathy important?

If we understand our audiences' real hopes, aspirations, wants, needs,
and fears, we will have far more success in motivating them to do
what we want.

Evie and me. She knows
me so well...

My youngest daughter Evie is the most empathetic person I know. It's uncanny; she can walk into the house after a few months away and instantly know how I'm feeling. A typical encounter would be as follows:

Evie: (*despite my smile, detects low mood*) "You're feeling sad Dad, why?"

Me: (*defensively*) "No, all good."

Evie: (*not convinced*) "Sure?"

Me: (*insistent, but reveal something in voice*) "I'm fine honestly."

Evie: (*knows something is up*) "Everton lose?"

Me: (*concedes*) "Yup."

Evie: (*smiles, gives me a hug*) "Knew it."

Evie is not a marketer, but with her uncanny sixth sense, she would make a bloody good one.

Possessing emotional empathy is a crucial component of being an effective marketer. Understanding how others are feeling gives you the ability to create messaging that feels more relevant and targeted. The greater the empathy you can show with your target audience, the more they will be drawn to engage with you. The following case study shows how easily even professionals can ignore this fundamental marketing principle.

In the 1990s, Brainstorm Publishing produced an annual supplement called 'Presentations', which offered direct marketing agencies the opportunity to advertise themselves to potential clients. Each agency was given a double-page spread – one page to list their people, media split, and clients, the other to showcase their creativity.

I was given the task of producing something for Chapter One, my agency at the time, and looked forward to showcasing our fantastic track record in achieving results. To help shape my thinking, I thought it wise to have a look at the previous year's supplement. I'm glad I did. It revealed that instead of offering new insight into their services and what they might offer prospective new clients, most agencies had chosen a different path.

The entire publication was clogged with, as one of our creative team referred to it, 'wafflewank'. A fifty-page supplement stuffed full of self-satisfied drivel, delivered with a level of insincerity guaranteed to choke every emotional impulse except mistrust and despair. Wading through it would have been akin to being stuck with the party bore, someone keen to talk about how great they were, but with scant interest in you. Rather than showing empathy with their audience, all the agencies had done was alienate them.

WAFFLEWANK [WOH-FULL-WAN-KUH] *NOUN.*
TALKING ABOUT ONESELF INCESSANTLY, WITH LITTLE REGARD FOR THE AUDIENCE.

'If you prefer to deal with people with a realistic attitude to business, we will be delighted to welcome you as one of the four new clients we shall take on this year.'

Amherst Direct

'You won't be able to categorise us as either traditional or new wave. No such limited description can satisfactorily describe our delivery.'

DDM Advertising

'What a pity most agencies don't have such style. We are constantly questioning, evaluating, and honing our craft.'

DDM

'The star in our logo isn't just a striking piece of design. It's there to emphasise our credo – together we can be the winning stars of your marketplace.'

RSCG

'It is new ground. It is a way of thinking – one that results from a unique mix of conviction and calculated experimentation.'

DMB&B Direct

'Our growth has been extremely heartening, but we're looking to expand. We'd like to sink our teeth into some food. A good drink would also go down well. And heaven only knows how long we can manage without a deodorant.'

Sutch Webster WMGO Direct

To avoid this gluttonous fate, we produced an idea which we felt would tap into the authentic needs of the readership. We wanted to show that we appreciated the concerns of the marketers we served, that we understood what they required from their next agency partner: less bullshit, more delivery.

Clients aren't really interested in how agencies do things; they don't care whether we are 'new wave or traditional' or that we are 'constantly honing our craft'; they just want to know if we can bring them the success their last agency couldn't. So we chose to show them the prize at the end of the Chapter One rainbow – the money we would make for them.

Playing the empathy card paid off. The concept helped the agency win two substantial pieces of business and picked up an award for best agency ad of the year.

LOADS OF LOVELY LOLLY.

(ISN'T THAT REALLY WHAT YOU WANT FROM YOUR NEXT DIRECT MARKETING AGENCY?)

Cash, dosh or dough; loot, lolly or filthy lucre. Call it what you will but money is what you really want.

Grand strategies and dazzling creative work are all very well but they're all worthless if they don't bring in the profit.

And pots, heaps and piles of money are the kinds of rewards our clients reap when they invest their Direct Marketing budget with us.

In 1991 clients of ours were repaid with paybacks as high as 123:1, 88:1 and 77:1.

So you won't be surprised to learn that Chapter One won all three cost-effectiveness prizes at the BDMA awards. In fact no other agency even had a finalist.

So, if you want to turn your hard-earned readies into even bigger bags of booty ring Morgan Edwards or Trevor Rodgers on 0684-850040. Or write to Chapter One Direct plc, Green Lane, Tewkesbury, Glos. GL20 8EZ.

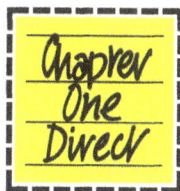

Chapter One Direct

EUROPE'S TOP CREATIVE AGENCY 1988/1989/1990/1991

% BDMA AWARD WINNERS 1984, 1985, 1986, 1987, 1988, 1989, 1990, 1991.

dma DMA AWARD WINNERS 1988, 1990, 1991.

EDMA AWARD WINNERS 1985, 1986, 1987, 1988, 1989, 1990, 1991.

Empathy is a building block of morality. For charities aiming to create a rapport and affinity with their audience, it is a particularly important keystone in any meaningful supporter relationship. With thousands of good causes jostling for the same emotional space in people's heads, that is easier said than done.

You can't expect empathy simply by including a needful image or writing anguish-laced copy starting with the phrase 'Imagine if you...' It requires true creativity to stand out.

The following campaign for Help the Aged is a good example.

The idea of elderly people in our country dying from the cold is, to say the least, appalling, yet every year thousands of pensioners struggling in poverty lose their lives due to cold-related conditions. We felt we had to raise awareness of the issue to help combat the problem.

While exploring ideas in a client workshop, one of their team (a young lad who hadn't said a word for the previous two hours) stood up and sheepishly stuck a yellow Post-it note on the wall. It contained three words: **HEAT OR EAT**.

Immediately loving it, I asked if he had just thought of the phrase. No, he said, people in the Help the Aged office had been using it for months.

Whoever originally came up with it will probably never be known, but it was genius, framing the issue in a fresh and totally relatable way. 'Heat or Eat' ran successfully for several years, its abiding strength being that it made people truly imagine what it must be like to face the frightening choice between being cold or going hungry. It transported them to a place where they could instantly empathise with the beneficiary of their donation, normally a pre-requisite for all successful campaigns since fundraising began.

The DRTV ad was one of the simplest and inexpensive we had ever produced. Involving just the use of a single room and one actor. With a concept this clear, it didn't need anything more.

Script from Help The Aged DRTV ad

Every winter in Britain

Thousands of elderly people have to choose between heating and eating

They simply can't afford to do both

It means that in order to eat a simple meal, many have to turn off their heating

And risk dying of the cold in their own homes

You can help stop an elderly person dying this Winter by giving just £2 a month

Please help, we're waiting for your call

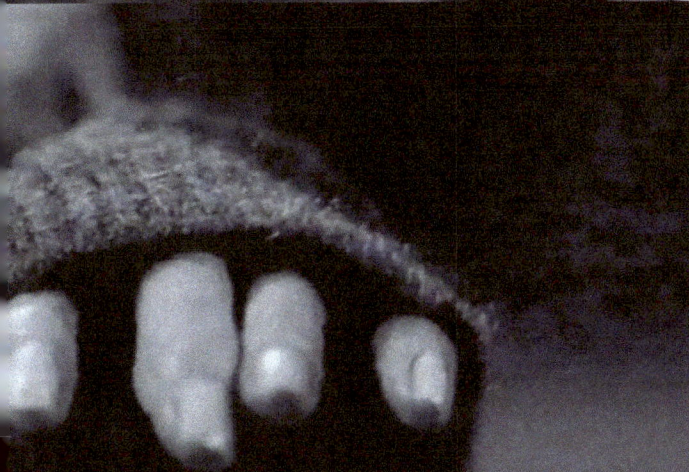

£2
a month
could save
a life

FEAR

Fear is a phoenix. You can watch it burn a thousand times and still it will return.

Leigh Bardugo

The oldest and strongest emotion of mankind is **fear**, especially fear of the unknown. Fear alerts us to the presence of danger or threat of harm. Fear can trigger an emotional response so powerful it can overcome even the strongest parts of our intelligence.

Why is fear important?

What people want most is an antidote for their fears – and invariably that is action. Good causes especially can provide an outlet to help people feel better by offering ways to overcome the most anxiety-inducing of ills, scariest of climate challenges, dreaded of diseases, and most evil of social injustices.

This ad we produced for WCRF alerted women to the prevalence of breast cancer and a proactive way of reducing their risk.

Growing up, I was an avid reader of comics, especially those featuring Batman and Spiderman. The tall buildings they leapt and the mean streets they tamed were all part of the impossibly glamorous faraway land called America. One day, I promised my young self, I would see it up close.

I finally got my chance in my mid-twenties when my boss, David Strickland-Eales, told me to get on a plane to Washington to meet the directors of a potential new client. The World Cancer Research Fund (WCRF) had developed a new proposition for the cancer market, one built on the premise that anyone could substantially reduce their risk of the disease by modifying their lifestyle. Conceived after medical studies showed that 35% of all cancer deaths could be attributed to poor diet and lack of exercise, WCRF had enjoyed sensational growth in their home market. Now they wanted to see if they could establish a foothold in Europe, hence the meeting with yours truly.

Travelling the short distance from my hotel in downtown Washington to their offices uptown, the boy in me marvelled at the size of everything; the roads, the trains, the cars, the buildings, the people. They were all enormous. This was the epitome of all-you-can-eat living, first-world gluttony on an epic scale. Even with my rose-

Are you killing your kids with kindness?

tinted eyes, it was plain to see they had an obesity problem, possibly explaining why WCRF's idea was doing so well. The charity's colonnaded head office was supersized too, with a car park full of gleaming, open-top Mercedes sports cars.

Their blond-haired, charismatic leader Marilyn Gentry was energetic, welcoming, and open-minded. She had personally contacted the agency (Chapter One) because we were recognised as the leading fundraising agency working with European non-profits. From the very first moment we met, we got on like the proverbial house on fire. She was the perfect client, sure in her proposition but willing to give us room to interpret it in our own way for new markets.

Postscript: Marilyn Gentry is now President of the American Institute of Cancer Research and the WCRF global network.

We all know someone who has been directly affected by cancer, so the disease is an emotionally loaded subject. Bearing this in mind, our launch strategy centred on targeting parents with a primary message suggesting that some foods they may be feeding their children could, in the long term, be putting them at risk. Alongside a low-key call for donations, we offered respondents a free guide to reducing their cancer risk.

The 'fear meets antidote' approach helped deliver staggering results, establishing a viable new territory for the charity's work within weeks. The campaign clearly demonstrated that (when applied sensitively) fear can be one of the strongest emotional motivators for action; when combined with the potent and visceral love of a parent for its child, it can be irresistible.

To mitigate the potential negative perception of this and subsequent approaches, like the example on page 61, we developed an empowering strapline to run alongside all the advertising, which is still being used by the charity today:

STOPPING CANCER BEFORE IT STARTS

You're Scum.

You're Filth.
You're Worthless.

How do you make someone feel the dread experienced by a person who has just been arrested simply because of the views they hold? This insert we produced for Amnesty shows how it can be done. The cover screams out the first threat and when the reader ventures inside, they are hit with another.

It might seem counter-productive to insult your readership; here the tactic worked because it was pertinent to the story we were telling. The copy in the middle of the piece explained all.

'They say that words can never hurt you, but when those words are accompanied by beatings, electric shocks, hammer blows, rape... they can become even more painful. Because they start to ring true. Maybe your life is worth nothing. Maybe nobody cares. Maybe you have been forgotten. Thousands of people around the world live with this daily fear.'

Far from being turned off by the creative approach, it was one of Amnesty's highest performing recruitment campaigns.

55

GRATITUDE

Gratitude is not only the greatest of virtues, but the parent of all others.

Marcus Tullius Cicero

Gratitude is a positive emotion associated with several mental and physical health benefits. Gratitude is being thankful for what we have (as opposed to focusing on what we don't have) and acknowledging the goodness in our lives. In the process, we usually recognise that the source of that goodness lies at least partially outside ourselves.

Why is gratitude important?

Being grateful helps people connect to something larger than themselves as individuals – whether to other people, nature, or a higher power.

When we experience gratitude, we respond with feelings of kindness, warmth, and other forms of generosity.

Thank you for making **THE HEROES PROMISE**

"A PROMISE IS SOMETHING VERY SIMPLE, BUT VERY POWERFUL."

Living in an affluent, law-abiding country, we Brits have a lot to be grateful for. I count my blessings every day. Working in the non-profit sector I have heard first-hand what it means to live in grinding poverty, to grow crops on land with no water, to attempt sleep with bombs dropping all around, to be fearful of being swept away by a flood.

According to CAF's (Charities Aid Foundation) 2022 report, the UK is 7th in the list of most charitable countries in the world. With the second highest donation rate (after Myanmar), a helping strangers rate of 60% (8th overall), and a volunteering rate of 30% (24th), the nation has a long philanthropic tradition stretching back to Tudor times. It's reassuring to see that it remains strong.

There but for the grace of God go I. It is accepted that guilt and gratitude are powerful unseen motivators behind much charitable giving. We realise our good fortune in not being in the same situation as others less fortunate; this triggers sympathy and compassion, and in turn compels us to help.

When this equation is combined with a sense of duty and the desire to right a wrong, the urge to give is especially potent. This was the case for one of the most extraordinary fundraising phenomena of the past 25 years, Help for Heroes. Formed in 2007 by Bryn and Emma Parry; it was a reaction

I MADE A PROMISE TO YOU.

WILL YOU MAKE ONE TO ME?

to what they perceived to be a lack of specialist provision for injured servicemen and women returning from Afghanistan. In just two years, thanks to brilliant publicity (and enormous support from The Sun and The Sunday Times) they raised £35 million and were able to open four specialist recovery centres across the country.

It was an amazing success story, but with the eventual scaling down of military operations in Afghanistan, the charity's public profile dipped, and with it, their income. So in 2018, we were asked to support their first direct marketing-led fundraising drive.

Our first campaign 'Promise', made recipients aware of the gratitude we should feel for the sacrifices our armed forces continue to make to preserve our peace.

Showing gratitude costs nothing. For all charities, appearing energised, eager to please, and hugely grateful for all gifts should be natural things to convey, especially when corresponding with people they rely on for their existence – their donors. Sadly, this is not always the case. As part of a mystery shopper exercise on legacy marketing and responsiveness, we contacted several leading charities for information on leaving a bequest to see who were the keenest. The results were mixed: one answered in 24 hours, most took around a week, three took longer than a fortnight, and two ignored us. Most sent a booklet, a short letter, and little else.

The best response came from The Salvation Army, which included this letter from the marvellous Margaret Meldrum.

Dear Mr Webster,

Thank you for your recent enquiry, I am happy to be in touch with you. It is very much appreciated that your Mother is considering including a bequest to The Salvation Army in her Will and I would like to thank you for taking the time to get the information necessary so far.

Your Mother's interest in our work and the desire to support through making a bequest is greatly appreciated and I hope the enclosed pack will be useful to you and also her solicitor or Will writer.

Part of the privilege of my job is not only to pass on information about making a bequest to The Salvation Army but also to keep in touch with friends who support in this way, and it would be lovely if your Mother so desired, to meet her personally when I am visiting in the Cheltenham area.

I can be contacted by email or my mobile should you wish to speak with me. Thank you again for getting in touch with us and if I can be further assistance please do not hesitate to give me a call.

With many thanks and God bless.

Margaret comes across as genuinely humble and, better still, very, very grateful.

She voices her thanks and appreciation no less than eight times. She is happy, privileged even, to deal with the request. It's a masterclass in gratitude.

Now compare her letter to this response from a leading medical charity, received after a glacial three weeks.

Dear Mr Webster,

Regarding your enquiry regarding leaving a gift in your mother's Will.

Find the enclosed booklet which offers some information and guidance on the process.

If you require any further information, please do not hesitate to contact our department again.

The letter was unsigned.

In 2019 The Salvation Army received over £60 million in legacy income, the medical charity just £8 million.

HAPPINESS

The happiest people are not those getting more, but those giving more.

H. Jackson Brown

Happiness is a state of emotional well-being we experience when good things happen in a specific moment, or more broadly, as a positive evaluation of one's life and well-being.

Happiness is characterised by feelings of joy, contentment, and fulfilment.

Why is happiness important?

Happiness has been shown to predict positive emotions and actions. When we are happy with a brand or cause, we stay with them. Happy people are more inclined to share their good fortune and give more generously.

This is not rocket science; happiness is an *included and appreciated donor.*

Although fundraising is essentially about laying bare the world's woes, inadequacies, and injustices and asking others to make it better, it is important for a charity to keep a warm, contented glow going among their supporter base.

Normally the best way to achieve this is by conveying lots of love and employing a little surprise and delight. The most successful non-profits routinely engineer these qualities into their communications to keep the goodwill going. I am a big fan of New York based **Charity: Water**, who are excellent in this regard. It keeps supporters in a happy place with such goodies as on-the-spot live feeds of new well drills or heart-warming films of the moment a remote village receives clean water for the first time.

We have endeavoured to create similar feel good moments for supporters to help cement loyalty. While sometimes a client may baulk at the cost of these 'donor love' activities, in my experience they are always well received and invariably result in increased giving.

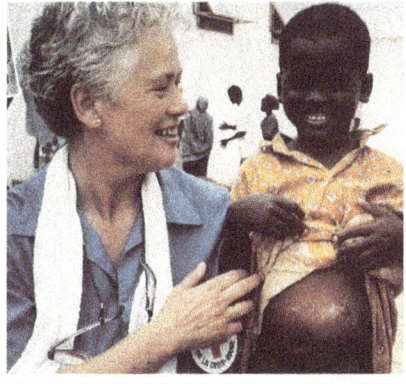

We regularly gave high-value British Red Cross donors the chance to visit overseas projects or opportunities to meet a royal at a House of Commons reception. Both offers were always heavily oversubscribed.

At the lower end, we always updated donors on projects they had supported; especially popular were detailed outcomes from their Tracing service, a brilliant resource that helps reunite families separated by conflict or disaster. Even though we could rarely show the individuals themselves, their heart-warming stories were especially well received. Here, my Dad and I stand in to illustrate a story of a father and son separated by the conflict in former Yugoslavia and reunited after ten years apart.

Left: Dad and I show 'our happy' for the British Red Cross.

O happy day: Ypres, Belgium. 11 November, 2008.

10th JULY 2005

John Hawthornthwaite, National Chairman

After every major anniversary campaign we produced for the British Legion, we ensured the happy results were relayed back to each participating supporter, along with personal messages from veterans and current serving personnel.

Legion supporters loved to receive pictures of the incredible displays they helped to create. Especially memorable were the 65,000 message flags that adorned Nelson's Column in Trafalgar Square in London for the 60th anniversary of D-Day (*shown above*) and the over 100,000 poppies, each containing personal messages of thanks, in Ypres, Belgium to commemorate the 90th anniversary of World War One (*shown on previous page*).

For pet charity Wood Green, we produced numerous short films; showing how they were helping abandoned cats and dogs find new, loving homes. These good news stories would be sent to their animal-loving supporters at regular intervals, keeping them constantly appraised of the importance of their contribution and the impact they were having.

Under-promising and over-delivering works. As in life, doing something nice without always asking for something in return can be very uplifting. Engineering surprise, inspiring wonder and connection, ensures donors are happier and, crucially, happy to give.

In need of a lift? The BBC's enormously popular Repair Shop is the place to turn to. Sentimental, kind-hearted and packed with lots of happy outcomes. It represents what most people want from a good cause.

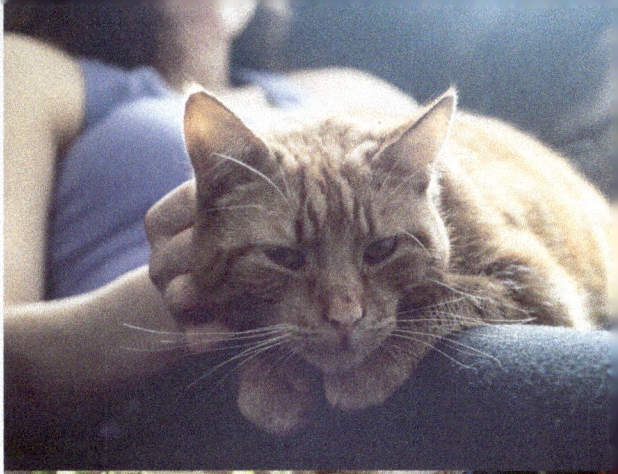

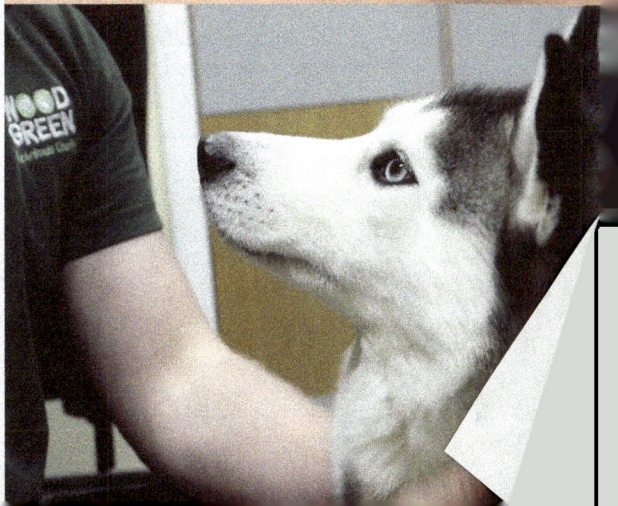

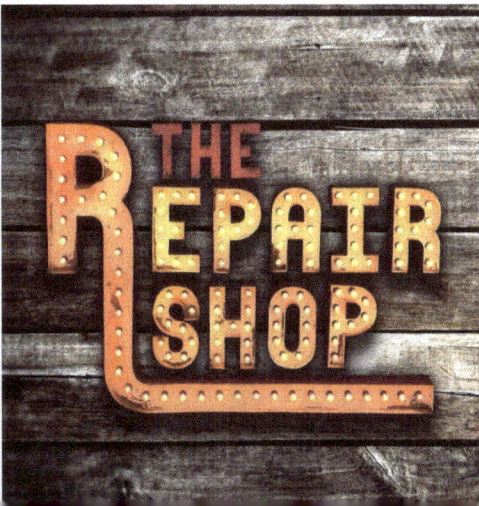

HOPE

Hope is the thing with feathers that perches in the soul and sings the tune without the words and never stops at all.

Emily Dickinson

Hope is perhaps the greatest form of optimism and pushes us forward. When things don't go as planned, hope is our belief that things will get better. Hope makes us feel more optimistic, confident, and in control.

Why is hope important?

Hope is a way of thinking that propels us to take steps to create a better tomorrow. Research has found that when people have hope, they're more likely to take the action needed to bring their goals to fruition.

At the opposite end of the scale, hopelessness is a feeling of despair that life can never get better.

Hope for the future. For Stroke Association, we have found it is the one thing above all else, that donors want to hear about.

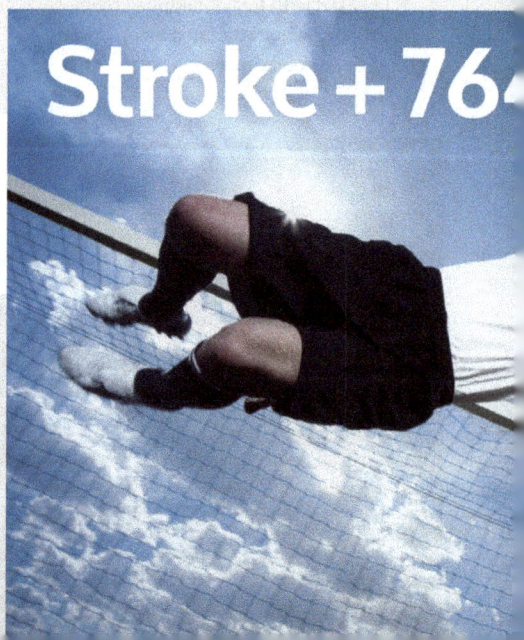

Stroke + 76

My first day at infants' school at just five years of age was a horror show. Traumatised by my mother abandoning me at the iron gates of the red-bricked Victorian building, I spent most of the day trying to hide. Halfway through the afternoon, it reached a low point and, thus far, the biggest humiliation of my young life. Sitting in class after a liquid lunch (a quarter pint of milk and an orange juice from memory), my undersized bladder was protesting. Unsure of how to get the teacher's attention to be excused, I started to panic. This had never happened before. At home it was easy. I didn't need anyone's permission.

I tried dropping my pencil on the floor – not a flicker from the demi-god at the front of the room. Mr Morse was too busy chalking up the two times table. Next, my exercise book was thrown down onto the parquet flooring, landing with a thwack.

Surely that would do the trick? But still nothing from the balding teacher in the herringbone jacket with leather elbow patches. Squirming in my agony, I started to whimper then sob. Finally, he turned. I stood ready to speak; alas the movement was enough to dissolve any control I had over my urethral sphincter. It wasn't my finest hour. The harrowing event triggered months of bedwetting, thoroughly perplexing my parents. Their five-year-old son had regressed from happy, carefree 'dry' child into incontinent, nervy wreck. Worse, back in the early 1960s, there was no support nor even much sympathy from the medical profession; Mum and Dad were simply told 'he will grow out of it.'

Today, bedwetting (now referred to as nocturnal enuresis) is known to affect around half a million children and teenagers in the UK. Despite its recognition as a significant condition, it remains a problem many families find difficult to talk about openly. It can take a toll on family life and ruin a young person's self-esteem and emotional well-being.

More encouraging is that there is an organisation that can offer support – ERIC, the children's bowel and bladder charity. By chance, I met their chief executive, Jenny Perez at a conference and over a coffee she talked me through her challenges. *'Our biggest barrier is projecting a positive message to encourage people to get in touch. Parents get beaten down by the perceived humiliation and choose to go through it alone. They develop a kind of bunker mentality. We want to be here for everyone going through this.'*

Inspired by Jenny's vision and with my own experience of the problem, I agreed to help gratis. To give some insight into how ERIC can help, she put me in touch with parents they had supported, many of whom had struggled for years before seeking help. One mother told me how her teenage son had been driven to attempt suicide because of the isolation he endured. A tearful father told me how his son's 'shame' had made him bunk off school for months. It was heartbreaking to hear, and clear evidence that showing families the merits of coming forward sooner should be our priority.

We drew inspiration from ten-year-old Ben, whose young life had been blighted by severe bullying because of his bedwetting. Thanks to the support of ERIC, he was enjoying a normal happy life once again. Ben was so grateful he wanted to help others going through the same challenges. His positivity and optimism formed the cornerstones of our idea – that bedwetting can be beaten and that young people can be the hero in their own story.

'Dry and Mighty' and 'Banish the Wee Horror' helped get a new message out to families, those working with children, and other health professionals – the message that they can feel hopeful about the future. The campaigns, timed to coincide with a Radio 4 appeal, increased helpline calls by 25% and helpline contacts by 31%. They also significantly raised ERIC's media profile, resulting in 37 separate pieces of coverage, three national radio interviews, and a national reach of over 10 million. The work was also recognised with a Third Sector excellence gold award for innovation.

BANISH THE WEE HORROR
Call 0845 370 8008

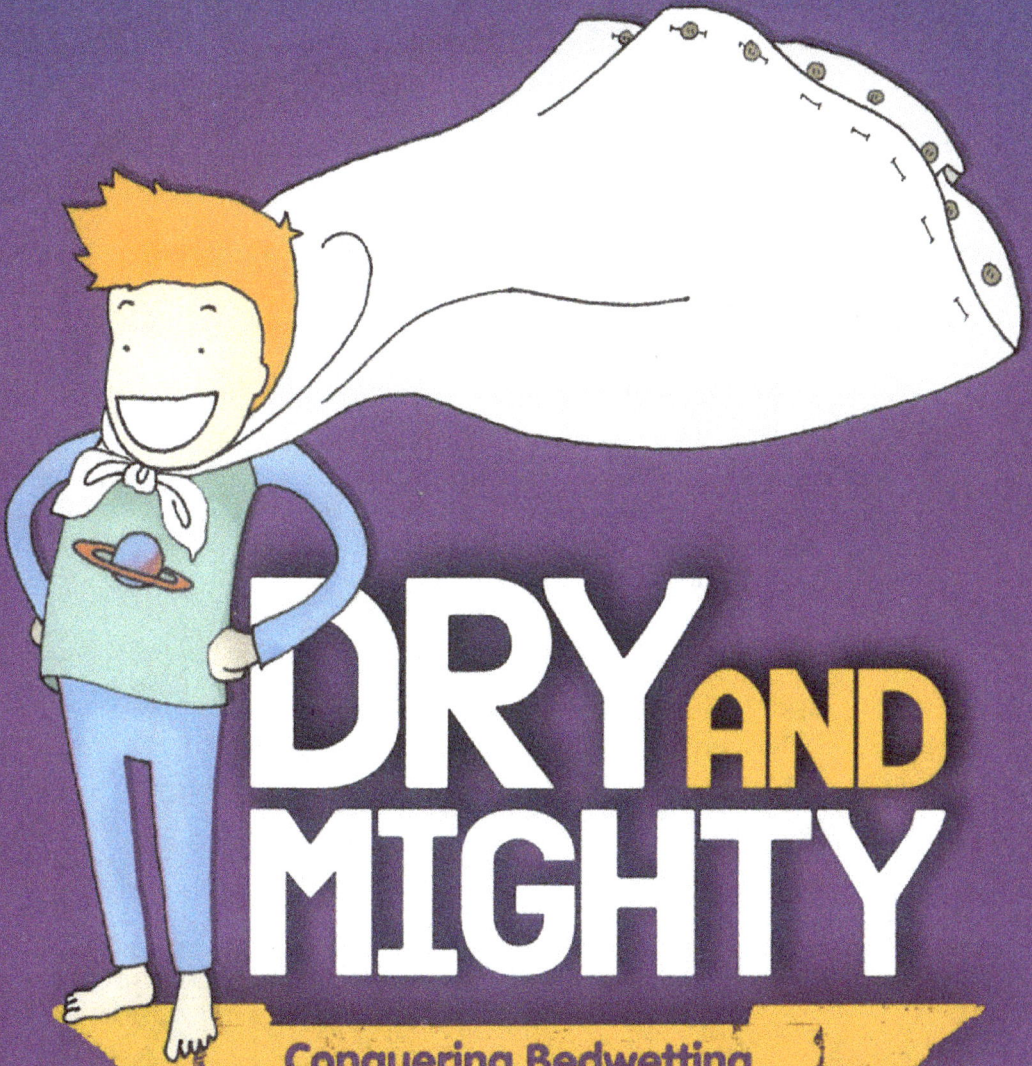

DRY AND MIGHTY

Conquering Bedwetting

INSPIRATION

Inspiration and motivation may come from others, but true inspiration comes from within.

Catherine Pulsifer

Be it through art, music, nature, film, or sports, **inspiration** can be found in anything, anywhere, anytime. Inspiration as a result of witnessing something that moves you deeply, can lead to increased focus and greater motivation.

Why is inspiration important?

When inspired, people experience a sense of certainty and clarity. Inspiration is likely to cause them to take some purposeful action and motivate them to do something new.

Peter Townsend, guitarist and principal songwriter of The Who. A massive inspiration for me. He showed how will power, hard work and talent can overcome any obstacle.

Similar to ERIC, another instance that showed how a positive outlook can shed new hope, optimism and inspiration on what might previously be seen as insurmountable problems was a campaign we produced for Victim Support.

Many crimes such as theft, fraud and assault can affect people for years, especially if they have occurred in the home. Victim Support offers free advice to those who have suffered from such traumatic incidents. We were asked by the charity to help encourage more victims of crime to seek its support. Our concept used inspirational stories of people who had found the resilience to recover and lead normal lives again.

The story of Ted and Winifred from Yorkshire was especially memorable. Walking back from an evening ballroom dancing class, a thick-set man, face hidden by a black balaclava, confronted the couple with a knife and demanded money. When Ted refused, he was savagely beaten. The assault only stopped when, after hearing the noise, a neighbour came out of his house with his two large two Dobermans and the man fled.

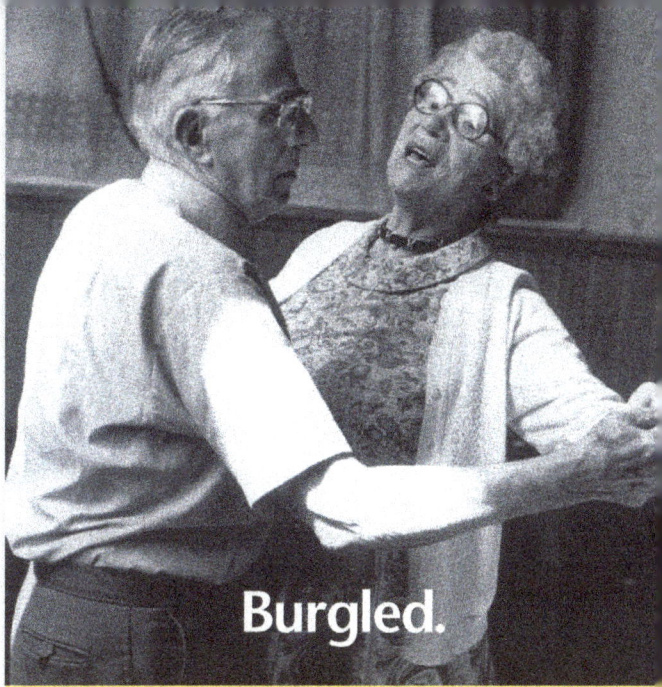

Burgled.

(but not broken.)

Last year in Gloucestershire we helped 49,000 people conquer the effects of crime.

Please help us do even more this year.

Victim Support   0800 000 000

Thanks to sympathetic medical care and the excellent counselling they received from Victim Support, the stoic couple eventually felt well enough to continue with their passion for the Foxtrot and Viennese Waltz. Their account, along with other similar inspirational stories of triumphing over adversity, provided new awareness of Victim Support's work, encouraging more people to come forward to seek its advice.

JOY

I don't think of all the misery, but of the beauty that still remains.

Anne Frank

Joy is a momentary emotional response that arises when something positive has happened to you or to someone important to you. Joy is the emotion associated with feelings of elation and happiness. It makes life worth living.

Why is joy important?

The benefits are extraordinary. The feeling of joy helps people know what's important to them and makes them seek more of it. Make your brand a joy bringer and people will seek you out too.

Although all fundraising should present a clear and immediate need for money, that doesn't mean the message has to be downbeat. In periods of uncertainty (at the time of writing, this has been caused by the Ukrainian war and economic recession) people generally want to engage with things that make them feel better. It is during these gloomy moments that more joyful marketing can really hit the spot, as was the case for campaigns we produced for RNIB and UNICEF.

RNIB's Talking Books do something magical. They bring stories to life for blind and partially sighted children and adults. However, only a fraction of new titles are available in audible format, meaning thousands of wonderful books are out of reach.

We wanted to inspire RNIB supporters to fund new recorded stories and so developed a concept that engaged them through a key feature of the service itself – the joy of storytelling.

To achieve this, we needed a central character to provide an emotional heart and represent the beneficiary group. We eventually found Lily-Grace, a nine-year-old young service user. Blind since birth, she adored stories. Our idea put her on a fantastical quest to track down a Talking Book

she wanted more than any other, the classic tale of *The Nutcracker*. Using a colourful, storybook format for the direct mail appeal, we portrayed Lily-Grace as an intrepid explorer, pluckily searching for stories and characters that would fire her imagination.

To add an extra dimension, we also brought her journey to life in an animated digital film, along with a video of her discussing her love of Talking Books with her mum. We also gave supporters the opportunity to vote for a favourite story of their own which they felt should be recorded.

How did it all end? Very joyfully, with RNIB's best ever results. A core channel ROI of 3.70:1 was achieved, 17,000 voting forms were returned,

Lily-Grace was the perfect heroine, both in the real world and the imagined.

and social activity reached 342,450 individuals. The films were viewed over 70,000 times. This meant that 25 new Talking Books titles could be made available for the very first time, including *The Nutcracker*.

The second slice of joy came through our work with UNICEF.

Over many years, the humanitarian aid charity had developed a successful formula for TV fundraising. This generally entailed running a country-specific urgent appeal, utilising powerful authentic images, and incorporating dialogue delivered (to camera) by an A-list celebrity such as Ewan McGregor, Olivia Colman, or Sir Andy Murray.

Wanting to explore alternative approaches to expand responder profiles, they developed a subscription product to showcase their work in a new way – Paddington's Postcards. For £8 a month, subscribers would receive postcards from Paddington Bear sent from UNICEF projects around the world. Designed to be fun, engaging, and educational, the product would

still convey the depth and value of the charity's life-saving work.

We were asked to develop the concept for DRTV, using the unique personality of the world's favourite bear to recruit a new type of audience for the charity. Primarily aimed at parents, the script gave us the opportunity to explore joyful adjectives rarely seen or heard in the fundraising sector.

Despite the constraints of filming through the pandemic, we managed to produce two different commercials. They proved to be UNICEF's best performing of the year and continue to do good business. Joy indeed.

Paddington's Postcards 60 second script

Paddington Bear loves hearing about the world through his friends at UNICEF... now he'd love to show your child all the wonders they have shown him.

This is a wonderful way to help your child explore the world and see how other children live.

They will see such wonders as the amazing Pygmy Hippos and the city of Petra.

Imagine their delight when one of Paddington's adventures drops through the letterbox – just for them!

Start your child's adventure today.

Greetings from **BANGLADESH**

Banglade

LONDON

WAY D ON VOYAGE

DELIVERED BY **2** ROYAL MAIL

123 Humble Home

Fern Road

Bushy Way

Porthill

EE11 2AS

FOR EVERY CHILD unicef

HOW TO USE OUR TRAVEL JOURNAL

UNITED KINGDOM

MUM DAD

BROTHER

LOVE

Love is bigger than anything in its way.

U2

When it comes to positive emotions, there is none more powerful than **love**. Our brains have been wired to seek affection and love. When we experience it, we feel connected and elated.

Why is love important?

Love is usually accompanied by the most intense emotions, particularly around protecting loved ones. Many people give to good causes to help make the world a safer place for their children and grandchildren. Under the spell of love, we will do almost anything; risk our lives, commit heinous crimes, or even go to war.

We produced multiple campaigns for the Remember a Charity consortium to keep the message fresh. This is one of my favourites, what better reason do you need to leave a gift in your Will?

Keep the love alive

IT'S WHAT YOU DO THAT MATTERS

THE SALVATION ARMY

Giving is loving.

While altruism can involve the assuaging of guilt (*for one's good fortune*); self-interest (*curing cancer, slowing climate change*); inheritance (*leaving behind a better world*); nostalgia (*yearning to create a better, bygone age*); ending a tyranny (*child cruelty, torture of political prisoners*); and a host of other motivations, it always has an element of love.

Humans have need for intellectual communion, but we all harbour a much deeper wish – to ***love and be loved***.

Above:

Work we created for the Army's Red Shield appeal illustrated its unique, hands on approach.

I can cite three clear examples where I believe love itself was the prime driver to give.

One of the best known 'loving organisations' in the non-profit sector is The Salvation Army. It holds a special place in the hearts of millions as the embodiment of goodness, kindness, and selflessness. During our twenty-year fundraising relationship, it always actively encouraged us to highlight

GOODNESS
LOVE FAMILY HOPE TRUST
SACRIFICE
FAITH CARE FRIENDSHIP
COMMITMENT

the loving values and beliefs that drive its work.

Several times, I observed this first-hand, accompanying its officers as they brought comfort to the poor, the elderly, the homeless, and the lonely, throughout the UK. Thousands of people forsaken by society knew they could rely on the tireless benevolence of The Salvation Army.

This remarkable 150-year-old charity believes passionately that no one is beyond hope, that everyone deserves the chance to be happy and should be recognised and valued. Its proposition to those who supported it was always the same:

Your love can put our beliefs into action.

For one hugely successful appeal we produced, these beliefs became the concept itself.

We wrote them large on the envelope and continued the theme inside. The focus of the appeal was about helping those in need, but equally important,

For the love of God

Put us where we need to be this Christmas

THE SALVATION ARMY

(leaflet text, partially visible):

...le need our love,
...there

...happy people this Christmas,
...ll be their only friend. That's why,
...less, we need to offer them food,
...re older people are all alone, we
...Where children suffer neglect and
...tect them. Please put us where we
...g your Christmas donation today.

...e a Christmas box to a family in need,
...food and a modest gift for each child.

...or five lonely older people to enjoy a
...ristmas dinner and friendship at a
...Army community centre.

...vide 24 hours of care, protection and love
...ld in a Salvation Army residential home
...dren who have nowhere else to go.

£63 ...ovide a homeless person with one week in a
Salvation Army centre, and a hot breakfast - which
could be the first step towards keeping them off the
streets for good.

£72 will pay for a 'meal run' giving hot soup and
sandwiches to people sleeping rough on a cold
winter night

£250 will keep a Salvation Army drop-in centre open
over the Christmas period.

Yes, here is my Christmas gift for people in need.

In order for us to process your donation efficiently please complete your details below.

Title (Mr, Mrs, Miss, Ms)   Name
Address   Postcode

Here is my gift of: £19 £28 £45 £63 £72 £250

I prefer to give: £

Make your credit card gift by calling

0800 389 8282
Lines open 24 hours

Please make your cheque/postal order payable to The Salvation Army or fill in your credit/debit card
details below.

Credit/Debit/CAF Card No. (We are unable to accept AmEx or Diners Club cards.)

Start date   Expiry date   Maestro Issue No.   Security code*

Signed   Date

giftaid it Tick here if you would like us to send you details about Gift
Aid to increase the value of your donation by almost a third.

Please return this form with your donation to The Salvation Army 201,
FREEPOST NAT21852, REIGATE RH12 0BR.

thank you!

---

it was about preserving age-old values such as love, faith, sacrifice and family.

By responding so enthusiastically, supporters indicated that in troubled, self-seeking times, these values were more important than ever.

When you love as selflessly and freely as The Salvation Army does, people are inevitably drawn to you.

With this simple insert (above), we proved that even in our largely secular society, people will still give for love in a religious context. This four-page insert has performed fantastically well for years on the strength of a very simple and heartfelt proposition.

The Salvation Army's reward for all the loving? A huge supporter base of loyal supporters and a scale of fundraising success which remains the envy of the sector. During our long association, we regularly made a profit from recruitment activity with supporter campaigns consistently achieving an 8:1 return on investment.

As fundraising ideas go, child sponsorship is genius. It combines two elements that supporters absolutely adore: tangibility and emotional connection. World Vision has utilised it brilliantly over the past 70 years to become one of the largest charities in the world. Today, it operates in nearly 100 countries.

But as with any successful idea, it has to find new markets to keep growing. Research we conducted for another child sponsorship specialist, Plan International, revealed that while the monthly giving product enjoyed general appeal, it was liked by different cohorts for distinctly different reasons. For example one cohort, 'active parents', used it to educate their own children about difficulties other children faced in the developing world. Another cohort, 'busy workers', rarely looked at the information they received, simply deciding that sponsorship was an effective way to help children in poverty.

A further cohort identified, but which had not been specifically targeted, was 'maternal empty nesters'. These became sponsors to assuage parental yearning. They enthusiastically engaged with all correspondence and actively supported their sponsored child's progress; demonstrating that for many parents, maternal and paternal instincts retained a lifelong gravitational pull.

I remember the feeling when my own first child Jessica was born and how in that moment, fatherhood aligned every inch of my head, heart, and gut.

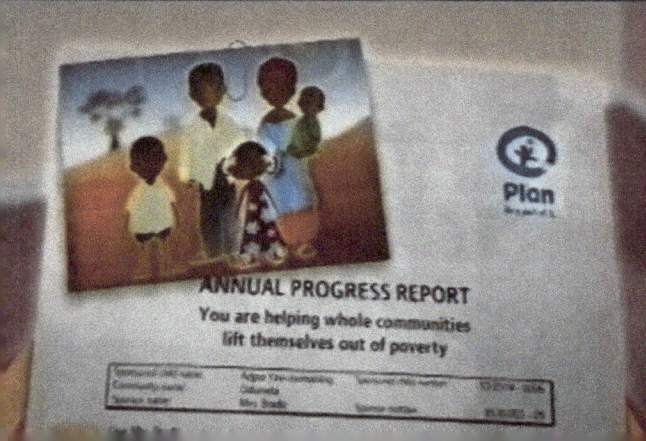

ANNUAL PROGRESS REPORT
You are helping whole communities lift themselves out of poverty

Being a parent has been described as the most beautiful emotion in the world. This feeling can be lost when the child grows and moves away, so it is only natural to try to replace this unrequited craving to love in some other way.

We felt these factors represented an excellent opportunity and created a specific proposition and DRTV concept to target empty nesters. The script empathised the strong bond the sponsor could expect, even portraying the sponsor and the child holding hands. The beautiful and sensitive animation treatment hit the maternalistic emotional bullseye perfectly and opened up a lucrative new market for the charity.

Plan International 60 second DRTV script:

If you want to get something different out of giving, feel like you're really involved,

Sponsor a child with Plan.

It's such a meaningful way to give.

Letters from your child will make you feel like you're really there – really part of it.

Thousands of Plan sponsors are experiencing this exciting way of giving.

They're seeing communities building new schools brick by brick.

Water pumps in villages where children have never drunk clean water before.

Crops being harvested so no-one will go hungry.

Become a Plan sponsor... it's a very special experience.

You'll be part of turning a child's world into a better place.

0800 282 242

NOSTALGIA

I'd trade all my tomorrows for one single yesterday.

Kris Kristofferson

Nostalgia refers to sentimental feelings that surface when you recall significant experiences and relationships of the past. It involves the cognitive process of remembering events and emotions attached to them. Often the feeling is bittersweet, recalling happy instances of a bygone age, but knowing they're gone forever.

Why is nostalgia important?

Often, nostalgia inspires positive emotions – a sense of connection and optimism. There are positive effects of being nostalgic, which include calmness, creativity, and inspiration. Retro is a theme that brands can incorporate into their marketing and strategies because the consumer market loves nostalgia.

The author as a young man. I still have those comics and that Triang jeep.

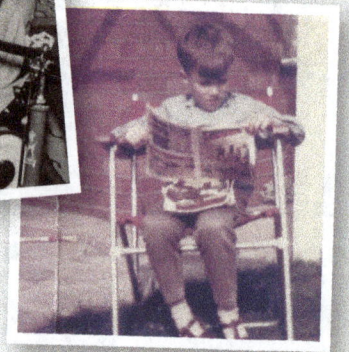

Leave it as you loved it.

As someone who is constantly looking to his past, I know nostalgia is an emotional force to be reckoned with. I have a nagging desire to return to my carefree, fun-seeking, tree-climbing, jumpers for goalposts, pre-pubescent years. To maintain an emotional bridge with this perceived golden age, I have re-purchased the toys and board games I once enjoyed and re-collected the bubble gum cards, football programmes, and comics I used to love. My study is testament to this near obsession, it is full of my *then* rather than my *now*, the eternal and unblemished 'good old days'.

Nostalgia is useful for marketers too, because it is an emotion that unifies. It can give a sense of who we are, remind us where we have been, and bring people together in common purpose to preserve what we perceived as a better time or situation.

When we researched Wildlife Trust donors to help formulate a motivating legacy proposition, we discovered that above all other considerations, people lamented the loss of nature as they remembered it. Many recalled earlier times of 'lanes lined with thick hedgerows', 'fields teeming with wildlife', and 'skies filled with birdsong'. They yearned to return to the countryside of their childhood where the spectre of climate change didn't exist.

The concept we produced reflected this powerful sentimental urge, managing to simultaneously direct people to think about past and future. Its success proved that we managed to hit the mark.

OPTIMISM

Optimism is the faith that leads to achievement.

Keller

Optimism goes beyond seeing the bright side of a situation or expecting good things. It is proactive; it is 'challenge accepted'. Optimism is feeling that a situation will have a good outcome. People who are optimistic tend to see the best in everything, despite their troubles.

Why is optimism important?

It strengthens us to try again rather than give up, allows us to keep motivated and work towards our goals. In a world cluttered with negativity, people are attracted to optimistic brands and people; creating a positive message can trigger people to commit to finding a solution. Be a source of optimism and people will follow.

The work shown is helping to create a more assured and accessible position for Practical Action.

Reg. Charity No. 247252

The pumpkin that proves

WE CAN DEFY CLIMATE CHANGE

Want to know how?
Visit practicalaction.org

Practical ACTION

If optimism can galvanise actions, pessimism can paralyse them. As I write this in 2022, there is mounting gloom around the lack of action to slow climate change. People are losing hope, which is dangerous. The world doesn't need heads in the sand, it needs clarity and new ideas. Fortunately, there are organisations that can bring these qualities forward to focus on this enormous challenge, one of which is the fabulous Practical Action.

Founded by radical economist Fritz Schumacher to help people overcome poverty and environmental challenges, it is fuelled by a belief that human ingenuity and cooperation can conquer any problem. It walks the talk too. Using brilliantly simple engineering solutions, it has helped hundreds of communities on the climate change frontline to produce food sustainably, generate reliable energy, access safe water, and build robust waste management systems.

Yet despite this impressive track record, it had been struggling to recruit donors, in part because the brand was still relatively unknown, but also because its marketing was often overly technical and verbose.

It was clear it needed to project a more confident voice and be recognised as a climate champion.

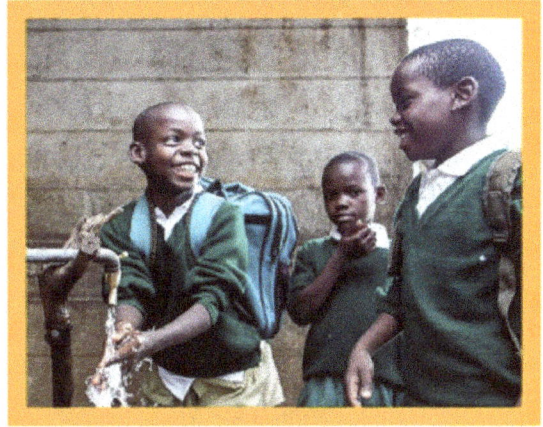

Practical Action
Sponsored · Paid for by Practical Action
ID: 698617247824164

Think it's impossible to solve the world's problems? Think again.

In an often thoughtless world,
JOIN THE THINKERS

Join the thinkers today
JOIN THE THINKERS TODAY

Learn More

Practical Action
February 14 at 20.20 ·

Derek's a man after our own hearts. Like so many of the people we help around the world, he's growing things where really nothing should grow. #impossiblegarden

PRACTICAL ACTION.ORG
The man who grows veg in his van

With such prevailing negativity around, the climate and people desperate to see someone actually doing something about it, we knew 'optimistic action' would be an attractive proposition.

Our first campaign proffered a galvanising call to action: '**Turn the tables on climate change**.' The work was punctuated with plain-speaking, eye-catching headlines, and engaging real-world storytelling.

Here are two examples:

There is an Acacia tree in Sudan growing near Eid El Beida village that shouldn't be there.

Just four years ago the land where it now sits was a lifeless desert.

Soon it will produce valuable gum arabic, so will 500 others planted alongside.

Their roots will continue to bind together and prevent soil erosion.

Practical Action is helping communities overcome climate change by planting new forests to stabilise land ravaged by changing weather.

It's just one of the ways we're helping people in poverty transform their world.

So now in Eid El Beida, where there was desert, there is green.

Where there was despair, there is hope.

Help more people turn the tables on climate change by calling 0800 000 000.

Reg. Charity No. 247257

The tree that should
NEVER HAVE GROWN

Want to know how?
Visit practicalaction.org

Practical
ACTION

For as long as people could remember in Wadi El Ku in Sudan, the rains always arrived in June.

By the time they had left in September, the wadi was lush with vegetation.

Food was plentiful. Forests part of the landscape.

Today, climate change means the rain doesn't come as much.

And when it does, it lands on hard, degraded soil – and just runs away.

Practical Action is helping farmers in Sudan to capture rain and preserve every precious drop.

Helping them reshape their land to irrigate their crops and grow food all year round.

It's just one of the ways we're helping people in poverty transform their world.

So now in Wadi El Ku, where there was desert, there is green.

Where there was sterile dirt, there is life-giving water – as far as the eye can see.

Help more people turn the tables on climate change by calling 0800 000 000.

The water that
DIDN'T RUN AWAY

Practical
ACTION

The new, positive approach worked like a charm, with the campaign beating all targets and raising over £3.46 million. It was the start of a happy run of success we had with this fantastic cause, clearly demonstrating that a cocktail of optimism, energy and great ideas, might well be all it takes to save our beautiful world.

Footnote:
*I was so exasperated by inaction on climate change that I felt moved to write a novel on the theme. It covers some radical ideas on how a future, less sentimental generation might tackle humanity's most pressing issue. **Cull 2031** is available on Amazon.*

OUTRAGE

Every normal man must be tempted, at times, to spit on his hands, hoist the black flag, and begin slitting throats.

H. L. Mencken

Outrage is an intense feeling of anger and shock. The emotion has now become a familiar part of everyday life, particularly on social media. Twitter, TikTok, and Facebook are awash with irritated indignance. Millions of people, vilifying each other for the woes of the world.

Why is outrage important?

On the surface, outrage seems like it should be an adverse, negative emotional state, but invariably it moves people to right the wrong and improve the situation.

Social media in particular, rewards shock and outrage.

I've always relished the challenge of press advertising, particularly the fundraising test, colloquially known in marketing circles as the 'twenty double', so-called because it measures just 200mm high by two columns – usually around 90mm – wide. Despite their diminutive size, they can be incredibly effective.

To be successful, the first objective of a small space press advertisement is to be seen. Not an easy task as it will sit amongst distractions such as the news of the day, features, and other advertising, so it needs an image with some wow factor. Humans respond to visual data far better than any other type of data. The human brain processes images 60,000 times faster than text, so in terms of stopping power they are hugely influential.

One of the best performing I created was for WSPA, (now World Animal Protection) supporting its campaign in Eastern Europe to free 'dancing bears'. The barbaric practice which causes great suffering raises money from tourists who pay to watch the poor animal's grotesque performance as it is pulled by a chain in its nose.

After agreeing our concept we set ourselves to finding the right image, luckily we had access to WSPA's own extensive photo library, collected from sources around the world. After a lengthy search, we finally came across a

£IO BUYS A CHAIN CUTTER

He's chained up through his sensitive nose and made to walk on **red hot** plates, whilst the back of his legs are **hit** in time to music. Onlookers **taunt** him and force him to drink beer. Why? Because they're teaching him to 'dance' for tourists who pay to watch his **agonising** waltz.

The World Society for the Protection of Animals (WSPA) rescues 'dancing bears' and takes them to sanctuaries where they can be free of pain and suffering. But we can't carry out our **life-saving work** without the support of people like <u>you</u>. **Your gift of just £10, or whatever you can afford, will help cut the chains of innocent animals.** So please send your donation <u>today</u>. He's counting on <u>you</u>.

YES, I WANT TO CUT THE CHAINS!
Please fill in your details below

Name _____

Address _____

_____ Postcode _____

Here is my donation of £_____
(Please make cheques payable to WSPA or complete the credit card details below.)
Visa/MasterCard/Switch/Eurocard/CAF CharityCard   (Please delete as applicable)

Card No. [ ][ ][ ][ ][ ][ ][ ][ ][ ][ ][ ][ ][ ][ ][ ][ ][ ][ ]
                          (If using Switch, please use the number printed in the middle of your card)

Expiry date ___/___   Switch issue no _____   Today's date ___/___

Signature _____

☐ Tick here if you would like a free information pack.
Please send this completed form and your donation to: WSPA, Dept AL355, Freepost NH2604, Northampton, NN3 6BR. No stamp is needed. THANK YOU. Reg Charity No. 282908

CALL 0990 214 214 NOW
TO MAKE AN INSTANT DONATION   WSPA World Society for the Protection of Animals

picture with the power and connection we were looking for. Putting it all together we knew we had something strong. Through a single image and five words, the execution had created an emotional bridge with the potential donor, and provided everything they needed to decide whether to engage. If they did, 120 words of supporting copy gave the details required to make a donation. In less than a minute, from possibly not knowing anything about dancing bears, a donor could be reaching for their credit cards. This particular ad ran successfully in the UK and many other WSPA territories overseas for several years.

A 2009 research study conducted by three US universities entitled 'Charitable organisations' storytelling influence on donors' emotions and intentions' called it a 'perfect piece of communication for the genre'. They described it as follows:

The viewer initially responds to the bear with the chain pulling painfully at its face, the image made more visceral because the animal is looking directly at the camera. This immediately provokes negative emotions – outrage and anger.

Next, the viewer registers the headline and proposition and these feelings convert into anticipated positive emotions when they are given the opportunity to help the animal in need. In this instance, they can free the bear for a specified amount of money.

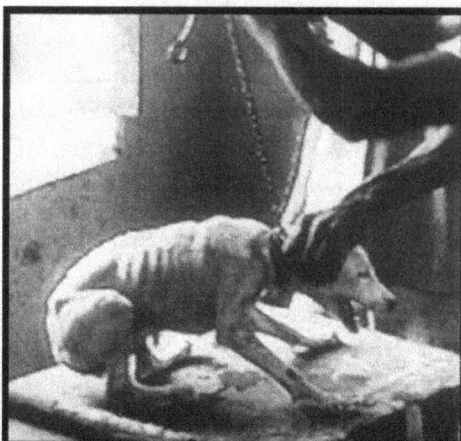

PREPARE TO BE SHOCKED.

A minute after this photo was taken, the dog was beaten, soaked with water and electrocuted.

Her crime? To be born in Asia where dealing with the world's biggest stray dog problem is a cruel affair.

Sometimes, the power supply is not strong enough to kill dogs like this. So some are buried alive.

The World Society for the Protection of Animals is working with local authorities and animal welfare groups to convince them to neuter not kill. We're helping by supporting shelters and supplying vital veterinary equipment.

£10 is all it takes to humanely neuter and care for one dog. You can help us save dogs like this and other innocent animals. Please send what you can now. Thank you.

Please return this coupon with your gift to the address below today.

Name _____

Address _____

_____ Postcode _____

Here is my donation of £_____

(Please make cheques payable to WSPA or complete the credit card details below.)

Visa/MasterCard/Switch/Eurocard/CAF CharityCard (Please delete as applicable)

Card No. [ ][ ][ ][ ][ ][ ][ ][ ][ ][ ][ ][ ][ ][ ][ ][ ][ ][ ]
(If using Switch, please use the number printed in the middle of your card)

Expiry date ___/___   Switch issue no _____   Today's date ___/___

Signature _____

☐ Tick here if you would like a free information pack.

Please send this completed form and your donation to: WSPA, Dept AP48, Freepost NH2604, Northampton, NN3 6BR. No stamp is needed. THANK YOU.   Reg Charity No. 282908

CALL 0990 214 214 NOW TO MAKE AN INSTANT DONATION   WSPA World Society for the Protection of Animals

Footnote:

'Chain cutter' was the first in a series of other equally successful 'fast hit' press advertisements we created for the animal charity.

PLEASE HELP THIS DOG TO FLY

It's his only chance of escape. He's trapped in a desolate landscape of ash and rock. Chained to the ruins of his owner's house. There's nothing to eat. Nothing to drink. And the volcano that destroyed his home is still active.

WSPA have just undertaken an animal airlift for the deserted pets of Montserrat. But many are still stranded - cut off by falling ash and debris.

If we're to help them, we need you to help us.

I WANT TO HELP WSPA'S DISASTER RELIEF
Return this coupon with your gift to the address below

Name _____

Address _____

_____

_____ Postcode _____

Here is my donation of £ _____
(Please make your cheque payable to WSPA or complete the credit card details below)
Visa/MasterCard/Switch/Eurocard/CAF CharityCard (Please delete as applicable)

Card No.
☐☐☐☐ ☐☐☐☐ ☐☐☐☐ ☐☐☐☐
(If using Switch, please use the number printed in the middle of your card)

Expiry date ____/____ Switch issue no _____ Today's date ____/____

Signature _____

☐ Tick here if you would like a free information pack from WSPA.
Please send this completed form and your donation to: WSPA, Dept AW10, Freepost NH2504, Northampton, NN3 6BR. No stamp is needed. THANK YOU. Reg Charity No. 282908

CALL 0990 214 214 NOW
TO MAKE AN INSTANT DONATION
WSPA World Society for the Protection of Animals

See the sport on TV last night?

Last night on Channel 4 News a new report highlighted the barbaric sport of bear baiting in Pakistan.

It described how day after day, bears are dragged into a bloody arena to face pairs of cross-bred bull terriers. Each bear has had his teeth ripped out and claws blunted, leaving him at the mercy of the dogs' vicious teeth. The trainer won't let him be killed, but the bear doesn't know this. *Over and over again,* he is fighting for his life.

Over 2,000 bear-baitings take place each year in Pakistan, despite the fact that they are now banned by law.

Our Libearty campaign frees captive bears and returns them to a safe natural habitat, campaigns to enforce laws protecting bears, and fights ignorance with training and education.

Please help us end this barbaric 'sport'.

PLEASE HELP WSPA'S CAMPAIGN AGAINST BEAR BAITING
Return this coupon with your gift to the address below.

Name _____

Address _____

_____ Postcode _____

I enclose my donation of £ _____
(Please make cheques payable to WSPA or fill in your credit card details below.)
Visa/Mastercard/Switch/Eurocard/CAF CharityCard (Please delete as applicable)

Card No.
☐☐☐☐ ☐☐☐☐ ☐☐☐☐ ☐☐☐☐
(If using Switch, please use the number printed in the middle of your card)

Expiry date ____/____ Today's date ____/____ Switch issue No. _____

Signature _____

☐ Tick here if you would like a free information pack.
Please send this completed form and your donation to: WSPA, Dept AP68, Freepost NH2604, Northampton, NN3 6BR. No stamp is needed. THANK YOU. Reg Charity No. 282908

CALL 0990 214 214 NOW
TO MAKE AN INSTANT DONATION
WSPA World Society for the Protection of Animals

PRIDE

Our struggles make a person we can be proud of.

Avijeet Das

Pride simultaneously focuses on the self and on others. It is often considered a negative force – the opposite of humility and a source of social friction. But taking pride in ourselves inspires us to be the best we can be, motivating us to work hard to gain approval from others.

Why is pride important?

Taking pride in others is a positive driver for good, an indication to ourselves that we are behaving in a way congruent with the values of society. Giving to military charities is an example of this. By taking pride in those who fought for our freedoms, we are doing the right thing, not only for society but also for our nation.

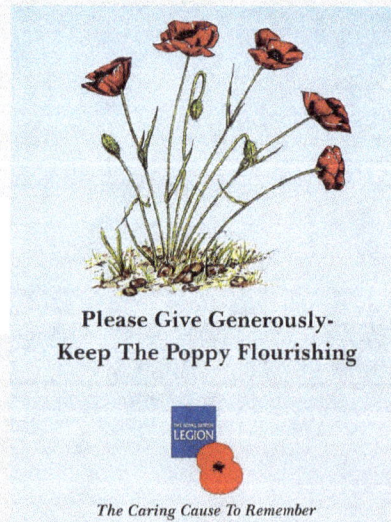

An example of the Legion's previous woeful advertising.

Please Give Generously- Keep The Poppy Flourishing

The Caring Cause To Remember

Hard to imagine now, but twenty-five years ago the Royal British Legion was in trouble, income being in such decline that they were struggling to meet their commitments to the armed forces. To improve the situation, the charity recruited a fundraising genius – Russell Thompson – someone we knew well from the Red Cross. Within weeks, he had invited us to help out, beginning one of the most rewarding and successful working partnerships of my career.

At our first meeting in the Legion's offices in the Mall, Russell spelt out the enormity of the task. He told us the organisation was viewed as 'old fashioned and irrelevant' and that the supporter database amounted to around '10,000 records in a shoebox'.

He wanted to give the Legion a leadership position and a new connection with supporters and the public. We proposed a three-pronged approach to strategy and messaging:

- **Establish the need**. Be more explicit about the struggles of veterans and lack of care for those leaving service.

- **Find a stronger voice**. Inject bolder and more overt patriotism into the messaging.

- **Create more moments to engage**. Devise new and more interesting ways in which the public can get involved, in both the November 'window of Remembrance' and at other times of the year.

Russell agreed to test the approach and we got to work. The tactics bore fruit immediately, revealing a pent-up desire amongst the British public to be given 'permission' to express pride in their nation's armed forces. They were hungry for new outlets for this powerful emotion and Russell and his rapidly expanding team were more than happy to provide them. Over the next two decades, we introduced novel ways to give to the Poppy Appeal (including a Westminster Abbey Field of Remembrance and virtual poppies), as well as creating other anniversaries where the public could express gratitude to their national heroes.

We devised a model which offered the chance for hundreds of thousands of people to say their thank you (through a personal message) in a location which had special significance. For example:

- For the 60th anniversary of the D-Day landings (below), 65,000 messages written on small Union flags planted on the sands of Sword Beach in Normandy.

- For the 100th anniversary of the end of World War One, 70,000 poppies with dedications planted at the Menin Gate in Ypres and the Thiepval Memorial on the Somme.

- For the 70th anniversary of the Battle of Britain, 25,000 messages written on paper propellers at the Battle of Britain memorial at Capel-le-Ferne in Kent.

- For the 65th anniversary of VE Day in Trafalgar Square in London (right), 65,000 victory pennants suspended from Nelson's column. Before we were allowed to pull off this stunt, we had to sign a form stating that we understood we could be jailed if we damaged the ancient monument.

I recall two of these special anniversary appeals for very different reasons.

November 2008, 90th anniversary of World War One, Ypres, Belgium.

The beautiful Belgium market town of Ypres had become the centre of fighting on the western front during the 1914-18 Great War. After five years of constant bombardment, the town had been pulverised. Almost nothing remained. Houses, shops, municipal buildings, schools, the cathedral, churches, the famous Cloth Hall had all gone; only the road and an endless pile of rubble remained to suggest it had even existed. Miraculously, within twenty years, using original town plans, Ypres was rebuilt exactly as it had been. As part of reparations, the Menin Gate Memorial to the Missing was built at the north end of the town, engraved with the names of 55,000 British and Commonwealth soldiers who had perished and whose graves are unknown.

We had produced an appeal to mark the 90th anniversary of the conflict and were in Ypres to plant 80,000 message poppies in the steep grass banks around the Gate to provide a visual showpiece for residents, tourists, supporters, and the media. The official event was scheduled for that Sunday,

so we arrived with a team of Legion volunteers two days beforehand to complete the job. By early evening on Saturday, the task was done and it looked fantastic. Russell was so delighted, he booked a restaurant in the town square to treat us to 'as much Belgium beer and frites as we could handle'. The night was going well with the very strong ale flowing freely when Russell tapped me on the shoulder. He looked worried.

'Seen the weather outside, Nicholas?'

Russell rarely fretted about anything, so I knew something was up. I went to the door and had to push hard to open it, the scene outside was sobering – a biblical storm was howling through the town. Great ribbons of rain lashed

across the square causing multiple gushing rivers to stream across the cobbled roads and pathways. Then, a thunderous crash as water that had gathered on the Cloth Hall roof, emptied onto rows of bikes below, collapsing them into a flattened, forlorn heap. As I watched transfixed, the marquee near the outside of the restaurant uprooted itself from sandbag weighted moorings and tumbled down the street, people desperately scattering to get out of harms way.

I suddenly feared for our beautiful poppy display. Caught in this maelstrom, I felt sure all our hard work must have been undone. Deciding there was nothing to be done until the morning, we ended our carousing and agreed to meet early to assess the damage.

The carnage that greeted us at six the next morning did nothing to soothe my hangover. At least a quarter of the poppies had been uprooted and blown into the adjacent town moat, virtually all of those remaining had been flattened to the ground. Luckily, we had replacements and set to work with the help of local schoolchildren whose teacher had heard of our predicament. After four hours of toil, we managed to repair the damage, just in time for the official ceremony at 11am. The next day, this image of stoutly erect poppies appeared in the British, Belgian, and French papers. Storm – *what storm*?

Saturday, 8 May, 2010, 65th anniversary of VE Day at Horse Guards Parade.

Once again we had run a successful campaign, collecting over 60,000 messages of 'Thanks for Victory'. Our plan on this occasion was to display them at the famous Whitehall parade ground, then invite the Prime Minister and Prince Charles along to meet armed forces veterans as a mark of solidarity and support. We were delighted when they both agreed to attend, little knowing that this particular day would prove to be one of the most turbulent in recent political times.

Two days earlier in a dramatic general election, British voters had delivered a hung parliament, the first in 36 years. It was not clear which Prime Minister would show up.

The question was still unresolved when the time came for the event to start.

At the designated time, as we looked over to the garden of 10 Downing Street which fringed the parade ground, three figures appeared and slowly walked towards us, heads down, two metres apart. Rather than letting the incumbent Gordon Brown do the honours, David Cameron and Nick Clegg had also decided to show up. Far from being the joyous occasion we were hoping for, the three men looked as if they would all rather be somewhere else. When Russell eventually got them to the veterans' reception he had to usher them through in different directions. Brown motored round as did Clegg; both gone within five minutes. Cameron to his credit (particularly after his disappointment at the election result) lingered longest and looked genuinely pleased to be part of the occasion.

Prince Charles was the real star of the show, staying for over an hour, talking enthusiastically to everyone. I took this image below of the Prince and Russell enjoying a joke after the three political

heavyweights had departed, the topic of which I couldn't possibly divulge.

Public appetite for these anniversaries remains high. Every November, thousands of poppies continue to be planted outside Westminster Abbey to remember the fallen from all wars.

By employing pride as the primary emotional motivator to action, these initiatives have helped the Legion grow its income during Russell's tenure from £35 million to over £110 million per annum.

INDEPENDENT

NEWS | SPORT | VOICES | CULTURE | LIFESTYLE | TRAVEL | PREMIUM | MORE

News > World > World History

D-Day 70th anniversary: Seven decades on, a band of brothers meet to pay their respects one last time

As world leaders head to Sword Beach, John Lichfield reports on the private ceremonies the pages of history

John Lichfield · Friday 06 June 2014 09:21 · Comments

METRO

Western Mail
A salute to the fallen

Daily Mail
MONDAY, JUNE 7, 2004   40p
D-DAY 60 YEARS ON SOUVENIR ISSUE

A FLAG FOR EVERY HERO

The Daily Telegraph
DAY 2014

REVELATION

Creative scientists and saints expect
revelation and do not fear it.
Neither do children.

Madeleine L'Engle

A revealing of something not previously known
or realised, a revelation is when you learn a fact
that changes the way you look at a person, an
organisation, or even the world.

Why is revelation important?
Revelation makes us look at things in a new way
and be more open to connection, engagement,
and support.

This poster, produced for the new look Salvation Army
may look antagonistic, but it referenced the best
known and least contentious Christian prose of all –
the Lord's Prayer.

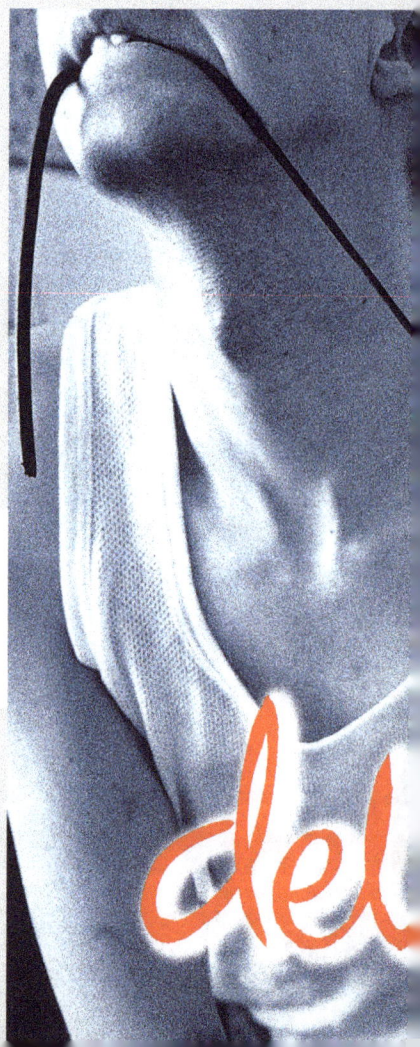

I've already referred to The Salvation Army, but there is one thing I didn't mention about this unique organisation – it is the UK's second largest social services provider.

When I first heard this fact from Julius Wolff-Ingham, the then Head of Fundraising, I was dumbfounded.

Its services covered homelessness, youth and children, older people, employment, modern slavery, and even debt advice. Far from being the quirky, bible bashing irrelevance I believed it to be, the 'Sally Army' was, in reality, hugely important to society and hundreds of thousands of people in need.

Now Julius and our Target team discussed how we might raise more income to support its ever increasing workload. He decided the charity must cease being the sector's best kept secret and should start shouting about what it does and why it needs support. He threw us the challenge all creatives want to receive from a client, but rarely do: 'Let's break the mould, let's get talked about.'

MAKE US FAMOUS.

Naturally, we eagerly set to work.

THE SALVATION ARMY

er us from evil

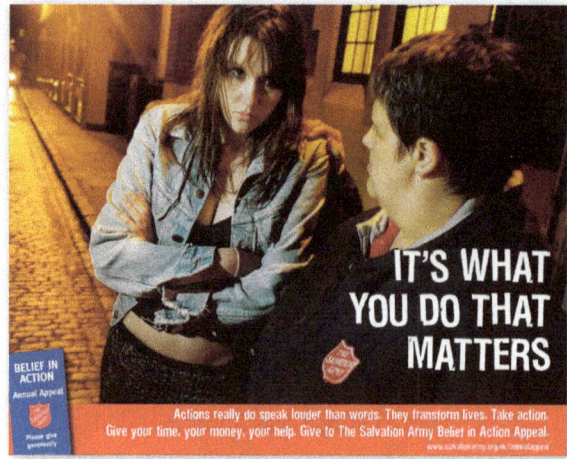

IT'S WHAT YOU DO THAT MATTERS

BELIEF IN ACTION
Annual Appeal

Please give generously

Actions really do speak louder than words. They transform lives. Take action.
Give your time, your money, your help. Give to The Salvation Army Belief in Action Appeal.
www.salvationarmy.org.uk/beliefinaction

Perversely, the charity's greatest operational strength – the range of services and beneficiaries reached – was its biggest weakness in terms of fundraising. Its immediate competitors – Age UK, Barnardo's, British Red Cross, Centrepoint, Crisis, and NSPCC – all better known brands, had much simpler fundraising propositions.

While it was evident the Army needed its own distinctive USP, we felt the first priority was to inform people about what it actually did. Most work carried out by its officers in communities up and down the country is done literally out of sight. Work such as aiding a young homeless person find a safe place for the night, supporting a drug addict off their dependency, visiting an elderly person to give much needed company, or imparting advice to someone deep in debt on the helpline.

To project the charity as a true force for good in the modern world, we needed to instil new drama and immediacy. The poster (right) was part of an initial series we produced demonstrating this new intent, simultaneously revealing the type of gritty places the Army operated in while inviting the viewer to participate.

Its power and honesty was a revelation for those who saw it around towns and cities, but initially it caused disquiet amongst the Army's senior management. They weren't used to such raw depictions of their work; when Julius pointed out the dramatic improvement in awareness and fundraising performance, the doubts faded away.

Although we were getting more marketing traction with the bolder direction, we felt we had to tackle the enormous elephant in the room to make the next leap forward – religion. The Salvation Army was an evangelical part of the Christian Church, how should we position these religious roots? What was the best way to convey a godly narrative without alienating a largely secular target audience and society?

Our solution was to focus on promoting universally accepted Christian values (love, family, trust, selflessness, sacrifice, goodness, etc.) rather than pushing Christianity itself. We decided the first expression

Be an angel

No other charity would have allowed us to produce this brand for a legacy campaign.

of the idea should reference the best known Christian prose of all – the Lord's Prayer.

Again, to his absolute credit, Julius went with the idea. When it worked its magic with even more audiences, we adopted the approach across all communications. By revealing the true substance and importance of its mission, these campaigns lent new credibility to The Salvation Army brand. In doing so, they provided a platform for one of the most successful fundraising programmes in the sector.

As humans, our greatest common denominator is our values: the vast majority of people, whether religious or not, are essentially good. By championing kindness and goodness, the Army has been able to reach and secure a place in the hearts, minds, and wallets of hundreds of thousands of people. This is especially true during the season of goodwill where the Salvation Army has become the 'Nation's Favourite Christmas Charity'.

The money it raises within the yuletide window runs to tens of millions, outperforming all competitors by a wide margin.

The Army's work is now so well understood, there is little to do to ensure further success beyond showing the officers doing their amazing work in action.

One piece of creative work that demonstrates this best of all is the first Christmas DRTV commercial we produced. Shot over three days, it featured real officers helping real people in need around London. It had no voice over, the only sound being a rendition of 'Silent Night' performed by the Army's own brass band (which we recorded in their own studio) playing throughout. It worked so well, it ran for several years.

Footnote:

I have known Julius for over 30 years as both friend and client. He is someone who has never been afraid to be bold and even controversial if he felt it was in the best interests of the charity. I was delighted to hear that he had been recognised with an OBE for services to charitable fundraising. On numbers alone, this was well deserved; having raised hundreds of millions of pounds, he must be one of, if not the UK's most successful professional fundraisers.

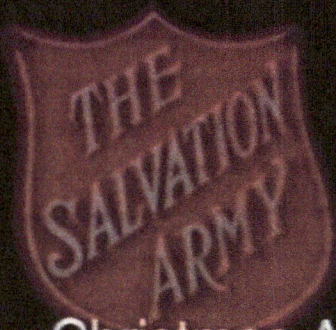
Christmas Appeal

Christmas Appeal

Christmas Appeal

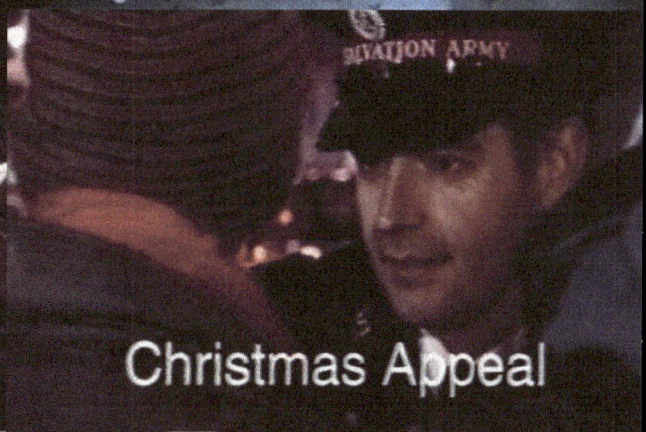
Christmas Appeal

Christmas Appeal

0800 202 500

0800 202 500

Please help us
to keep on caring

Do young homeless people really lack the will, energy, and ambition to change their situation? Are they really content to be sleeping outside in the cold, vulnerable to abuse and violence?

According to research we conducted for Centrepoint, that was the prevailing view of a surprising number of people. As some charities know (disability and overseas causes especially), if beneficiaries are perceived as undeserving, their fundraising will suffer as a result. To help Centrepoint move forward, we had to debunk this unhelpful myth.

In a second phase of research, we talked directly to young homeless people themselves to understand more about their experiences and the future they wanted for themselves. From this fresh insight, we created a series of propositions for judgement. When the results came back, one shone out as a clear winner:

'Homeless young people have the same dreams as everybody else, you can provide the support so they can reach them.'

To bring the idea to life, we created a film showing three young homeless people who wanted to fulfil their

dreams of becoming a footballer, a chef, and, most memorably, an astronaut. The five-minute film also featured a highly emotional interview with a young woman forced to leave home at 15 years of age and helped by Centrepoint to find a home and a new career.

Alongside this, we produced a personalised DM campaign for supporters and a press and digital campaign for cold audiences.

Please leave a
gift in your Will
to Centrepoint.

0300 330 2732

centre point give homeless young people a future

The approach proved a revelation for audiences and client alike. The digital ads and film attracted over 100,000 views and resulted in 9,000 visits to Centrepoint's legacy-giving webpages. The campaign itself received pledges with a value of £3.575 million.

The supporter appeal generated a further 73 enquirers and 547 considerers, with a potential total value of £6.175 million.

SADNESS

Tears shed for another person are not a sign of weakness. They are a sign of a pure heart.

José N. Harris

Sadness is a transient emotional state characterised by feelings of disappointment, grief, hopelessness, and a dampened mood. Feeling sad is an essential feature of our emotional mind; it lets us know we need to grieve and seek out those who love and support us. We all occasionally seek ways to experience sadness – by listening to sad songs, watching sad movies, or reading sad books.

Why is sadness important?

Research suggests that sadness can help people improve attention, reduce judgmental bias, and promote generosity. Sadness can increase motivation, operating like a mild alarm signal that triggers efforts to change the unpleasant state.

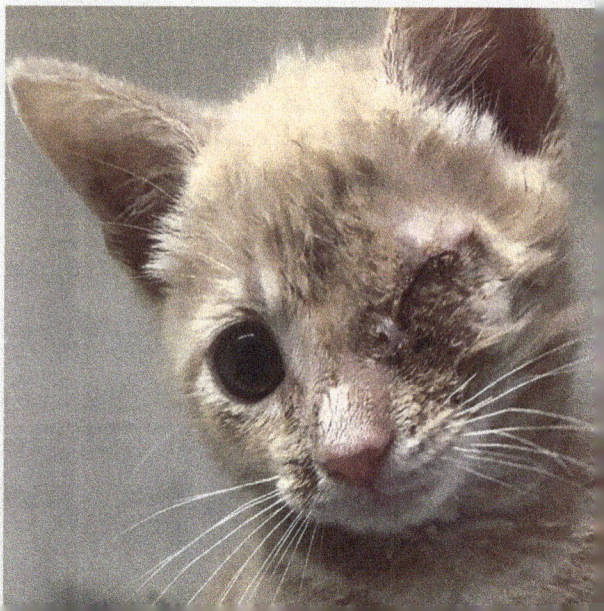

When I told a colleague I was writing a book on emotional marketing, he asked me a question:

Of all the emotions, which would I choose to perform best for a charity?

Easy, I replied. **Sadness**. People give most when their heart is grieving.

In one sense, the third sector itself presides over a great unspoken sadness. Sadness that so much suffering, injustice, and poverty exists in the world and that it is largely down to the goodwill of individuals and charities to make it better. Sadness is the base emotional currency every fundraiser has to work with; its proven power to move should always make it the first emotion to be considered.

For fundraising, I have always believed the strongest way to transmit sadness is in the most direct way – straight from beneficiary in need to potential donor. Throw in a great image, a clear call to action, and you have the ingredients for fundraising magic. For creatives, achieving this perfection is often easier than we care to believe; we just have to allow the focus of the appeal to do the heavy lifting.

The examples shown here that we produced for Wood Green and World Horse Welfare both used this elementary formula and ran successfully for years.

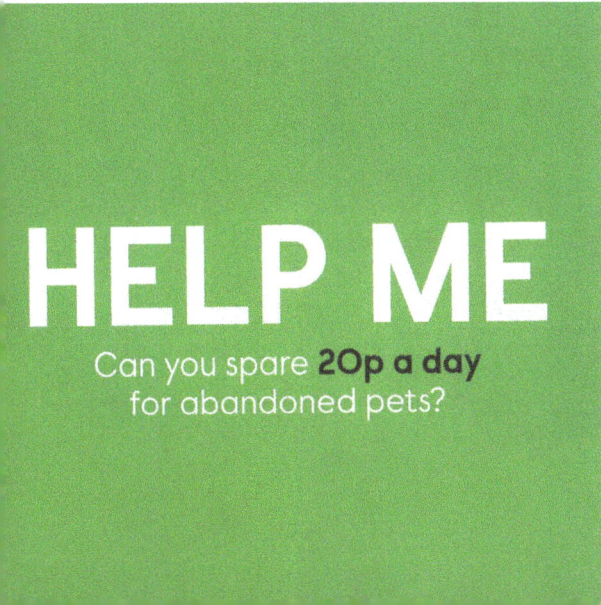

Help me

Every year 100,000 terrified horses are packed into trucks and driven thousands of miles across Europe for slaughter. Bruised, bleeding and enduring temperatures of up to 40°C, they become desperate for food, water and rest.

With your help, **World Horse Welfare** is determined to break this cruel trade.

Please make a donation by calling 01953 497239, completing the form below or visit www.worldhorsewelfare.org/donate

Here is my gift of £20 ☐ other ☐

☐ Cheque/postal order made payable to World Horse Welfare
☐ Visa/MasterCard/CAF/CharityCard/Maestro (delete as appropriate)

Start date___/___   Expiry date___/___   Maestro issue no___

Security code ☐☐☐ (last 3 digits on signature strip)

Signature _____

Title ___ Name _____

Address _____

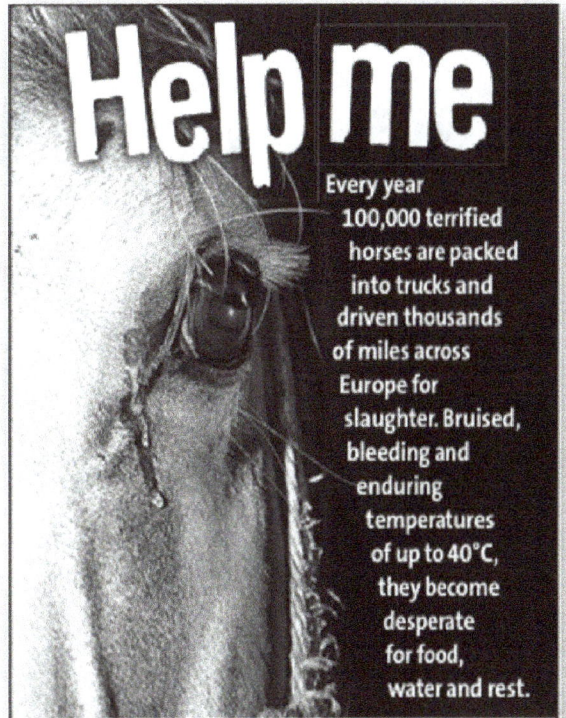

HELP ME

Can you spare **20p a day** for abandoned pets?

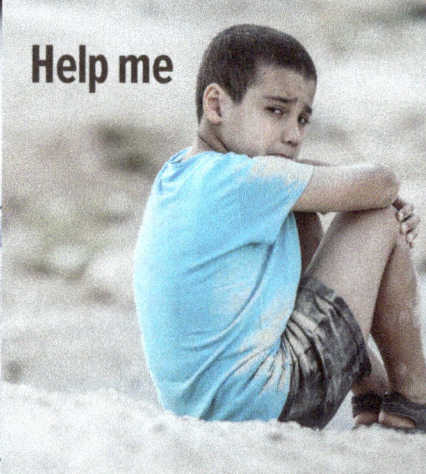

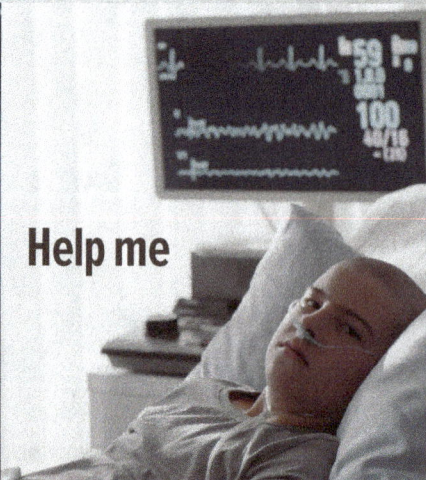

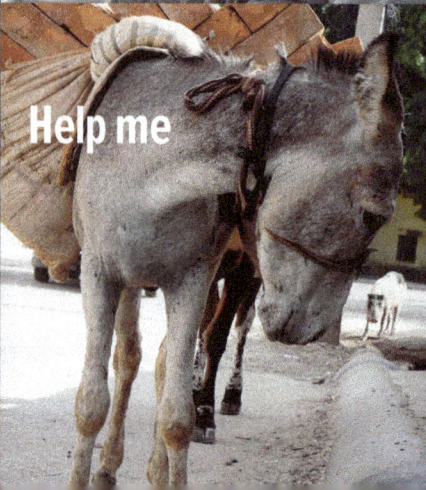

In fact, if the image is powerful enough, this approach could work for virtually any cause from overseas aid to elderly and homeless charities.

It is asking for support at its most authentic and human. No charity, no brand, no witty headlines. Just beneficiary and benefactor. While hardly sophisticated, it can move people to action, simply because it makes them sad.

Sometimes, the only way to appreciate and convey the anguish of heart-breaking sadness is to experience it for yourself. To gain new material for overseas charity Help the Aged (now HelpAge International), I travelled to India to seek out frontline case studies. Today the South-Asian country has the fifth largest economy in the world, whereas twenty-five years ago when I went, it was wrestling with the demands of an antiquated transport infrastructure, poor balance of payments, hopelessly outdated business practices, and a rigid social caste system.

On arriving in the capital, New Delhi, I was struck by the contrast between the opulent buildings, broad boulevards, and grand designs of faded colonialism, and the grinding poverty of the people who filled its landscape. My hotel, the regally named Imperial, was situated in the east of

the city. Standing four floors high, walls painted brilliant white, it stood conspicuously in well-manicured, palm fringed grounds. Surrounded on three sides by the slums of the suburbs, it towered over the single-storied frail clay houses and pinched alleyways just metres away, a visual metaphor for the cheek-by-jowl inequality.

Every day, my guides would arrive in the rather tired but always game white VW minibus to take me into the neighbouring countryside and the villages where Help the Aged carried out its life-changing work.

Without exception, I was received warmly; before being allowed to collect my stories, I would often be taken to see the community leader. I remember one in particular, a Hindu elder with the surname of Babu, meaning 'father'. His wind- and sun-sculptured face creased into a broad two-toothed smile as he shook both my hands enthusiastically. Leading our party into a dark, humid hut, he signalled for us to sit. As we did so, his wife solemnly passed around tall glasses containing a thick, pale-orange liquid. I was about to ask my interpreter to enquire what it was, when Babu spoke.

'It is Lassi. Made with oranges, honey, and nuts,' he said in perfect English.

'Now tell me, have you ever been to Anfield to see Liverpool play?'

It transpired that Babu listened intently to the football results on the BBC World Service every Saturday and had developed a passion for the Reds.

Hard places are usually where you find good people and those I encountered in the villages of Gotra, Noorpur, Rataul, and Sunehra were some of the kindest I've ever met. They gladly shared what they had and remained cheerful despite their privations, premature cataracts, and the expectation of lives being cut short by wholly preventable diseases. For two weeks, I gathered my interviews and took my pictures, every night returning to my air-conditioning, three-course meals, cold beer, fluffy-pillowed haven. It felt surreal to say the least.

One of the saddest things I saw on this trip concerned a woman beggar. No matter what time I left my hotel in the morning, or returned in the evening, she was there, on the paving slab to the side of the black iron entrance gates. The driver told me her name was Meera, she had travelled from Uttar Pradesh and been outside the hotel for several months, making money from residents.

One night it was so humid, even the large ceiling fans in my room couldn't cope, so I decided to go for a walk. It was around 2am and aside from the chattering crickets, even this most vibrant of cities seemed to be sleeping. Venturing through the hotel gates out onto the pavement I noticed Meera was awake, sitting cross-legged under an ornate Victorian street light.

Recognising me, she held out her hand and smiled, revealing a full set of immaculate teeth. After giving her a handful of rupees I asked why she remained in the same spot. Meera told me that the paving slab no larger than two square metres, was her home. The proximity of the hotel and its generous guests made this a lucrative location. If she left, it would be taken

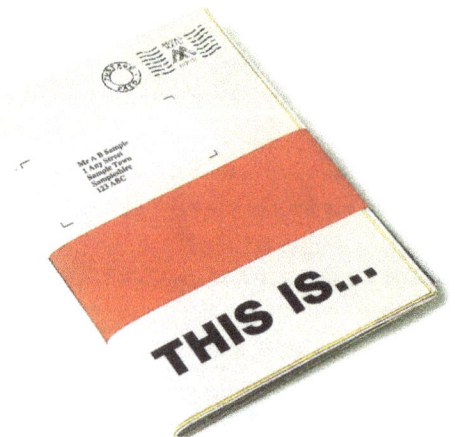

by another beggar. Every other day, around noon, her sister would take her place for a few hours to enable her to rest and eat. Most of what Meera earned, she sent to her elderly parents who still lived in her home village. This beautiful woman, with no children of her own, was sacrificing her future and health to support her family. It was a moving story and eventually became the inspiration for a very successful recruitment campaign for the charity's work in Asia and Africa.

To graphically demonstrate the issue for people like Meera, we created a mailer which started out at A5 size and could then be folded out to accurately represent the diminutive size of the homes of many of those who are poor. The example shown here was produced for Ethiopia.

SHOCK

There is only one kind of shock worse than the totally unexpected: the expected for which one has refused to prepare.

Mary Renault

Emotional shock is a reaction you may have to an unexpected event or incident. In 2016, researchers studying people viewing graphic versus non-graphic content related to cigarette packs, concluded that the feeling of shock imprints itself more permanently on the mind, and can lead to more long-term behavioural change.

Why is shock important?

Shock advertising and content is intended to startle and break through the advertising noise. It has been proven on numerous occasions to significantly increase attention and positively influence behaviour. Presenting an issue in a shocking way can prompt people to re-evaluate norms, create mental tension, and instil a desire to resolve that tension and correct it.

Sometimes it takes courage to shock.

This ad, produced by Susie Henry and Bill Thompson, upset a few people but sold a lot of slimming drinks.

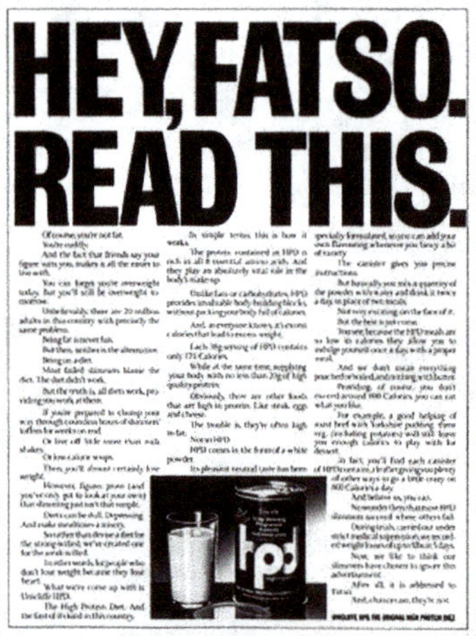

HEY, FATSO. READ THIS.

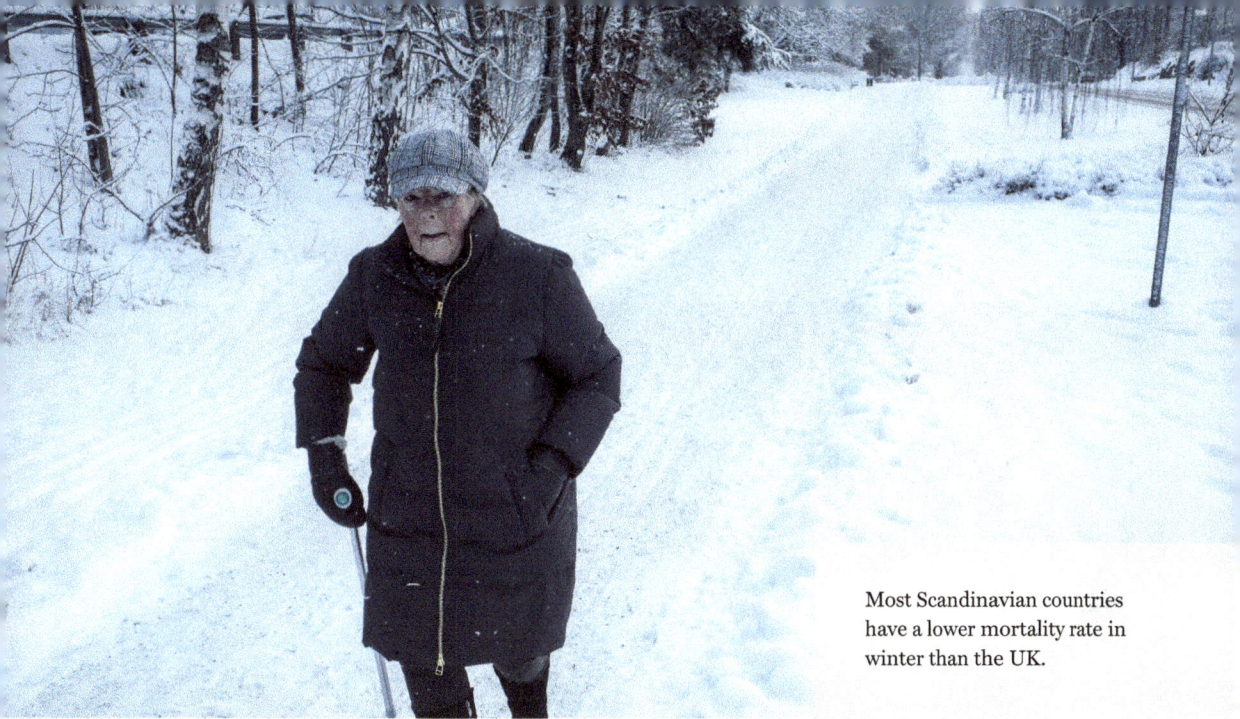

Most Scandinavian countries have a lower mortality rate in winter than the UK.

When striving for emotional clout, it is better to risk a negative feeling than no feeling at all. So it was for another campaign for Help the Aged, when we utilised shock tactics to generate the impact we wanted.

To boost the charity's vitally important winter appeal, we needed to raise new awareness of the dangers facing elderly people when temperatures fell. During research, we unearthed a disturbing statistic – more than 21,000 pensioners die from cold-related causes every year in the UK. This was a far greater number than in so called 'cold countries' such as Iceland, Norway, and Sweden; more damning still, it was one of the highest mortality rates in Europe. The story was even worse in poorer households; the client felt this was totally unacceptable and should be made public. We agreed that a properly coordinated PR and advertising campaign could achieve the critical mass of coverage needed to positively influence the fundraising.

The creative brief was simple and direct: Do whatever it took to get noticed. After pushing it around the agency for a few days, we were confident with our approach. Initially, the organisation struggled with the image and confrontational tone. Chief executive, Michael Lake only agreed to get behind the campaign if we shared our thinking with internal stakeholders first. Thankfully, the reaction was overwhelmingly a big 'thumbs up', with many suggesting that Help the Aged had a moral obligation to take the initiative. And so, the now infamous 'dead feet' campaign was born...

On the eve of the campaign, we sent hundreds of journalists and news commentators at major media outlets

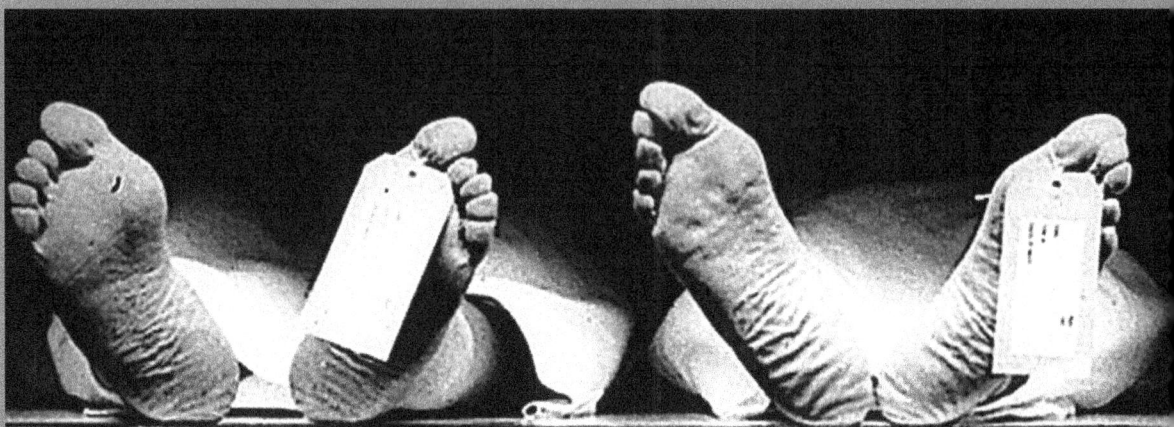

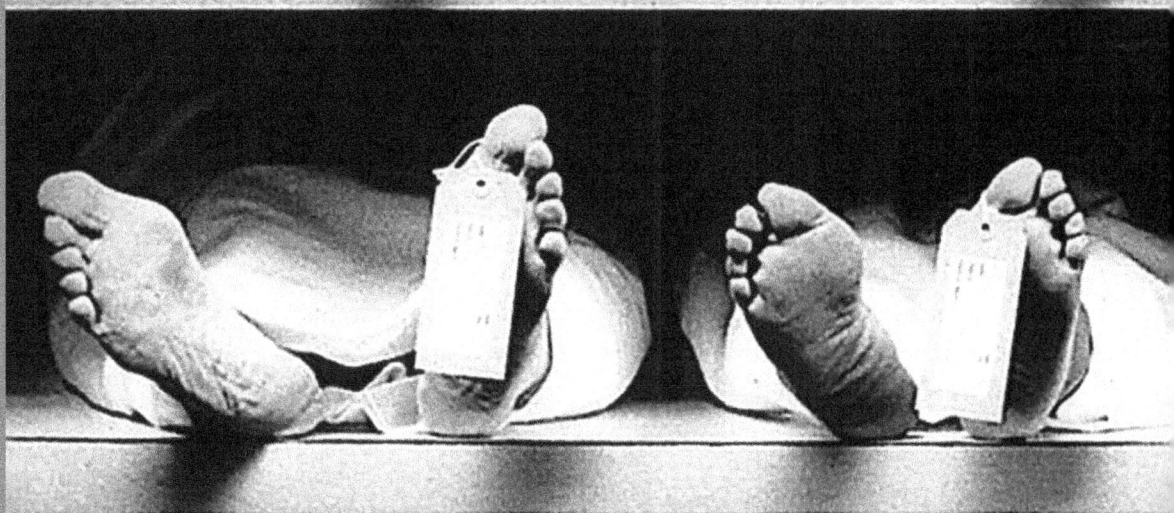

THOUSANDS OF ELDERLY PEOPLE WILL STO

Don't let the winter kill. Call 0800 75 00 75

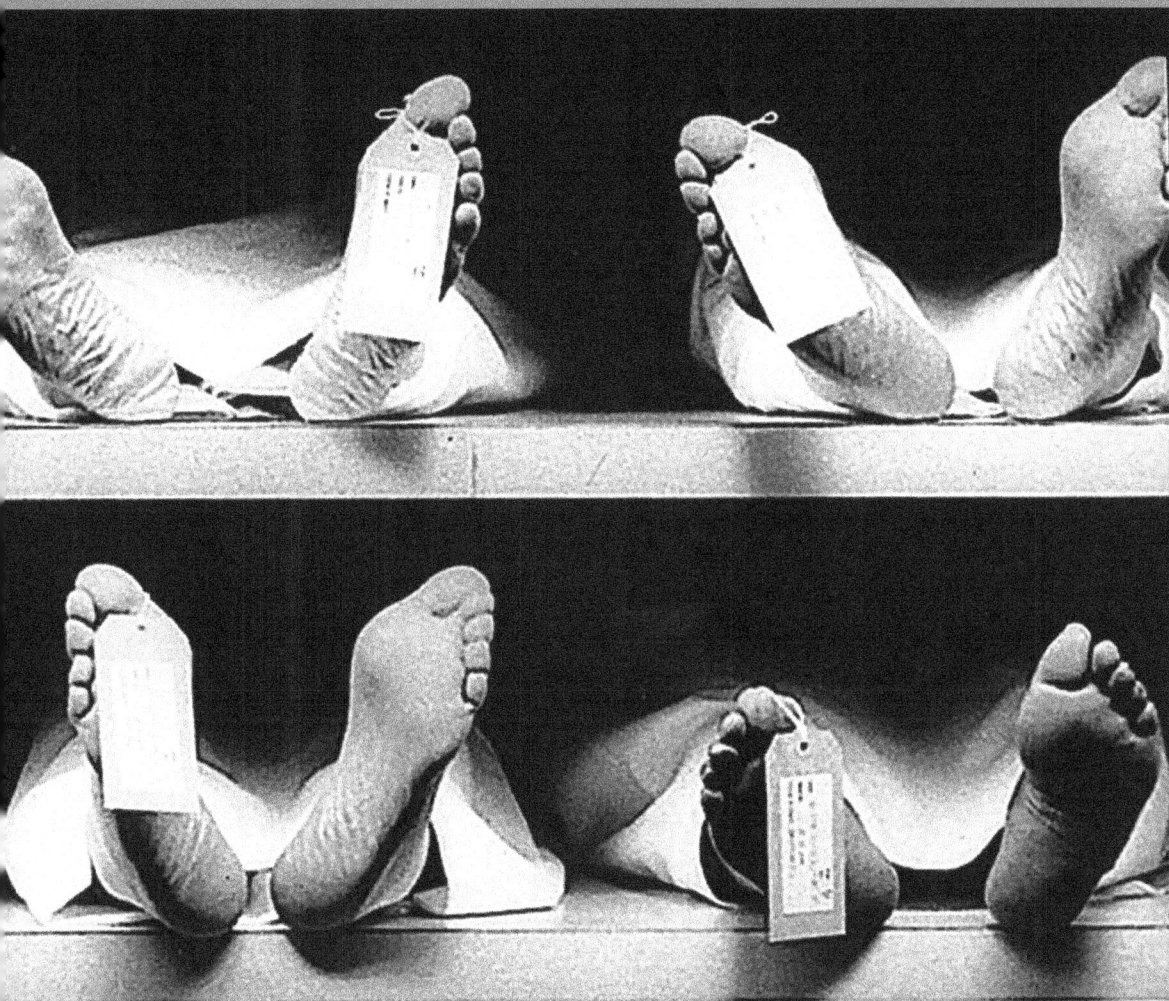

EELING THE COLD THIS WINTER

Help the Aged

a brown cardboard box. Inside was a pair of second-hand shoes wrapped in tissue paper. A handwritten message declared: *21,000 elderly people won't be needing these after this winter*. Also included was a press release outlining the aims of the initiative, a disc containing statistics, and a copy of the poster from the marketing campaign.

Force-feeding the media with the facts they required worked extremely well; when the campaign broke the following morning it attracted huge coverage in the newspapers. The Times, Daily Mail and Telegraph refused to run the advertising, but still ran large news features showing the concept, raising even more awareness.

At 4.30pm that same day, just as it was getting dark, an intrepid team (including our brilliant clients Helen Wright and Maddy Clay) projected the 'dead feet' image on to the Houses of Parliament from a small boat in the Thames. Despite the choppy waters and the wobbly projection, this ran as lead story on both the BBC and ITV's main news channels at 6pm.

Initially, reaction was one of outrage and Lake was bombarded with demands to pull the work. To his credit, for the days the campaign remained in the news, he remained resolute during numerous TV and radio interviews, stoutly defending the charity's right to expose 'this national scandal'.

Proving the maxim that all publicity is good publicity, over time it became clear the dead feet had worked. Help the Aged may have made some enemies, but results exceeded all expectations, recruiting thousands of new donors and raising £2 million.

THOUSANDS OF ELDERLY PEOPLE WILL STOP FEELING THE COLD THIS WINTER

It generated an estimated extra £3 million of awareness for the charity's work and resulted in government legislation to award heating grants to the elderly.

How far is going too far to raise awareness and funds for a deserving cause? In recent times, charities have lowered the threshold considerably and become over wary of using shock tactics to provoke action. I believe this is fundamentally flawed; leading charities should stand up for their beneficiaries. As in all walks of life, not speaking out about injustice can be perceived as acceptance, worse still betrayal. This case study demonstrates that, used appropriately, shock can be effective and even advantageous. Backed by credible statistical evidence, and the willingness to stand by them, being outspoken can revitalise a cause. In the case of Help the Aged, we persuaded a client to ruffle some feathers and it paid off handsomely.

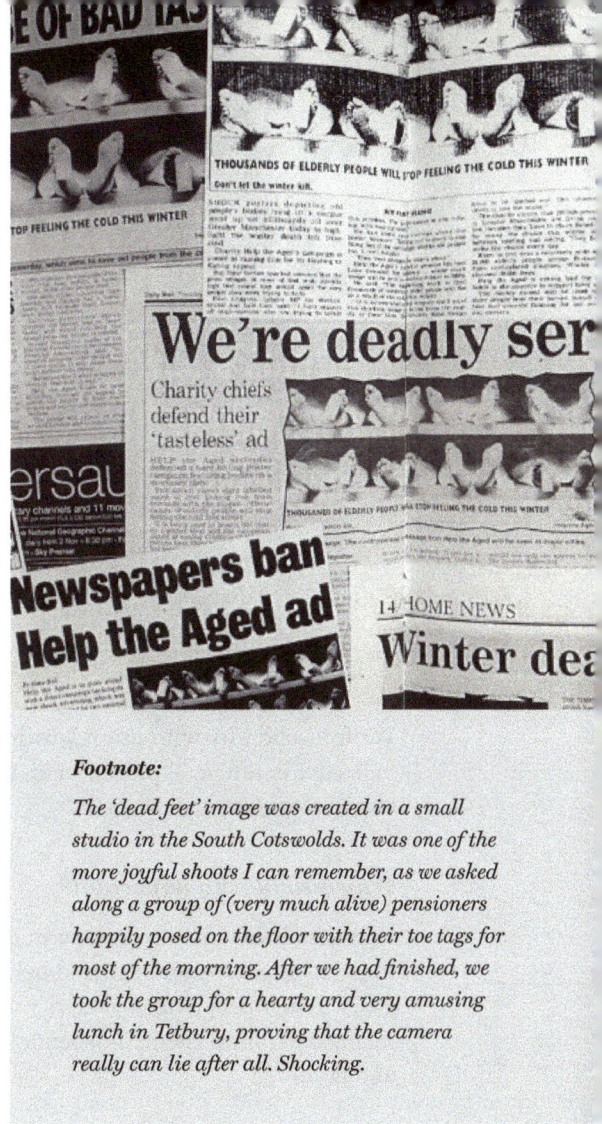

Footnote:

The 'dead feet' image was created in a small studio in the South Cotswolds. It was one of the more joyful shoots I can remember, as we asked along a group of (very much alive) pensioners happily posed on the floor with their toe tags for most of the morning. After we had finished, we took the group for a hearty and very amusing lunch in Tetbury, proving that the camera really can lie after all. Shocking.

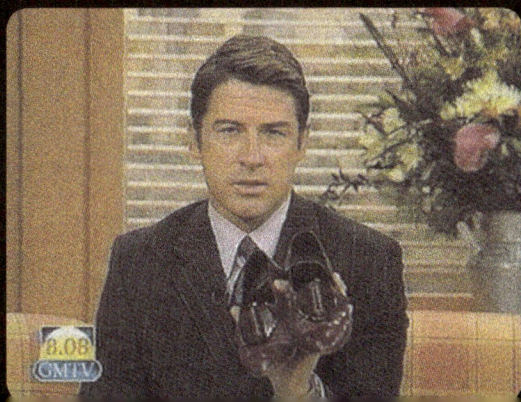

SOLIDARITY

Solidarity isn't merely a task, it is a pleasure and the best assurance of security.

Erich Fromm

We feel solidarity with our fellow human beings in what is called a 'reflective emotion'. Typically mediated by thought and belief, it has a strong ideological component.

Why is solidarity important?

Emotional solidarity is a sense of closeness that is forged between individuals as a result of shared beliefs, having the same interests or goals. When people feel solidarity with a person or brand, they are inclined to follow them, independent of consequences based on fear and desire.

CTC was seen as clinging to the past, members did not want to move away from the organisation's heritage and especially its winged logo.

Fuelled largely by the stirring success of the British Cycling Olympic team, hundreds of thousands of people in the UK have been getting back on two wheels.

This should have been good news for the Cycling Touring Club (CTC), the oldest, most established cycling club in the country. But no. Although other cycling groups were experiencing a new surge in interest, CTC's membership was declining.

New chief executive, Paul Tuohy was given the task of finding out why and rejuvenating the charity's fortunes. After researching perceptions of the organisation's offer and brand, the message was clear – CTC was viewed as old fashioned, irrelevant, and elitist.

By contrast, younger organisations like British Cycling and Sustrans were seen as 'of the moment', family friendly, and welcoming. With falling numbers also meaning that CTC was struggling to get the representation needed to influence external organisations and government, Tuohy decided radical action was needed if it was to survive. He invited us to give the brand and proposition a complete overhaul.

Following a consultation and co-creation process with staff, trustees, members, and external stakeholders, we concluded the organisation urgently needed to move on from its past and create a fresh vision and name to give it the platform to attract new support.

we are cycling UK

Along with a new name and brand, we created this manifesto of intent:

Imagine a country where cycling is given equal priority to cars.

Where parents are happy to allow their children to cycle to school.

Where people feel safe to experience the benefits and exhilaration of being in the saddle.

Cycling UK will make getting on a bike natural once more.

We shall make roads safer for cyclists, open up new countryside routes.

Create new cycling communities and support disadvantaged people to access cycling.

Join us and let's make cycling the joy it should be.

Our aims for Cycling UK were also bold and unequivocal:

To be the nation's voice for cycling and for change.

To empower the UK to cycle through becoming a movement.

To champion the benefits of cycling to more people.

we are Cycling UK

Feel the bike effect

The wind in your hair and a sense of freedom. Getting on your bike can have an amazing effect on your wellbeing. There's nothing like it.

Whether you're new to cycling or want to get back into it, you can be part of Cycling UK'S mission to get a million more people cycling.

Find out more at **cyclinguk.org/bikeeffect**

Without exception, the vision and aims were accepted by Paul and the executive; however, the second part of our recommendation was a far harder sell – changing the name and binning the old logo.

The Cycling Tourist Club's winged wheel logo, created in 1878, was still popular among hundreds of long-standing members; they did not want it dropped.

Many members weren't impressed by the research, our rationale, or even their own leadership's support for change. They seemed determined not to lose these ties to yesteryear.

A former CTC council member even attempted to gather members to petition against the rebranding

and stop the process. In a letter to members, he wrote:

'We are petitioning the CTC to demand a poll so all members will have the opportunity to endorse or overturn the motion. It is our opinion the entire decision-making process was flawed and any dissent was ignored.'

It all came to a fiery head when we were asked to present our recommendations to the membership at the organisation's AGM. The crackle of dissension and muscle-rub lay heavy in the air as we made our way through the packed hall to make the case for revolution. Heckled from the start, our ideas were called (among other things) 'derivative', 'popularist', 'a waste of money', and 'plainly crap.' We had to stop our presentation repeatedly to address specific objections.

Even so, gradually, point-by-point over the course of the debate, together with Paul Tuohy, we began to win the dissenters around. The key point with which the membership couldn't disagree was the urgent need for a new unifying persona. One barrier to modernising and attracting new members was the abiding negative perception of CTC's current membership which was seen as consisting of over-enthusiastic, slightly belligerent, middle-aged men and women in undersized Lycra. To the 'new cycling generation', this was divisive and unattractive. They simply didn't want to associate with it.

In the end, reason overcame emotion for once. If CTC was to survive, solidarity and unity was accepted by all as being crucial non-negotiable components. 'Cycling UK' was eventually voted in and adopted. Four years later, the new unifying vision and name has helped membership grow from 52,000 to over 80,000. As a result, the organisation's ability to attract the corporate sector and influence government has grown considerably.

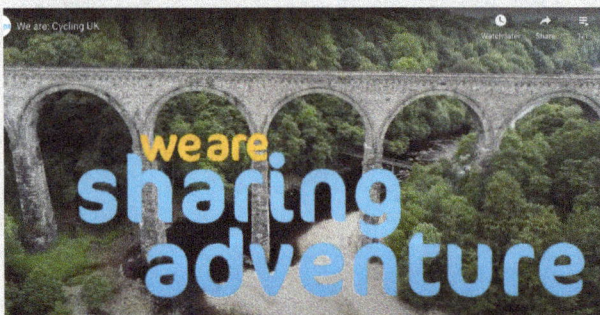

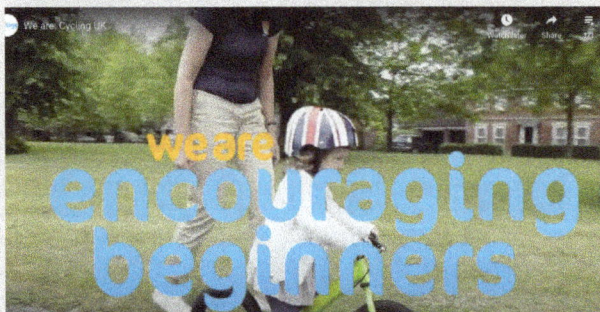

we are sharing adventure

we are supporting members

we are encouraging beginners

we are campaigning

we are
cycling
UK

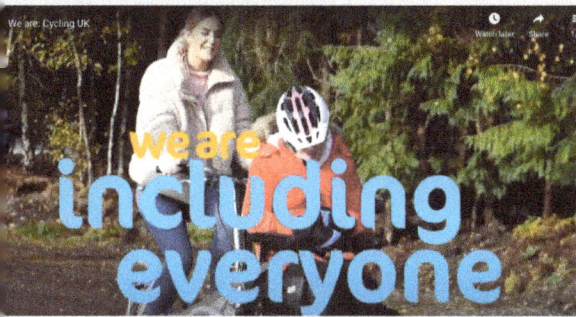

we are
including everyone

we are
active

we are
teaching

we are
cycling
UK

SURPRISE
(BETTER STILL, AMAZEMENT & DELIGHT)

There is no surprise more magical than the surprise of being in love.

Charles Morgan

Surprise is the briefest of all emotions; its function is to focus our attention on determining what is happening and whether or not it is dangerous. Surprise as an emotion can be both positive and negative, depending on the specific nature of the surprising event.

Why is surprise important?

Humans need surprise. The delight it can engender works on the dopamine system in our brains, helping us focus attention and look at a situation in new ways. It is important for bringing vitality to our lives and providing a pathway to further engagement and wonder.

Surprise changes behaviour. It introduces us to new stimuli, which we then reconcile with shifts in our beliefs and behaviour. It's been known by scientists for a long time that unexpected events in particular, drive learning.

Mr A B Sample
1 Sample Street
Sample Area
Sample Town
Sampleshire
WX1 2YZ

9999999   9999

Thank you!

INTERNATIONAL RED CROSS MOVEMENT

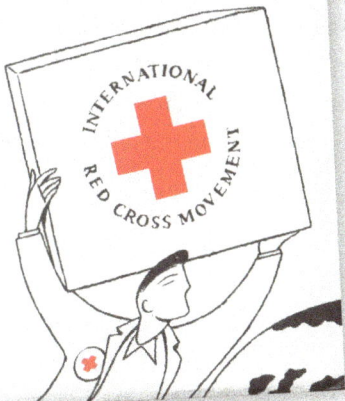

AN OPEN LETTER FROM THE DIRECTOR-GENERAL OF THE BRITISH RED CROSS

British Red Cross

National Headquarters
9 Grosvenor Crescent
London, SW1X 7EJ

CRISIS IN EASTERN EUROPE

Dear Telegraph Reader

Over the last few months, this newspaper has given pages of coverage to the bloody fighting in Bosnia.

Today I appeal to you personally to help the people whose miserable suffering you have read about. By supporting our Crisis in Eastern Europe Appeal.

Please - I urge you to read on, to see why your help is so desperately needed. And how effectively we will use it.

In just a few months, we've seen Bosnia turn into a bloodbath. The charred, dismembered bodies of innocent people litter the streets. Like those who were shelled as they queued for bread in Sarajevo. Even Red Cross workers have fallen victim.

A mother of two, Edina Gorasanovic, said she had gone outside twice since the war started. But how much longer can she shelter her children from random shelling?

The Red Cross is reaching out to people like Edina all over Eastern Europe. Already we've provided blankets and £100,000 worth of medical supplies to Bosnia. The latest form part of a £1.3 million programme for the republic's 19 main hospitals. In addition we've sent drugs worth £2 million to the former Soviet Union - and aid to Albania.

BUT NOW BOSNIA BRINGS THE GREATEST CHALLENGE

The failure of ceasefires, constant shelling and bombardment is too much for Bosnians to bear any longer.

They are fleeing from towns and villages in droves. An expected 1.5 million will be on the move - the biggest refugee crisis in Europe since the Second World War.

That is why my task today is to boost our Eastern European Appeal. So I appeal to you NOW to help the Bosnians and their neighbours in Eastern Europe who are in desperate need of food, medicine and shelter.

It costs so little to help: £36 will feed a child for a year, a pack of 10 bloodbags costs just £20, a bale of blankets is £100.

Please give what you can now. Use this opportunity to help the Eastern Europeans in the most practical way possible.

Yours sincerely

Mike Whitlam, Director-General

PS   We rely on public donations. And millions of people rely on us. Currently the British Red Cross is working in 44 countries worldwide. From Cambodia to Somalia. PLEASE HELP NOW.

HELP THE CRISIS IN EASTERN EUROPE

YES, I want to help the Red Cross save lives. Here is my gift to help the latest victims of war and disaster. My cheque/Postal Order is enclosed (tick) [ ] for

£200 [ ] £100 [ ] £75 [ ] £50 [ ] £30 [ ] £20 [ ] Other £ [   ]

OR Please debit my Visa/Mastercard/ Amex/Diners Club Card Number

Name
Address
Postcode

Expiry Date
Todays Date
Signature

Please fill in this coupon then return it with your gift to: British Red Cross, FREEPOST, London SW1X 7BR.

TO HELP THE VICTIMS OF WAR AND DISASTER NOW, CALL THE
RED ALERT HOTLINE ON 0891 234222
Calls are charged at 36p (inc. VAT) cheap rate and 48p (inc. VAT) at all other times.

When it comes to disaster and emergency response, the British Red Cross has always been important, but in the 1990s it was a particularly big deal. Conflicts in the former Yugoslavia, Rwanda, and Angola, combined with its pre-eminent role in helping refugees, meant its media profile had never been higher or its fundraising more crucial to the organisation's ability to respond.

Being its agency partner during those halcyon days, we created dozens of appeals through all available channels to keep the charity at the forefront of public sentiment and giving. The work was relentless and required fast turnaround; the knowing environment in which it appeared meant that invariably it worked, raising millions of pounds.

As part of a thank you to fundraisers and volunteers, I was invited to a reception at the Palace of Westminster. This was memorable for three reasons. Nosing around the green-benched House of Commons and being amazed at how small it was, apparently there are only 427 seats for 650 MPs. Meeting the charismatic Princess Diana on the terrace bar, feeling slightly weak-kneed when she shook my hand. Enjoying indiscreet gossip with a very worse-for-drink Richard Branson in the press bar.

It all felt pretty rock and roll and it was great to work with such a high profile brand. But over time, the high volume of coverage it was getting started to work against them and us. With numerous appearances in the daily news, dozens of press advertisements, and millions of inserts falling out of magazines every week, the brand was becoming too ubiquitous. Overfamiliarity meant we were losing the ability to surprise.

Gradually, fundraising performance started to tail off due in part, to donor fatigue, but also, as research revealed, because many people felt the Red Cross was so assuredly omnipresent it would prevail whether they gave or not.

To galvanise new interest, we developed an idea to dispel the unhelpful myth that the Red Cross was rolling in money.

We asked Mike Whitlam, the charity's Director General, to suggest the Red Cross would be forced to do something it has never done before.

Here's an extract...

Because of the enormous demands on the organisation, and after saying YES to every person in desperate need for the past 125 years, the Red Cross may for the very first time, have to say NO.

NO to 30,000 people in the former Yugoslavia who depend on Red Cross soup kitchens for their only meal of the day.

NO to thousands of accident victims in the UK who, every year, depend on Red Cross First Aid teams to tend to their injuries.

NO to countless displaced families in the former Zaire in desperate need of humanitarian aid.

British Red Cross

POSTAGE PAID

ROYAL MAIL

HQ 4611

Mr A B Sample
123 Sample Street
Sample Area
Sample Town
Sampleshire
WX1 2YZ

SAMP/9999

NO.

The tactic worked extremely well, particularly in recruiting new supporters. It showed the value of introducing the unexpected to an ask. While it is crucial to help a donor understand the good they can do when they give, we should leave them in no doubt as to what the impact might be if they stop giving.

Illustrating the consequences of not responding can be surprising and function as a pressing reason to act. One of the biggest barriers to profitable fundraising is inertia; this is an effective tactic that can be employed to make sure that apathy does not win out.

The Salvation Army has always understood the value of surprise and delight. It commissioned us to produce a series of authentic images to reveal the true nature of its work and the uniquely close relationship it has with the people it helps. For donors, they provided a extraordinary new insight into this fascinating organisation.

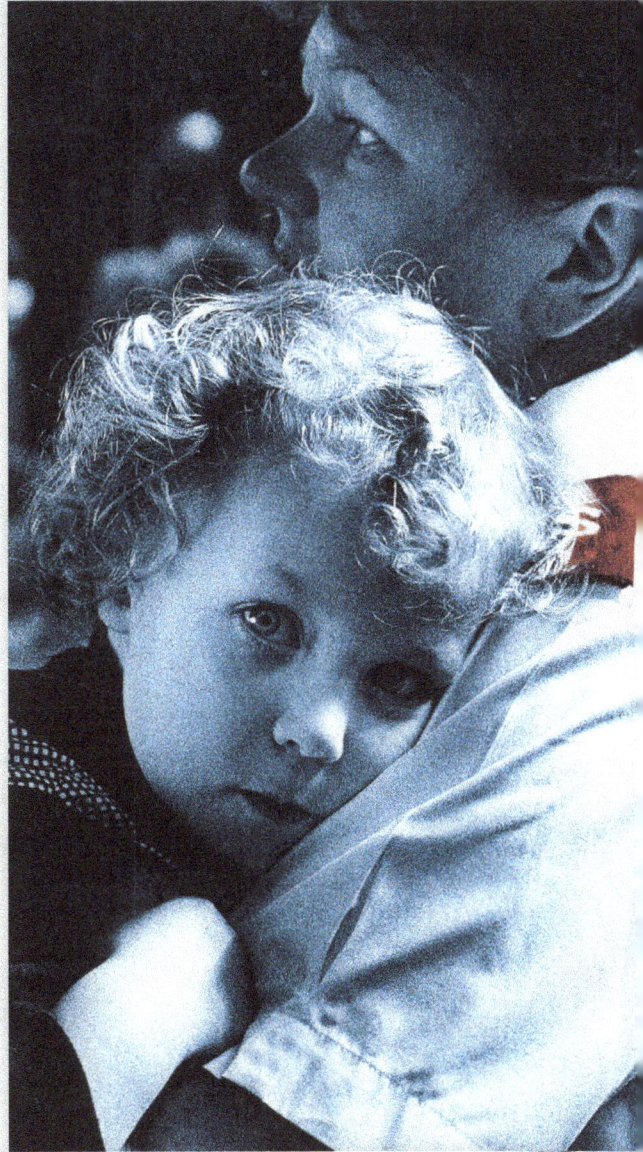

For the love and support you give...

we are truly grateful.

THRILL

The thrill of new beginnings is immensely alluring!

Avijeet Das

Being thrilled is a temporary but powerful emotion. An emotional state marked by enthusiasm, excitement, or anticipation; the heart rate increases, the nervous system increases activity, the brain signals increase production of hormones. When we are excited, our emotions become more powerful and affect our decision-making abilities.

Why are thrills important?

Everyone loves being thrilled, particularly at the prospect of bagging a bargain. There is something uniquely exciting about getting the product you're after for a low price. It's instant gratification.

From left: Brian Waldron, John Allen, Susie Henry and Bill Thompson. For a short while, they ruled on the Brompton Road.

The euphoria and excitement of bagging a bargain drives the beating heart of consumerism. No matter how much wealth we have, deals still hold a special attraction. It seems all of us adore the feeling, however transitory, of being a successful shopper. The thrill of paying less than we might have. This abiding principle lies at the centre of this next case study.

I had just joined Waldron, Allen, Henry and Thompson in Knightsbridge, London. Their building was directly opposite Harrods and, housed in my own office, I thought I had arrived. I was wrong.

Until I had proved myself, everything had to be seen and agreed by Bill Thompson, my creative director. One of my first proper jobs was for Budget Rent-a-Car and I was eager to impress. Back then, Hertz was the biggest car rental company in the UK, followed by Avis with their 'We try harder' ethos.

The brief we received from Budget, a relatively recent entrant to the market, was clear and ambitious: *'**Make us the new challenger brand.**'*

Up to this point, as its name suggested, Budget's business had been built on offering low-cost rentals for low-end cars. To expand audience appeal, it wanted to test a move into the more lucrative executive car sector, with an aggressive pricing strategy pitching it at an advantage against its competitors.

After working on the concepts for a day with creative partner Mike Brown, we were confident we had some strong stuff. Alas, I no longer remember what they were as Bill threw them in his bin.

'Fooking crap', he bellowed in his broad Geordie twang.

'Come back when you've got something worth me fooking time.'

Tails between legs, we sloped away. Over the next day this ritual played out several more times. He would be happy with the concept but unhappy with the headline, then satisfied with the headline, but exasperated by the copy; content with the image, but irritated by the layout.

I showed him a first draft of the copy typeset in a block of semi-justified type; unknown to me it contained two heinous typographic crimes.

A 'Widow' – paragraph ending line that fell at the beginning of the following page, thereby separating it from the rest of the text, and an 'Orphan' – paragraph-opening line that appeared by itself at the bottom of a page or column, again isolating it from the preceding text.

'Looks like a bird has shat all over the page,' he spat, throwing it back at me. Mature and supporting it wasn't and it drained the tiger blood from me.

After some midnight oil burning, finally we had something he was satisfied with. An idea that was big picture enough, Budget Rent-a-Car enough, looked good enough, and, more importantly, communicated the idea well enough. The idea that a Budget customer could enjoy the thrill of driving a middle-management Mercedes with that iconic star logo on the bonnet for the same price as a humble sales rep Vauxhall Cavalier.

I say Bill was satisfied because he signed it off, but you would never have known from his face or his parting comment.

'*Thank fook for that.*'

I may have found the experience chastening but the effort was worth it. The campaign smashed its targets and was a precursor to a long and fruitful relationship with Budget, helping it break the market domination imposed by Hertz and Avis.

Footnote:

I've already thanked Bill Thompson for his part in improving me as a creative thinker. When I became a creative director a couple of years later, I took forward the same determination as he did to get it right at every level of the concept. The biggest difference between us was I never ripped up lousy concepts in front of the creative team who had developed them. I always waited until they had left the room.

TRIBE

Everybody wants to protect their own tribe, whether they are right or wrong.

Charles Barkley

Humans are innately tribal. Belonging and maintaining relationships in a group is crucial to our wellbeing. Our sense of ourselves as social beings is more psychologically important than our personal identity. We discover who we are by discovering where we belong.

Why are tribes important?

Belonging is the power of 'we'. All movements begin with tribes, a group of people who care enough to do something. Everyone needs a tribe in their life to find real happiness, meaning, and purpose.

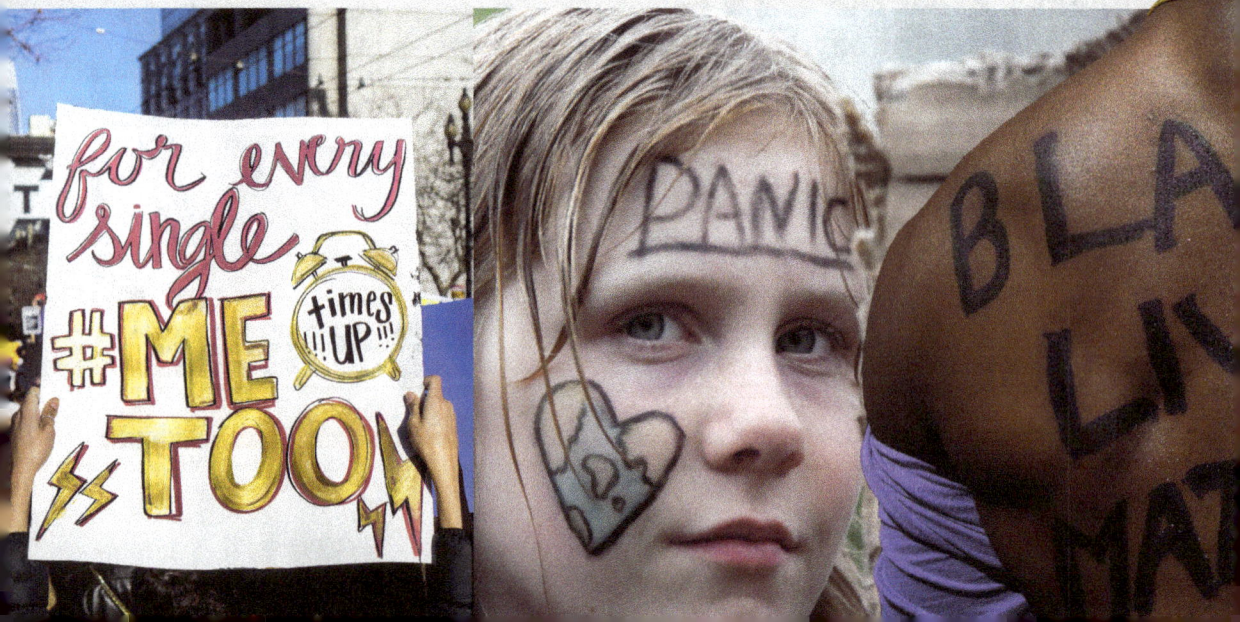

There is little to match the power of a tribe in full emotional unison. Harnessed for good, a harmonised group of focused individuals can achieve significant social change, such as Black Lives Matter, Schools Strike for Climate, and the #MeToo Movement. In its more malevolent form, such as the worst excesses of Trump tribalism, it can threaten the very heart of democracy itself.

Great causes build great tribes in their wake. Cancer Research UK and NSPCC have been successful in galvanising huge numbers of followers to unite behind defeating a heinous enemy. Both of these charities understand that tribes run on emotional connections to maintain momentum and purpose. With the

internet they have a powerful weapon to help them. Even the simplest web platform can develop relationships in a way that was impossible to do even five years ago. These connections, if sustained over the long term, can be incredible valuable. It is well understood that most legacy givers in the UK (market value £5 billion p.a.) have a close emotional bond with the charity to whom they choose to leave a gift in their Will.

Committed supporters remain the financial bedrock of the entire non-profit sector; treated properly, these kindred spirits will respond with virtually inexhaustible amounts of time, advocacy and money.

Therefore, when a closely affiliated group of 250 millionaires gathered together in one place, it represented

a fundraising opportunity too good to miss. The occasion – the Professional Footballers Association awards dinner. The venue – the Grosvenor Hotel, Park Lane, London. Thanks to a campaign we had run with football league clubs raising awareness of testicular cancer, Cancer Research Campaign had asked us to promote its first National Cancer Day at the event.

The evening was high prestige, strictly black tie and exclusively attended by men. Being the annual end of year bash, it had a reputation for being high-spirited and boozy, there was only a small window of lucidity in which to make our pitch.

We were not allowed to interrupt the awards ceremony to make any formal announcement about the aims of the campaign, so we decided to place our posters where they would be seen most often – the toilets.

At the start of the evening, I had managed to persuade Player of the Year winner, Alan Shearer and Young Player of the Year winner, David Beckham to mention the campaign (using hastily written cue cards) as they received their awards. I was particularly impressed by the 22-year-old Beckham's poise and delivery and remembered thinking 'the boy should go far.'

Thanks to endorsements from these tribal heroes and the perfect footballing chord we managed to strike with our messaging, we signed up several players to the cause on the night and raised thousands in pledges.

Come on United!

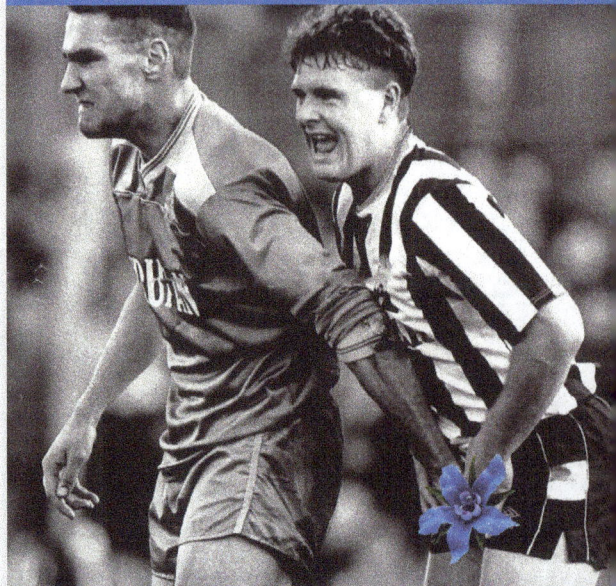

tackled

Our research has helped find cures for over 90% of testicular cancer cases. **Pick up a Starflower on National Cancer Day, Friday 23rd May** and you'll help us develop new treatments and cures to tackle cancer.

cancer research campaign

Registered Charity Number 225831

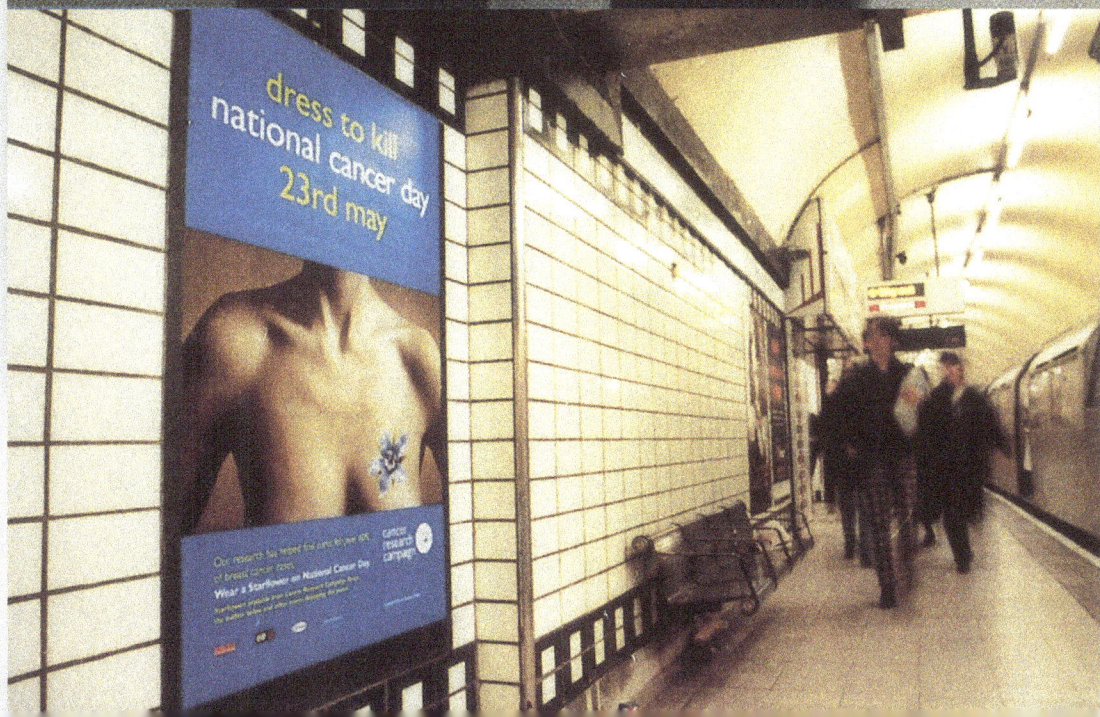

TRUST

The best way to find out if you can trust somebody is to trust them.

Ernest Hemingway

Trust means that you can rely on someone to do the right thing, you have confidence in their honesty or integrity. It provides a sense of safety and is essential to our welfare and happiness. Trust is the belief that someone is being truthful.

Why is trust important?

Trust is vital to a brand's livelihood; it will cushion the blow if organisational reputation takes a hit. When customers trust your business, they will want to do business with you. Trust results in greater advocacy, loyalty, and engagement but it has to be fought for and protected.

LET THERE BE BRAND

When I first started working with charities, I would generally find myself discussing strategy, tactics, and ideas with Directors of Fundraising, Heads of Marketing, Chiefs of Supporter Development and Managers of Recruitment, sometimes even the Chief Executive. This meant that all the skills and authority needed for planning and decision-making were present. Then about twenty years ago, a new person started to appear – the Head of Brand.

At first, this was still only the case for the bigger brands and generally their position was junior to the fundraisers. Gradually, their influence has grown; today these self-styled 'brand guardians' have inordinate influence over communications for most of the top 100 charities. In my experience as a marketer and fundraiser, this has had two detrimental effects. First, the lengthened chain of approval has meant the ability to produce speedy, reactive communications has been lost, such as responding to breaking news or extraordinary events, usually a hugely successful fundraising tactic. Second, because of heavily policed brand rules, everything has begun to look the same and wholly predictable.

I understand the benefits of a strong brand and am in favour of a brand protecting its core essence. However, when guidelines become too restrictive and inflexible, they kill proactive fundraising. Fundraising is ultra-competitive; to succeed, fundraisers must be given the latitude to express themselves, to move people towards their cause in any way they can within accepted boundaries of decency and truth.

Fundraising has become too gentile, too wary of offending, and far too worried about adhering to rules written with no reference or support for the task of persuading people to part with their money. In a perverse twist of logic, many brand guidelines I have encountered actually seem to positively discriminate against the fundamental tools a fundraiser relies on.

At a recent campaign planning workshop, I asked the assembled client team what they thought were the most valuable assets a charity brand can possess. One brand manager got to his feet and declared confidently:

'Five things: A great logo, consistency, distinctive colour palette, sustainability and inclusivity'.

His colleague, a fundraiser sitting next to him, gave a different view: *'Just two things: passion and transparency. I want to be a brand that speaks its mind and delivers on its promises.'*

From sitting in numerous supporter groups, I know donors care little for logos and colour palettes. They are wary of charities that appear as brand aware and slick as wealthy commercial enterprises. All donors seem to want from the causes they support is the feeling that their money is gratefully received and that they can trust them to use it to make a difference.

Impact is trust. Knowledge is trust. Trust is loyalty. The Royal National Lifeboat Institution understands this better than most. When we were asked by the charity to improve retention rates, we felt bringing the supporter closer to the life-saving work of its brave volunteers might do the trick. We produced a stream of communications following the same ten crew members for a whole year, sharing new insights into their training, their lives, and of course, their dramatic rescues. We presented the relationship between donor and crews as a true collaboration, a joint enterprise that relies entirely on the unwavering commitment of both parties. The significant uplift in results over the year clearly indicated RNLI supporters welcomed the deeper sense of belonging and trust this gave.

If a charity brand (or any brand for that matter), retains just one abiding attribute, it should be trust. Brand trust increases audience receptiveness, creates goodwill, fosters advocacy, and enables an organisation to weather any storm. However, trust is hard earned, it must be defended when threatened. Over the past 30 years, The Salvation Army has been rocked periodically by accusations involving financial irregularities, sexual misconduct, and even a perceived anti-LGBTQ stance. Each time it has responded decisively and with candour, and remains one of the UK's most trusted charity brands. Other organisations in the sector such as Oxfam, Save the Children, and even the Institute of Fundraising, have responded less well to similar accusations, appearing murky and evasive. Along with the reputational damage this caused, a Charities Aid Foundation survey at the time indicated that scandals had seriously eroded public trust in these organisations.

The sector must desist in keeping supporters at arm's length. For the vitally important and more demanding baby boomer generation in particular, this simply won't wash. The more distant charities appear, the more they will alienate. Our golden goose, the goodwill of supporters on which everything depends, could easily be slain along the way, which would be a disaster.

The question of how best to proactively infuse trust into fundraising and specific appeals can often come down to the choice of messenger. For the likes of Médecins Sans Frontières,

UNICEF, The Salvation Army, and the RSPCA, the message is best delivered directly from the people actually doing the work. The iconography of doctors, nurses, volunteers, and officers delivering help, is powerful. Using people actually 'on the frontline' means the narrative can be delivered with authenticity and raw emotion.

Without exception these carry more weight with the supporter.

Messages from senior members of the charity such as the chief executive can also be effective, particularly for urgent appeals where they lend gravitas and a 'sit up and pay attention' tone.

Well-known personalities are also worth considering, if relevant to the cause. UNICEF has found that using A-list celebrities in its DRTV appeals can often double the number of responses.

If the personality has a personal connection to the cause, they can have even greater effect.

When we cast around for a suitable spokesperson to front a legacy campaign for Alzheimer's Society, the charity put us in touch with Sir Tony Robinson. The actor and presenter had lost both parents to the disease and told us he would be happy to share his story to promote the appeal. He was the perfect choice: credible, charismatic, and trustworthy. Using a script that was developed almost verbatim from a piece of supporter motivation research, he delivered a compelling case for support whilst sitting in his home office in North London.

Alzheimer's Society 60 second Tony Robinson DRTV script

If you're over 65 like me, chances are you'll know someone with dementia.

This terrible condition took my mum and dad from me.

I don't want my grandchildren to fear going the same way.

That's why I'm leaving a gift in my Will to Alzheimer's Society.

They're supporting those living with the condition and working day and night to make the breakthroughs to keep dementia at bay.

But they need more money and more people peering down these [microscopes] to discover the answers we need.

I want to help create a dementia free future which is why I'm asking you to please consider making a gift in your Will to the work of Alzheimer's Society.

Life shouldn't end when dementia begins; your gift can help make sure it doesn't.

Leading the fight against dementia

Alzheimer's
Society

0370 011 0290
alzheimers.org.uk/tonyrobinson

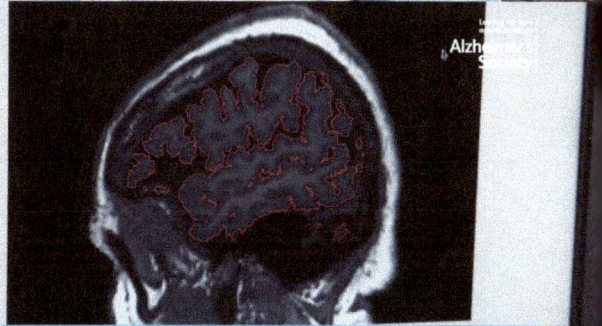

0370 011 0290
alzheimers.org.uk/tonyrobinson

Registered charity no. 296645   Company number 2115499

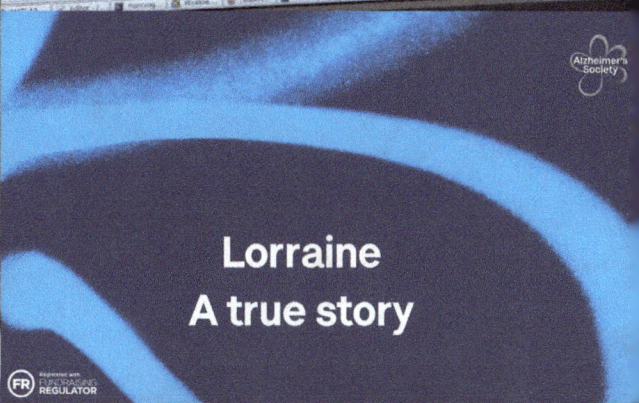

Lorraine
A true story

FR
FUNDRAISING
REGULATOR

Alzheimer's Society

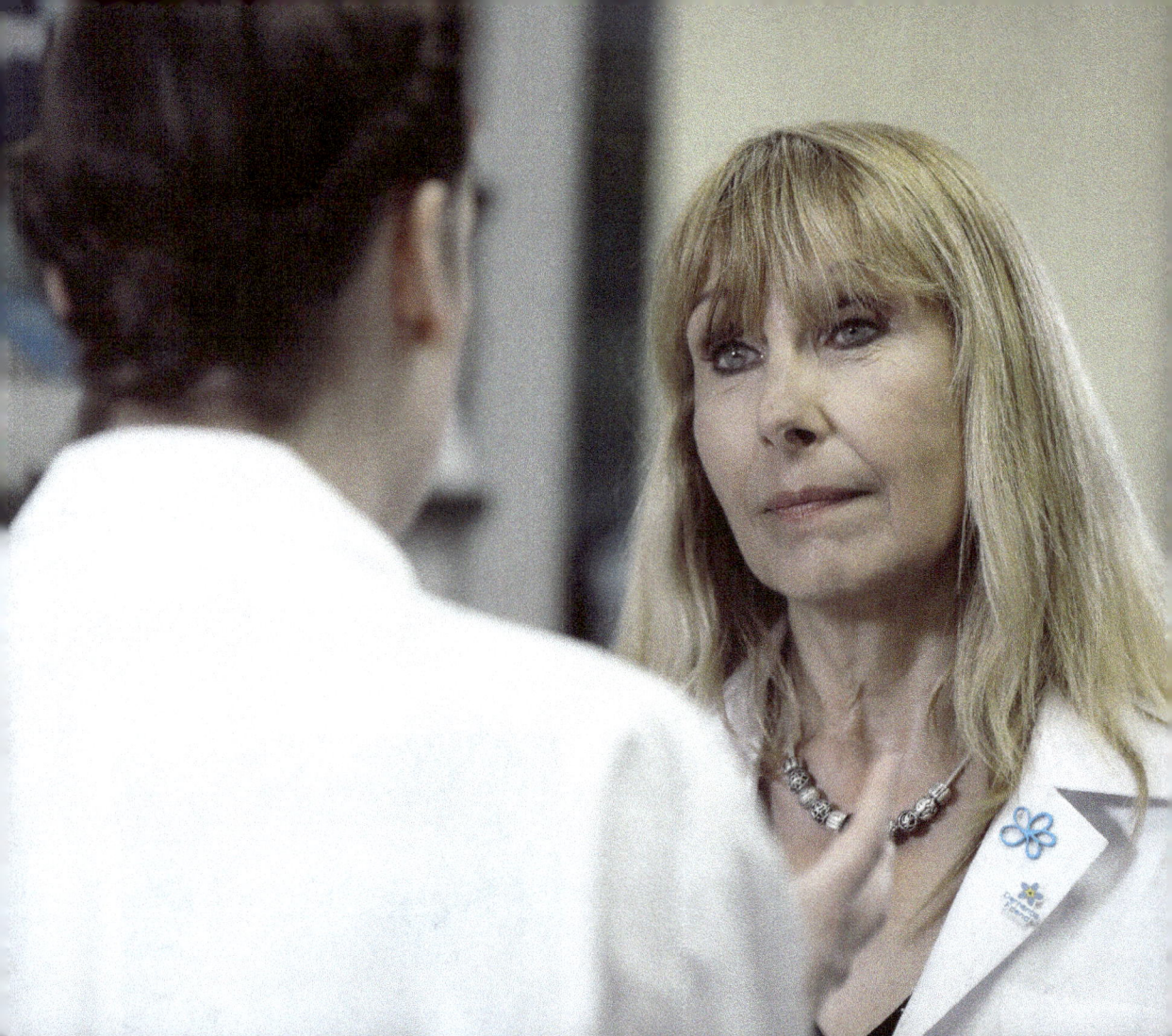

0370 011 0290
alzheimers.org.uk/tonyrobinson

We ran the campaign across various broadcast, press, and social media channels, and pulled in over £13.5 million in pledges.

After two years of successfully utilising Tony, we decided to use a different spokesperson and conducted research asking people for their opinions on various possible options. These included television personalities, a dementia scientist, the organisation's chief executive, a carer, and someone actually living with the condition. This latter option was the favourite, with a large number of participants stating that people actually going through dementia rarely featured and needed a voice.

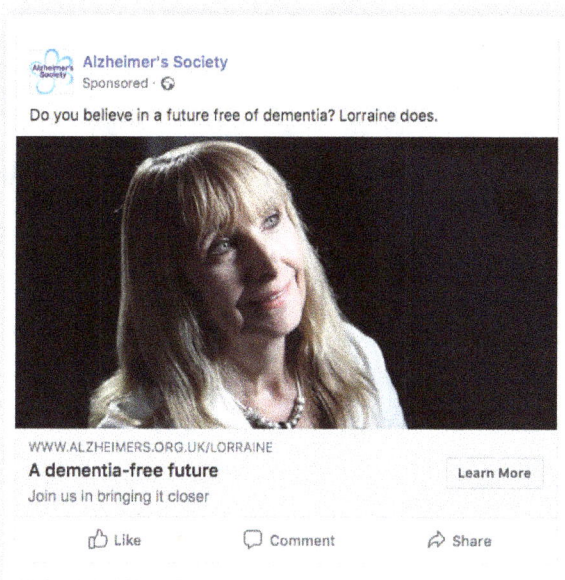

Alzheimer's Society 60 second Lorraine Brown DRTV script

After the diagnosis I was devastated.

It really didn't dawn on me that it would be dementia.

I just sat there and listened to it all, not really taking it in.

And that's when I went into this dark place for about a year.

It's a death really, you're saying goodbye to the life you had.

I decided that while I'm still able, I want to do something about it and make a donation in my Will to the Alzheimer's Society.

And put a stop to dementia.

So it was that our next campaigns featured the amazing Lorraine Brown, diagnosed with early onset Alzheimer's in her early sixties. Despite the hammer blow of the diagnosis and subsequent failure of her marriage, she was determined to remain positive, travel the world, and remain close to her children and grandchildren. Lorraine and her family were truly an inspiration. Speaking in her own words, she gave a revealing insight into an aspect of dementia, previously considered taboo.

Both campaigns, which ran across broadcast, press, and social media channels, struck a potent emotional chord with audiences. They seemed to have instinctively trusted and taken to heart two people with very different, yet equally poignant experiences.

VALUED

It's a great feeling when your work is appreciated.

Jacqueline Fernandez

We all want to be valued. This need has ancient roots, dating back to when, as isolated mammals, we were trying to avoid becoming lunch for faster, stronger animals. We learnt that forming social groups dramatically boosted our survival odds. To benefit from that protection, we had to add value. This survival mode explains why we get anxious when we feel less valued.

Why is this important?

To feel valued (and valuable) is almost as compelling a need as food; it can become the only thing that matters. If we can show customers and supporters how valued they are, they in turn will become more valuable to us through their loyalty. This can be achieved by thanking them or bestowing special benefits. A recent survey found 41% of consumers are likely to remain loyal simply on the basis of exclusive privileges with which they are rewarded.

I'm sitting on a picnic rug on a tightly cropped lawn, sipping tea and eating a cheese sandwich with The National Trust's director of fundraising, Gill Raikes. She is, as usual, in a good mood, chatting enthusiastically about the Trust's new £30 million acquisition, Tyntesfield House, whose impressive gothic façade is directly in front of us.

'Striking building isn't it? Built from bird poo you know,' she chuckled.

Tyntesfield's original owner, William Gibbs, had built his fortune and the house after securing a monopoly to export guano, nitrate-rich seabird droppings from the Chincha Islands off the coast of Peru. Vast piles of the valuable fertiliser had been deposited on its shoreline and at the peak of the trade, his firm earned £100,000 a year – a staggering £8,000,000 plus in today's money.

When Gibbs's great grandson, Lord Wraxall, died, the family decided to put Tyntesfield up for sale. To help buy the property, the Trust secured a £17 million contribution from the National Heritage Memorial Fund, its largest ever single grant.

'We'll need another £20 million for restoration but it will be worth it,' Raikes continued. *'Drink up, I'll show you round.'*

For the next hour, I was treated to a behind-the-scenes tour of the Victorian treasure trove. The house still retains a strong sense of the family's presence, furniture, objects, and paintings, all exactly as they would have been when the last owner lived here. Portraits of successive generations looked down inquisitively from their position high on the wall above the huge staircase. A pile of yellowing newspapers lay on a table in the snug, while a rocking horse in the hall waited patiently for its

next rider. It was as if the occupants had just popped out for a walk around the grounds and never returned. Hats on hat stands, cigarette lighters on sideboards, vintage port in crystal decanters, fox fur throws on sofas; all revealed an intimate frozen snapshot of life in an aristocratic country house.

I felt privileged to be given access to this vanished world; as we walked around it occurred to me that it also represented an opportunity for The National Trust.

'Why don't you invite people to view it, as part of a fundraising drive?' I ventured as we stood in the snooker room, marvelling at the still functioning electronic scoring system.

'You could offer exclusive access to the restoration work, a unique for-your-eyes-only experience not usually open to "ordinary" members. In return they would have to listen to a pitch about helping to pay for it.'

Raikes looked at me perplexed. *'Our restoration people wouldn't want people... poking about.'*

She walked back through the hallway and into the library without another word. I was starting to think she had dismissed the idea when she turned to me and smiled.

'Perhaps it doesn't have to be at Tyntesfield. We have plenty of other venues in which to offer a privileged tour.'

'Everyone loves being valued, part of an exclusive club,' I replied. She smiled again.

'I'll have a think, now come and look at the family chapel.'

Things rarely happen quickly at the Trust, even with a director of fundraising pushing them along. Four months later we were asked to trial a series of Legacy Promotion Days, marketed directly to the membership.

As we assumed, members loved the idea and the events were heavily over-subscribed. The programme helped raise tens of millions for this fantastic cause.

It appears the value of being valued can be significantly valuable.

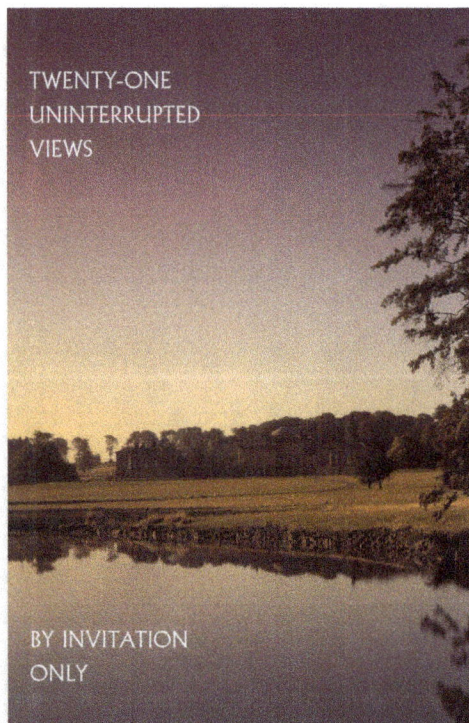

TWENTY-ONE
UNINTERRUPTED
VIEWS

BY INVITATION
ONLY

KEDLESTON

Derby,
Derbyshire

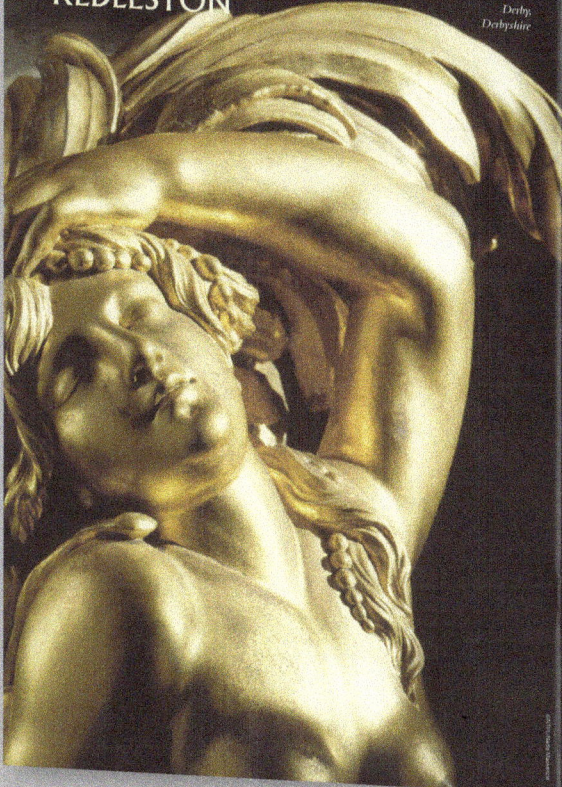

A neo-classical mansion, Kedleston was built between 1759 and 1765 for the Curzon family, who have lived in the area since at least the 12th century. The house boasts the most complete and best-altered sequence of Robert Adam interiors in England, with the magnificent state rooms retaining their great collections of paintings and original furniture.

You'll be given a fascinating talk by the staff of Kedleston on the property's silverware, with a particular focus on the dining room silver which was generously left to the Trust in a supporter's Will. You will even have an opportunity to don some gloves and join the experts in cleaning this precious silverware, so that it can be preserved for future generations.

After a tasty buffet lunch, you may wish to while away the summer's afternoon exploring the gardens which have been restored in part to an 18th century 'pleasure ground'. The topiary event has been especially arranged in order for you to enjoy the naturalised display of azaleas and rhododendrons which are an especial delight in June. The surrounding park, also designed by Adam, including a fine bridge, fishing pavilion and series of lakes and cascades.

Fiona Reynolds, the Director-General, will be the special guest at this event.

Photographs, clockwise from top: picture detail in the figure in neo-classically-designed alcoves in the Dining Room; the Saloon; the coffered interior in the ceiling of the Saloon; Fiona Reynolds, Director-General. Clockwise main: famous centrepiece on the North Front of Kedleston Hall.

14th June 2007

Itinerary

9.30am *Guests arrive. Welcome, introductions and overview of the day. Morning coffee.*

10.00am *Talk by Kedleston staff on the property's silverware, particularly that on display in the Dining Room.*

11.00am *We will all don gloves and have a fun and informative time cleaning silverware under expert tuition. (Gloves will be provided, though please bring aprons to protect your clothes.)*

1.00pm *A buffet lunch will be served in the restaurant.*

2.00pm *Brief thank you and speech on the importance of legacy gifts to the National Trust.*

2.15pm *Goodbye and depart.*

PECKOVER HOUSE

North Brink,
Wisbech,
Cambridgeshire

Peckover House is an elegant Georgian townhouse, on the centre of the River Nene in Wisbech. The property was bequeathed to the National Trust in 1943 by Alexandra Peckover, daughter of local merchant. The Peckovers were a family of bankers who built up a successful local banking business whilst showing great generosity to the local community.

As well as the house, where rooms on three storeys are open to the public, the property boasts an outstanding two-acre 'town' garden, one of the finest in the care of the Trust. It provides a fertile testing ground for new gardeners through the Gardening Schools. In addition, the Peckover Estate owns other property in the town, and approximately 50 acres of open land close to the House and Gardens, mostly leased to community sports groups.

We are pleased to welcome you to tour the property soon by morning coffee and chocolate in the 17th century Reed Barn Restaurant, where you will learn an interesting talk. Following this, you can wander on a two-hour tour of the house and gardens with the opportunity to see some fine 20th Property Manager and Gardener-in-Charge. Finish of the event with a light lunch back at the Reed Barn.

We look forward to welcoming you to this gem of a property.

Note on access arrangements: the garden has level paths, and a single-storey Folly pavilion inside, service is available to the public to share and request. This house has a beautiful external and is an opportunity for visitors to attend to.

14th June 2007

Itinerary

10.00am *Guests arrive. Welcome and morning coffee served in 17th century Reed Barn Restaurant with a talk on the National Trust's work.*

10.30am *Tour of the House with Property Manager.*

11.30am *Tour of the Garden with Gardener in Charge.*

12.30am *Light lunch in the Reed Barn.*

1.30pm *Brief thank you and speech on the importance of legacy gifts to the National Trust.*

1.45pm *Goodbye and depart.*

Following your morning at Peckover you might like to take the opportunity to visit Octavia Hill's Birthplace House in Wisbech (a visit the life and work of one of the founders of the National Trust. This birthplace house will be open 1pm until 5pm, free of charge, from 1pm and the Chairman of the Trustees will be delighted to facilitate you on the exciting opportunity ahead for the National.

Photographs, clockwise from top: exterior. The windows to the Drawing Room; tea, early 20th century portraits, view in the social; nearby townscape taken with gardens in The Cafe and the Reed or Plane.

WINNING

**Winning isn't everything –
but wanting to win is.**

Vince Lombardi

It feels good to win. Triumphing inspires a range of positive feelings from elation and excitement to pride and pleasure. People not only feel a positive emotion when they win; they also tend to express that emotion.

Why is winning important?

Our brain evolved to constantly compare itself to others. It rewards us with a good feeling when we come out on top or gain an advantage. Today we expect high levels of reward, so tend to follow people or brands that deliver this need.

Positioning the winning physical benefits over the spiritual enabled us to attract far more converts to Transcendental Meditation.

MORE TIME FOR BUSY PEOPLE.

OVER 3 MILLION PEOPLE FIND THE TIME AND ENERGY TO DO MORE BECAUSE THEY PRACTISE TRANSCENDENTAL MEDITATION.
For more information phone Karen Matthews free of charge on
0800 269 303.

TRANSCENDENTAL MEDITATION
Or write to: Transcendental Meditation FREEPOST London SW1P 4YY.

My first love wasn't a girl or a football team, it was a car. My mind can still conjure up the moment. I was seven years old and the object of my desire was parked directly outside the rear exit of Cavendish House in Cheltenham. As I emerged from the shop with my mother, the sight of it bewitched me – a Ferrari Dino 246 in Rosso Corsa red with silver Campagnola wheels. It was beautiful; I was smitten.

Of course this love was to remain unrequited, I could only fantasise about owning such grown-up exotica. But I could still get close through the pages of a motor magazine. Over the next thirty years, I devoured hundreds of reviews of the latest supercars in Autocar, CAR, Auto Express, EVO, Top Gear, and What Car?. I wanted to know how they were built, where they were built, the designer's name,

latest modifications and innovations, number of valves per cylinder, number of cylinders per engine, recommended motor oils, service intervals, even the depth of the shagpile carpet.

To feed my curiosity in more recent times, I turn to YouTube and videos for my car porn, lapping up the drama of such confrontations as Alfa GTV v Fiat Dino, Audi TT v BMW Z4, Honda Type R v Subaru WRX, and Volvo S80 v Mercedes E.

While gawping at all this rich content kept me entertained, invariably it carried a deflating residual effect. Rather than this hobby/obsession giving comfort, it left me feeling like a loser, feeling that I was driving a car clearly 'off the pace', that I must change it for something faster, more comfortable, better looking, more economical, or perhaps the same car in a trendier colour. I would convince myself (after more fraught referencing) that there was only one possible way to solve my dilemma – buy a different car.

This would work for a while, but within no time I would be hit by another attack of buyer's remorse and the cycle would be repeated. As a result, I have changed my car over 60 times. Lost in this agony of multiplicity, my search to find the perfect car has seemed never ending, never resolved. I'm not unique, millions suffer in varying degrees from the same gnawing doubts: Have they bought the best their money can buy or an over-priced dud? Can they really trust the self-appointed experts? Are they really as neutral as they appear?

Happily for myself and these poor souls there is a solution – Which? magazine. Its impartial reviewers test thousands of products to enable their subscribers to make more enlightened choices about where they should spend their money. It's a brilliant resource, especially for dithering consumers like me.

When we started working for the magazine's producers, Consumers Association, they were struggling to get this USP across and had resorted to recruiting subscribers via a banal prize draw and first-three-months-free offer. While initial sign ups were good, attrition rates – particularly in the fourth month – were high.

We felt a better way to cement loyalty lay in highlighting the real strength of the proposition – the power to be a winning consumer.

We created a commercial that showed the core target audience (middle-class home owners) enjoying life because, as Which? subscribers, they had a huge team of product experts working for them. The action takes place in their home, where white-coated testers whizz about at breakneck speed, testing hoovers, lawn mowers, TVs, wine, and even beds. Amidst the frenzy – led by an upbeat Hugh Lawrie voice over – our couple live out the ultimate consumer fantasy, serene in the knowledge that their hard-earned cash has been utilised for maximum effect and pleasure. To the like-minded audience we were targeting, they represented nirvana, the art of winning big with little effort.

The campaign smashed all targets, bringing in more subscribers and with a much higher propensity to remain loyal. From that day to this, Which? has junked prize draws and concentrated on adopting a product-led approach for all their recruitment.

Which? magazine 60 second subscription DRTV script

When it comes to getting the best out of life

Some people have a distinct advantage

As Which? Subscribers, they have an army of independent experts

Working just for them

They know that no matter what they buy

They'll always be buying what's best

All they have to do is make their own very individual choices

At Which?, hundreds of products and services are tested and suggested every month

So you choose the best quality, the best value

Whichever's best for you

Which isn't available in the shops so call for your free, no obligation trial

And start getting the best out of life

Footnote:

My search has ended, the itch has been scratched and calmed. I have bought one of Elon Musk's incredible Teslas; it is fast, comfortable and looks great in blue. I no longer need to seek out another oil burner, but I do need to get another hobby.

Plutchik's Wheel of Emotion

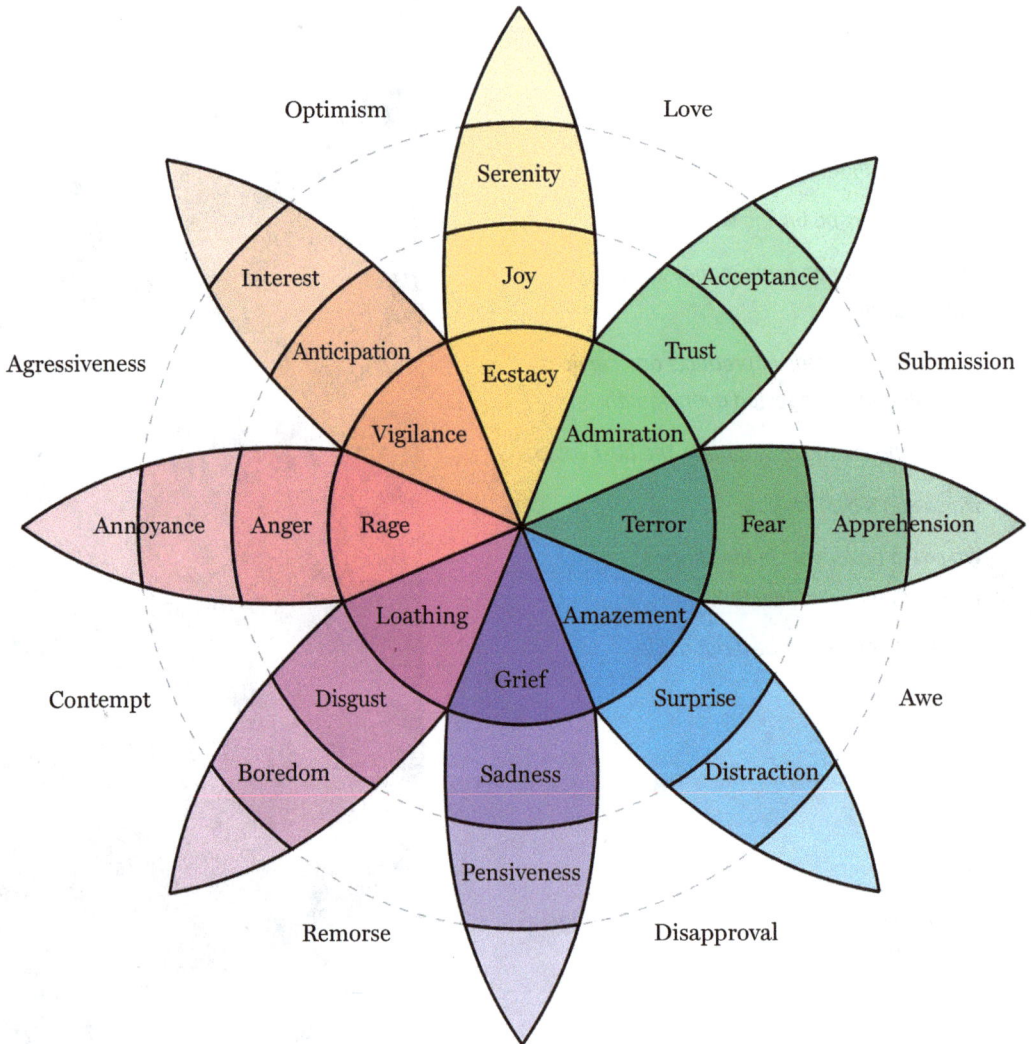

Optimism

Love

Serenity

Joy

Acceptance

Interest

Trust

Anticipation

Ecstacy

Agressiveness

Submission

Vigilance

Admiration

Annoyance Anger Rage

Terror Fear Apprehension

Loathing

Amazement

Contempt

Disgust

Grief

Surprise

Awe

Boredom

Sadness

Distraction

Pensiveness

Remorse

Disapproval

With over 34,000 distinguishable emotions, Robert Plutchik simplified and organized our instinctive state of mind in his Wheel of Emotions.

OUTRO

While we live our lives forward, we only truly understand them backwards. As a 22-year-old creative marketer, I wish I knew then what I know now; hopefully this book will help you avoid the pitfalls I couldn't.

My objective has been to illustrate the merits of making the emotional needs of your audience, your first consideration. Experience has shown me that when it comes to firing customers into action, it is THE essential component.

The exciting news is that the 30 emotions I've illustrated, represent just a tiny fraction of the emotional territory available.

When William James published *The Principles of Psychology* in 1890 on the importance of emotions, he proposed that there were just four – fear, grief, love, and rage.

Today, the psychologist Robert Plutchik believes that humans can actually experience 34,000 unique emotions. While most are obscure (for example *Abbiocco* – the sleepy feeling after a big meal; *Han* – a combination of love and hope; *Pronoia* – the opposite of paranoia) there are still hundreds distinct enough to be understood and, in a marketing context, exploited.

Emotions remain gold dust for marketers because they retain an inexhaustible ability to make us susceptible and suggestable. Despite the vast differences in culture around the world, the basis of all human DNA is identical, and there are few attributes more central to the universal human experience than the way we emote. The things that make us feel angry, sad, happy or joyful are essentially, the same things.

As I said in the introduction, Alfred Hitchcock understood this implicitly. That is why he remains one of the world's most successful and studied film directors. I highly recommend further investigation of his work.

Over this final section of the book, I'd like to share more insights, observations and experiences from my 40 years in the marketing business. I hope, after you've read them, they impart in you a feeling of *Kaifas.**

Relief from having completed something significant and being duly rewarded with something amazing.

YOU ARE NOT ALONE.

In writing this book, I've highlighted 30 emotions and explained how I've used them to simplify my message and connect with the intended audience.

All of these emotions will be familiar to you, but during my research I've come across more obscure emotional touchpoints which may also be of interest. Although possessing little-known names, they too seem to be part of the universal human experience. Here are a few that might interest you...

Trumspringa

The longing to wander off your career track to pursue a simpler life.

Déjà vu

Most know this one; the feeling you've been to a place before or you are repeating an event.

Ellipsism

A sense of sadness that you won't live to see the future. For example, not seeing a grandchild into adulthood.

Vemödalen

The fear that originality is no longer possible (I get this often).

Foreclearing

The act of deliberately refusing to learn scientific explanations in case it ruins the magic.

Liberosis

The desire to care less about things. Wishing you could be a child without cares and concerns.

Ozurie

Feeling torn between the life you want and the life you have.

Idlewild

Feeling grateful to be stranded in a place where you can't do much of anything, like sitting for two hours in an airport.

The kick drop

The moment you wake up from an immersive dream and have to quickly adjust to the real world.

Justing

The habit of telling yourself that one tweak could solve all your problems.

Ludiosis

The sense that you're making it all up as you go along.

Xena

Smallest measure of human connection, typically exchanged between passing strangers. A smile, a sympathetic nod, a shared laugh about an odd coincidence.

Scribedread

Frisson felt by writers on handing their book over for critical appraisal.

If you like these, you'll find more in The Dictionary of Obscure Sorrows by John Koenig.

THE SECOND CHEAPEST BOTTLE OF WINE.

Ever sat in a restaurant looking at the wine list, feeling slightly intimated by the endless complex choice of reds, whites, rose, and champagnes on offer? Your partner is waiting, so too is the sommelier standing at your shoulder. Just moments ago you were carefree, happy at the prospect of the meal ahead. Now in your anxiety, they seem to be judging your next move. Your partner looks relaxed enough but is transmitting a very clear message; *does he know what he's doing?* The smartly dressed sommelier is sending another vibe; is he a cheapskate?

Then you do what everybody does in the same situation, you avoid the cheapest bottle at £23 and opt instead for the one slightly more expensive at £25. With the deed done, you snap the wine book shut and hand it back to the impassive waiter. They seem to be smirking, but at least the ordeal is over.

Alas, according to the experts, choosing the second cheapest wine isn't the smart thing to do. Because restaurateurs know diners will take this option to avoid looking like a penny pincher, so they give it the highest mark-up. Ergo the second bottle of wine is usually the worst value.

Peculiar and idiosyncratic as this awkward social convention may be, there are parallels in the fundraising world, particularly at public charity auctions. In the heady atmosphere, bidders can be sucked into absurd acts of generosity either by fear of looking mean or a desire to appear wealthy. I have on occasion been caught up in this madness myself, paying over the odds for autographed sporting prints I didn't need or bespoke knitted jumpers I would never wear.

The act of giving as showing off has been well understood and exploited by charities for decades. The Battersea Coats and Collars Ball is an excellent example of this phenomenon. The great, the good and the wealthy are fleeced without mercy for the entire evening; most are happy to bid eye-watering sums; many go home with trinkets of dubious value.

The same is not true for individual fundraising, where people can ponder and rationalise the amounts they want to give in the privacy of their own homes. There is no auctioneer driving them on to give more, no crowd to impress. They can tick the first donation box, give the minimum amount, and still feel good about it. In this environment, the fundraiser has to employ other methods to upsell; normally, they don't have to be too sophisticated or original.

The recognition of a 'certificate of thanks' remains attractive, the incentive of an 'exclusive tiepin or brooch' for giving more has been known to turn the head of even the most parsimonious of donors. One example we produced that worked well in this regard was for WWF's Korup

Rainforest Appeal. Recipients were asked to give £20 to sponsor and protect an acre of the Cameroon rainforest, in return for which they would receive a certificate signed by conservationist Gerald Durrell. If they could stretch to £40 for two acres, they would also be sent a copy of David Attenborough's The Living Planet. This simple tactic helped raise the average gift by over 100%.

Using the same approach for the Whale and Dolphin Society, this time offering an exclusive T-shirt for donations over £25, boosted the usual gift level by 150%.

One of my favourite upsell successes was for the RSPCA's Operation Seal Rescue appeal. To add extra involvement to the act of giving, we included a strip of self-adhesive donation stamps, inviting recipients to select a stamp of the right value, tear it off, lick the back, and place it in the box on the form. Sneakily, we made the stamp with the lowest amount – £9.50 – the trickiest to get to, placing it in the middle of the strip.

Not beyond the dexterity of most people you might think, but just enough for the majority of responders to opt for the less fiddly £19 stamp, at a stroke doubling the usual amount given by donors.

£19.00
provides a seal with food, medicines and care for TWO DAYS.
Use one of these stamps to show how much you are giving to save our seals. Simply stick it on the donation form in the space provided.

£28.50
provides a seal with food, medicines and care for THREE DAYS.
Use one of these stamps to show how much you are giving to save our seals. Simply stick it on the donation form in the space provided.

£9.50
provides a seal with food, medicines and care for ONE DAY.
Use one or these stamps to show how much you are giving to save our seals. Simply stick it on the donation form in the space provided.

£66.50
provides a seal with food, medicines and care for a WHOLE WEEK.
Use one of these stamps to show how much you are giving to save our seals. Simply stick it on the donation form in the space provided.

£266
provides a seal with food, medicines and care for a WHOLE MONTH.
Use one of these stamps to show how much you are giving to save our seals. Simply stick it on the donation form in the space provided.

**Goodness is the only investment
that never fails.**

Henry David Thoreau

DAMN, THAT FEELS GOOD.

I can't lie, working for good causes can be a pain for a creative.

Limited money, very tight timescales, a reluctance to innovate, and overbearing trustees have been four constants. For the first ten years of my career, I worked for commercial organisations like American Express, BT, Coutts Bank, Cunard, Ford cars and Sony. Budgets and ambitions were generally far bigger and we always got plenty of time to make everything look beautiful.

So why have I spent the last thirty years working for the Third Sector?

The first reason is the challenge. As a creative, the intellectual poser of having to create value propositions armed with nothing more than emotions is hugely appealing.

The second reason is that it feels good. I enjoy taking money from strangers, happy in the knowledge that the wealth I've taken from people I'll never meet, has gone to deserving causes I love. It's nice telling your children that in your day job you do some good. I also like to think that by promoting the act of giving, I have helped the payer too.

Doing good can be its own reward. Many people feel a rush after performing a good deed. This 'helper's high' is produced when the brain releases endorphins, the feel-good chemicals.

It is well documented but not well enough promoted that humans are happier when they do the right thing; the more we do this on a consistent basis, the more we tend to like ourselves. By doing things like giving to charity we can create more positive emotions and a better self-image.

Conversely, when we don't do things of value to others we don't feel good, often without really knowing why, as if we are somehow letting ourselves down.

Perhaps in order to raise national and global well-being from its depressing low point, we should launch an initiative to shift public attitudes towards a more enlightened view of the benefits of altruism and selflessness.

We all fear irrelevance. Being part of something bigger than ourselves, such as curing cancer, combating poverty, or stopping animal cruelty, can help us feel more connected, more important, more significant. As the 21st century searches for alternative forms of inner fulfilment, helping good causes could provide an inexhaustible source of peace and happiness.

THE ONES THAT GOT AWAY.

One of the greatest thrills for a creative is persuading a client to run a brave idea. Going boldly where no one has gone before is a leap of faith for all concerned. This book highlights times when that has paid off handsomely. The 'dead feet' posters for Help the Aged; MSF's colour inserts; WWF's 'adultery' legacy campaign; the radical new interpretation of The Salvation Army's work.

Of course there are many times when salesmanship, enthusiasm, and a cogent argument, cannot carry the day and the idea is rejected. All commercial creativity has to have limits and those are set by those who pay the bills – your client. When this has happened to me, the discarded ideas are often confined to the bin, normally the one directly outside the client's office.

I have kept hold of a number of these unsponsored masterpieces. Perhaps in the vain hope I can convince someone of their merit at a later date.

Here are four of my favourite losers...

StepChange Debt Charity

Being trapped in debt is a dark place to be. Knowing that for many people asking for help can be traumatic, this concept highlighted the benefits of coming forward to experience the euphoria of freedom from the woes of owing money.

RNLI

The volunteer lifeboat crews who risk their lives to rescue those in peril on the seas are the nearest we have to real flesh and blood super heroes. In this concept for an animated TV commercial, we portrayed an RNLI crew member emerging from the seas like a benevolent version of the Greek god Poseidon, to lift a sinking fishing trawler out of danger. Despite the memorable iconography, the client wasn't convinced.

Christian Aid

Christian Aid posed us a question: Can we make them synonymous with giving at Christmas and grow income? We said we could if we were allowed to change their name for the whole of December to Christmas Aid. The fundraisers loved it, the brand police did not. Humbug.

RSPCA

We wanted to shock people into joining a campaign to stop the scrapping of the dog licence. The idea we created starkly illustrated the consequences of doing so, namely the death of more dogs. Although we thought it was pretty strong stuff, the client didn't agree and chose something even stronger from AMV BBDO, the famous 'dead dogs ad' shown on page 235.

#FindDebtZen

christmas **aid**

christmas **aid**

christmas **aid**

The one year old female Labrador is brought into the room. Shaking nervously, she is lifted onto the table. The vet approaches with a needle and injects the overdose of anaesthetic into her back leg. The animal gives a small whimper and closes her eyes.

Within seconds the animal is dead, placed in a black bin liner and put onto the heap with the others. In a hour they will be taken away for cremation. This no fantasy horror, this is reality. Every day RSPCA has to kill hundreds of healthy dogs and puppies this way because of irresponsible dog ownership due to the scrapping of the dog licence. Support our new dog registration scheme and end the slaughter today. Call 0800 400478 for details.

RSPCA

Trash the dog licence.
Trash the dog.

0 m.p.g.
RALEIGH

A guaranteed seat to work every morning.
The nippy ten-speed Raleigh Arena.
RALEIGH

0-20 in 9.2 seconds.
The nippy ten-speed Raleigh Arena.
RALEIGH

4.2 cu. ft. baggage space.
The smooth spacious Raleigh Nova.
RALEIGH

NO SENSATION. NO SALE.

Imagine the scene. You are twenty-one-years old, fresh out of art college. You are sitting in an enormous reception in a London advertising agency, so enormous you almost feel agoraphobic, certainly diminished. The space is over air-conditioned; you are chilly. The stiff collar of your brand-new, straight-out-of-the-box shirt is rubbing your neck. Your shoes vanish into the thick beige carpet. The whitewashed walls are covered with chrome-framed creative award certificates. They shout: this place is special, we hope you're intimidated.

Other walls are spotted with the latest masterpieces for Alfa Romeo, Bovril, Coca Cola, Brut aftershave, and British Airways. The year is 1980, so without exception, headlines are short and capitalised, body copy semi-justified, images full bleed.

You peer down the corridor, see glimpses of activity in the offices. Impossibly attractive people hurry by, carrying papers, folders, flipcharts, layout pads, chrome coffee pots.

You wonder. Perhaps here it is forbidden to walk around empty handed, to look unfocused, lacking purpose. Most of these industrious superhumans are young, probably no more than a couple of years older than you. But in their sophistication and your insecurity they appear a world away from you, nursing your oversized art portfolio on the deep-cushioned, low-backed leather sofa.

You're not the only one feeling the same way. Sitting with you are four more advertising students, like you also hoping for their big break, all looking as nervous as first day pupils. You've all been shortlisted for the prestigious Creative Circle award, with work deemed good enough to give you a crack at winning a full-time job at the extraordinary palace of advertising that is Ogilvy and Mather.

All you have to do to enter this promised land is convince the judges behind the oak-veneered boardroom door opposite that your concept is the best solution to persuade people to rediscover their love for bikes. In particular Raleigh bikes.

OK, you can stop imagining now. I've enjoyed a successful career, but it didn't start on that day in Ogilvy's.

While the judges liked my idea of presenting the benefits of bikes as a car manufacturer would do (original concepts shown here), they scored me down for my lack of passion in selling it. They said the winner appeared to want it more and sold their idea 'from the heart'. I remember one stinging comment in particular: 'He was passionate about his work, we didn't get that feeling about you.'

It was an early sighter of one of the most important lessons in advertising:

If you can't convince your client about the brilliance of your work, then it will never see the light of day. **No sensation. No sale.**

BETTER MARMITE THAN MEDIOCRE.

Last year, I was enjoying a break in Sorrento and noticed a Marc Chagall exhibition being advertised just off the main square, so went to have a peek.

Chagall was an early modernist painter famous for his fearless use of colour. Taking in his extraordinarily bold paintings, etchings, and glasswork, it was impossible to feel neutral about his work. While I was a fan, some around me clearly weren't. One middle-aged couple muttered displeasure about 'the crudity of line' and 'poor composition'. They promptly left shaking their heads. Chagall would have been delighted, as like all great painters he believed the role of art was to arrest, polarise, and create emotion. At the exit of the exhibition, I noticed this quote from the artist:

> *'If I can create from the heart, nearly everything works; if from the head, almost nothing.'*

I'm no Chagall but this neatly sums up my career as a creative fundraiser. When I've created work designed to get an emotional reaction, invariably it has succeeded; when I've created it from a rational point of view, it hasn't. At Campfire, we apply this philosophy to everything we do and generally our clients are happy for us to chase strong feelings to trigger a response, any response, even if that includes love or hate.

Sometimes this can be unsettling and raise blood pressure. I recall difficult conversations with clients and trying to soothe their worries. Telling them that early negative reactions were often a good sign, that the work was being seen, that this was usually a good indicator it would be successful. In most cases (thank goodness) I was right, proving that the most ineffective marketing is usually the type that nobody notices or even cares enough about to complain.

I've heard the lament that it's all too easy in these play-it-safe times to produce mediocre fundraising work, but I maintain it's extraordinarily difficult. You've got to be pretty calculated to produce work that doesn't register at all on someone's emotional Richter scale. In my experience, human beings are ready to emote with you at the slightest provocation. Not to arouse a flicker of feeling, a tingle of curiosity, or even to raise a single hair on the back of a single neck, must mean that you've either produced something totally derivative or completely devoid of passion. It's time to be bolder, more Marmite, and if necessary ruffle a few feathers. Fundraising is serious work, we're in the business of saving lives, alleviating misery, righting horrific injustices, saving our planet; we shouldn't concern ourselves with petty sensibilities when the stakes are this high. Because after all, if we can't get worked up about our cause, then why should anybody else?

PBS

Be a believer

In a few years time he'll be glad you did

Believe our mission to expose injustices and get to the truth should be protected?

Believe our nation's children should be able to access the best educational support and resources totally free?

Believe your community should be able to watch local, un-biased new reporting 24/7?

Then make a gift in your will to PBS and become a believer today.

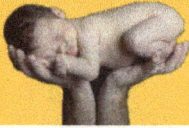

PBS

Never compromise

Why suffer poor drama when you can watch the best? Why settle for second-class educational shows when you can offer your kids first class?

Why accept biased news reporting when you can be given the unadulterated truth? Why put up with second-rate music when you can see it at the Met?

You shouldn't compromise in life, so don't accept it when you're gone. leave a gift to PBS and protect broadcasting without compromises.

PBS

Keep the big idea alive

Back in the sixties we had a groovy idea - to expand people's minds to breaking point.

We wanted to fill the minds of children with exciting ways to connect with numbers and literacy; to expose whole generations to wonderful new worlds of music, theatre and the arts; to bring incredibly diverse cultures into the living rooms of millions of homes and deliver true unbiased news programs free from commercial influence - for the first time in a long time.

We thought it was a big idea then and we still do now. By making a gift to PBS, you can help us keep the dream alive until the next time the sixties come around.

PBS

Give ignorance a tough time

Be against ignorance, darkness, illiteracy, innumeracy and innocence.

Be for enlightenment, intelligence and knowing.

Give just $5 a month to PBS (just over a dollar a week as you know) and help us continue to educate, astound and amaze millions of Americans near you.

PBS

Indiana pride

Stretching from Alabama to Wyoming, from the busy heart of New York to the remoteness of West Plains, Missouri PBS's commitment to quality and unbiased television touches virtually every citizen in out nation.

You can help protect our stake in the future prosperity of your state by making a small gift in your will to PBS.

If you do, we'll add your name to the Fame Wall at your local PBS station office, its dedicated to all those local citizens who helped protect free quality public broadcasting for the great state of Indiana.

PBS

GIVE A LITTLE GET A LOT!!!

We want to be straight with you - we're looking for money. We're not asking you for $30, we don't want $20, we're not even looking for $10 but just a miserly five bucks.

Actually, we're not even chasing that. We would like to ask you for just over a dollar a week.

We'll turn your dollar into something truly magical for millions of men, women and especially children in your state and beyond. Your dollar will help protect free quality broadcasting and bring the magic of Sesame Street and Downton Abbey into their homes.

PBS

Freedom is never free

But five bucks a month is about is pretty close

The price of freedom can be high, many good people have died in its cause. At PBS we believe in speaking truth to the American people, regardless of those who may not want us to.

Sometimes we have to rely on friends help protect these fundamental principals.Join them today by giving $5 a month, we hope you'll agree it's a small price to pay something as priceless as liberty.

PBS

1% of you can save 100% of me

What better cause can there be than protecting the education of American children and ensuring others can enjoy quality and un-biased programming totally free?

After looking after your nearest and dearest please consider giving just 1% of your estate to PBS. Just a small fraction of the value of your estate could mean your local PBS can continue to broadcast and provide a priceless resource to millions within your community and across America.

PBS

Keep this wolf from our door

When Romney came gunning for PBS it was a tense moment. If he had succeeded in cutting government funds it could have sunk us.

Meaning no more Sesame Street, no more Downton Abbey, no more bias free local news programs –and no more free broadcasting. Romney may not have got elected but there will be more like him in the future, eager to test our value and very existence.

Give $5 a month to protect our mission to bring the finest programming into your community.

PBS

When Saint Peter asks you at the Pearly Gates what gift you left behind you can tell him:

enlightenment

You can tell him by supporting PSB, you helped protect one of the most trusted news and current affairs providers in the United States.

You can also let him know (if he has time) you gave the gift of literacy and numeracy to millions of kids. That you took young and old alike around the world to sample new cultures and the arts.

Most of all you can tell him you gave people the truth and enlightenment they would have otherwise been denied, all totally free of charge. Amen.

ASK CUSTOMERS WHAT THEY WANT.
GIVE IT TO THEM. DUH.

Seems obvious doesn't it? But all too often, clients want to tell their audience what they want to tell them rather than what their audience want to hear.

I'm a big fan of research, especially stakeholder and supporter workshops. Managed properly, they can reveal what moves people in the real world to engage with a particular cause or brand. At Campfire, we run plenty of these workshops to help us deliver the best message with the right emotional pitch. We ask our audience direct questions. What really makes them feel happy, sad or mad? What really moves them or turns them off? What's the real reason they give? And as importantly, what's the reason they don't? We press for honest answers, we get nosey, we ask the same question in six different ways to get to the one truthful answer. As a further methodology to give us what we require, we produce polarising concepts to provoke a reaction.

The set of ideas (shown left) I put together for the Public Broadcasting Service in America provide a good example of this technique. The free-to-air television network was facing damaging cuts to its funding so had asked us to help it locate and recruit new donors.

Creating ideas in this detailed way meant we could explore propositions, images, and copy tone in forensic detail with the audience at which they were aimed. For a community based broadcaster like PBS serving 50 different states, many with polar opposite views, allegiances and political leanings, this was particularly important.

IBM, the American technology giant, expanded its business and remained customer relevant on its extensive use of research panels. Its philosophy was ludicrously simple:

1. Ask customers what they want.

2. Give it to them.

So, when preparing your next creative brief, don't ask:

'What do we want to say to our customers?'

Instead ask:

'What do they want to hear?'
'How do we want them to feel?'
'How can we help them?'

'WE CAN'T GET THE F*****G VAN OUT!'

5th June 2004, 2.40pm.

I'm driving a white transit van on the marble smooth A28 through north-eastern France. Life feels good, the sun is shining, I have my partner Heather by my side, and the back of the van is crammed to the roof with fundraising success.

We're on our way to the Normandy coast to fulfil our obligation to 100,000 people who participated in our D-Day appeal for the Royal British Legion. Along with their donations, they've all written a personal message on a flag in memory of the British and Commonwealth soldiers who died during the landings on 6th June, 1944. We've promised to plant every single one at Saint-Aubin-sur-Mer, the five-mile stretch of coastline more commonly known by military historians as Sword Beach.

We're in high spirits, the campaign has raised millions and we've got a few hours to enjoy the scenery before we have to get to work. Our plan is to plant our small lollipop-sticked paper flags in the sand the following morning and then inform the media of the position – giving us the best chance of making the front pages the next day. To add human interest, we've organised for a D-Day veteran, his son, and grandson to attend.

We arrive at the Sainte Mere Eglise campsite at 6pm, park up, and meet Ed our photographer who had come down earlier to find the best location for our picture. The site he's chosen is just two kilometres away and his test shots look great. After practising spacing the rows of flags, we enjoy an excellent dinner at the local creperie and retire early to our tents. The weather forecast is good and the media had been told where and when to arrive. *What could possibly go wrong?*

6th June, 3.30am.

We rise blearily from our tent. The sun is just edging up, the sky is clear, first box ticked. Resourceful Ed has already made coffee and bacon butties for later in the morning. We head for our vehicles, him to his small van, his lights, and cameras, us to the transit and our boxes of flags.

Horror. The empty car park from the previous evening is now a chaos of

vehicles. As is the French way, nobody has taken heed of where or how they have parked. The transit is completed hemmed in by lorries, trucks, and cars, with no way to find their owners and get it free. We have no choice; we must transfer everything to Ed's vehicle. After half an hour of frantic effort we decide we have to go, leaving at least half the flags and their messages still in the transit.

The media coach is due at the site at 8am, giving us around three hours to make our display. Ed, Heather, and I set to work wordlessly on the sands, planting the rows twice as wide as we had practised the night before to cover more area.

As we toil on our hands and knees, my watch beeps. 5.30am, the time the battle had begun 60 years ago. I stare out to sea, imagining what a bowel-loosening sight the invasion fleet must have been to the defenders. The entire horizon filled with warships, thousands of guns ready to turn you and your mates to dust.

A noise on the adjacent road nudges me from my daydream, whistling coming through the morning mist. As I continue to look in the direction of the sound, a British soldier emerges dressed in full khaki battledress, Lee Enfield rifle slung on his back and pushing a bicycle. He looks over and smiles before continuing on his way, disappearing into the murk, still whistling. Heads down on the sand, Heather and Ed have not seen this curious apparition, I decide not to interrupt them from their labours.

Two hours later we have covered an area of a football pitch, more than enough for a decent image. My phone rings – it's Andrew Jones, my client at the Legion.

'We're five minutes away, how we looking? No dramas, I hope?'

I didn't tell him about our brush with disaster and luckily he didn't count the flags either. The next day the Legion dominated the front pages with some fantastic coverage.

MOVED TO TEARS.

My father was an emotional man, but for the first eighty years of his life, I never saw him cry. He would laugh, get angry, jump for joy, even show anxiety, but the tears would not come.

Then one day as I sat with him watching a programme about a year in the life of a pride of African lions, it happened. As is the way with wildlife films, to help the viewer engage emotionally with their story, each lion had been named. The pride leader, Nala, had given birth to cubs Leo and Elsa and we followed their mother's struggles to keep them alive in the face of a severe drought and lack of food. In one scene, the adult lions were busy hunting an antelope when four-month-old Elsa became separated from the pride. Within seconds a lone hyena following the hunt had snatched the cub and killed it.

It was heartbreaking and the dam of emotional empathy I had built for these animals suddenly burst, the tears started flowing. As I reached for my handkerchief I looked over at Dad, he was sobbing like a baby too. It was a doubly poignant moment.

Film can trigger emotion better than any other medium and evoke feelings so powerful, viewers feel like a victim to them – like they have control over you and your response.

Charities have come to appreciate the potency of the medium and in recent times film has played a much larger part in the fundraising story. So much so that to help us handle the demand, we created a specialist film unit at Campfire, producing explainer videos, DRTV commercials, and digital content.

With its ability to convey authentic emotional punch from the perspective of staff, volunteers and beneficiaries, we have found that a good film can strengthen any fundraising ask. With advertising and marketing being so saturated with artificial or forced emotions, people have become expert at spotting fakes. But when asked in the right way, people on the 'charity frontline' can put across a quality of believable raw emotion guaranteed to melt the most cynical of hearts.

I remember interviewing four people in particular and being unable to control my tears as they relayed their story.

The young woman made homeless at 16 who was given the confidence to make a better life because the charity (Centrepoint) had believed in her.

For MNDA, the testimony of David who had lost his once vibrant, energetic mother to motor neurone disease in the space of just six months.

For Wood Green, the animal charity, hearing from Monika, a senior member of the care team, and her joyous account of seeing an abandoned dog finally find the love and new owner it deserved.

Sitting with Lorraine who had lost her marriage, home and job because of the early onset of Alzheimer's.

These stories contributed to films which all produced great results. In the case of Wood Green, it helped convert dozens of legacy enquirers into pledgers, generating hundreds of thousands of pounds.

Clearly I'm a fan of moving pictures. Properly harnessed, film is a wonderfully engaging medium and should remain an integral part of any charity's fundraising armoury.

After all, if it can move my stiff-upper-lipped father to tears, just imagine what it could do to yours.

SHOCK: CLIENTS SHOULD BE FRIENDS.

Eighteen months into my career, the big day finally came – I was going to meet a client. As a junior creative, I had been kept well away from 'the bastards who really pay your salary', as my then boss liked to refer to them.

I wasn't given a speaking role, I was instructed only to say something if directly addressed and to keep my answer short. I sat anxiously in the agency boardroom as the four-strong client team walked in; to me they looked stern, serious and utterly terrifying. My back was straight, my face smiling, only my shaking legs knew the real story.

In the event I wasn't asked anything, the whole meeting was handled by the agency account director, Miranda Bell. I quietly marvelled as she effortlessly sold my concept and persuaded the client (Coutts Bank) to buy it despite their initial misgivings. She and the senior client had great rapport, they seemed to genuinely like each other.

After the meeting, I asked Miranda how she had learnt to be so relaxed and in control. *'I knew it might be a tricky meeting, so I met the senior client with the concepts last night; we agreed on our approach over a bottle of Sancerre. That meeting was all show for her team.'*

She said she always tried to get to know her clients outside of the business environment; as in the case of Coutts, it always made selling bolder, riskier work easier.

'Most clients want maximum innovation with minimal risk. The impossible Holy Grail of an original idea that has miraculously worked before! Knowing your client well helps you get round that particularly tricky equation.'

Taking her advice, when I started to run my own agencies, I always attempted to transcend the formal buyer-seller client relationship and elevate it to one of mutual understanding and friendship. In short, act like a partner, not a supplier. It has not always been easy. I recall clients who have kept us at arm's length and treated their buyer position as something of a power trip. I remember vividly one unpleasant individual at a major charity who regarded us as if we were slime. But when I have succeeded, it has helped smooth the path to infinitely more innovative and effective work. Over my career, time spent in pubs, coffee bars, conferences, horse racing courses, football matches or doing whatever else floats my client's boat, has always been time well spent.

Generally as in life, the more people know you, the more likely they are to trust you. Of course, ultimately both sides benefit. The client gets an agency they can trust to go the extra mile and deliver. The agency gains a client who will respect them and stay around for more than just five minutes and the first free lunch.

Great relationships = great clients = great campaigns. Simples.

THE IMPORTANCE OF EMOTIONAL ESCAPE.

'*It's a kind of hopelessness I guess. Helplessness,*' said Ross Simpson, 22, from Glasgow. He's articulating how he and his friends feel about stopping the effects of climate change. Seeing so many negative stories of heatwaves, droughts, floods, and global temperatures on the rise, is crushing. Like many of his generation, he worries it's already too late.

'*What difference does changing your lifestyle make? Why do anything, if we're all doomed anyway?*' he bewails.

Noor Elmasry, 22, from Chicago, feels equally pessimistic.

'*Frustration manifests from people in power constantly disappointing you,*' she says.

Their anxiety is shared by many other young people around the world. Of 10,000 who were asked about climate change in a recent survey, three-quarters said the future was 'frightening', and more than half thought 'humanity was doomed.'

This is nothing new. Throughout human history, anxiety has been a constant, a persistent thorn pricking at our well-being. For our earliest ancestors, it was fear of sabre-toothed cats. For Anglo Saxons, concern of a Viking invasion. For Europeans in the mid-1300s, dread of the Black Death. For us today, apprehension is fired by sights such as the fracturing ice shelf in Antarctica, million of acres of newly infertile soil in Africa or the horror of unchecked forest fires raging across Europe, Australia and North America. All relentlessly beamed into our homes and accompanied by data so credible that even the most optimistic of observers wearing the rosiest, rose tinted sunglasses ever made, would conclude the end of human civilization was very nigh.

Of course, fear is best tackled by action, however small. For climate worriers, even prosaic things like recycling, changing to a plant-based diet, planting a tree, insulating a home, or going on marches, can soothe apprehensions and concerns.

It could also involve helping a good cause. The act of joining or supporting a charity has helped millions of people feel better about the future. It's one reason why the UK non-profit sector is worth over £50 billion. Whether out of a sense of morality, belief in a specific cause, religion, or personal connection, giving helps the giver.

If the sector can continue to hold the trust of the public and institutions to deliver change, it can grow in size and influence further still. If it can also help donors feel that doom is not guaranteed, then the sky really can be the limit.

A lot has changed over my thirty-five year career as an agency fundraiser. Some good, like the rise of the internet, which has presented new opportunities for innovation, targeting and relationship building. Some not so good, such as the hard silos that have grown between brand, media relations, and fundraising. Back in the 1990s integration was the marketing objective; not so now.

One of the biggest victims of this change has been the death of the 'humble charity' and in many respects, with it, the art of storytelling.

Far too often these days, I pick up a piece of communication from a top 100 UK charity and find it stuffed full of dense, self-obsessed language and third-sector banality. I'm not talking about an Annual Review (which being a corporate document you might expect some grandstanding) but frontline fundraising.

As an example, here's an extract from a recent cold DM appeal for a leading UK homelessness charity.

Dear friend,

*Right now, more and more people are feeling the sharp end of poverty as costs continue to rise. The services ***** offers are absolutely vital if we are to stop more people being pushed into homelessness. In my role as a coach I see how our strategy is working – helping people rebuild their lives, step-by-step.*

Our coaches are needed more than ever, with the number of people experiencing homelessness expected to rise dramatically in our present

cost-of-living crisis. Rising rents, energy bills, and surging inflation mean more people are struggling to keep a roof over their heads.

Homelessness can't be solved overnight; it's about being there with people day-by-day through one of the toughest times of their lives.

The job I do is really hard at times. You're helping people who are having some of the worst times of their lives, and it's hard to see. But it's so good to know you're making a difference.

Ask yourself:

Has this got the emotional power and case for support that would make you want to give? Do you really need to hear that there is 'a cost-of-living crisis and surging inflation'? Are you interested in the charity's strategy? Is being told 'homelessness will rise dramatically' helpful or simply overwhelming and demotivating? Are you concerned that his job is 'hard at times'?

The copy is almost totally devoid of authentic feeling and full of lazy clichés, such as 'helping people rebuild their lives' and 'making a difference'. Yawn.

There is nothing more certain to turn off the brain's willingness to engage than by showing it something it has seen thousands of times before.

The surest route to fundraising glory is often the shortest – the one between your donor and your beneficiary. This is the equation that most causes seem to find hardest to understand: donors give through charities, not to them.

The fact is that people aren't interested in how charities do things, they are only interested in what they achieve. I remember doing some research on behalf of the Marine Conservation Society which wanted to improve both its standout and fundraising. We started with some basic simplification.

For example, changing the way it described its key money handles...

From: £10 could help MCS to produce 10 pocket Good Fish Guides to help people make more sustainable seafood choices.

To: £10 could mean 10 more people choosing fish from sustainable sources.

From: £100 could allow MCS to spend an hour advising a fisherman on how to use wildlife-friendly fishing gear.

To: £100 can mean another fisherman using wildlife-friendly fishing gear.

From: £30 could help MCS provide all the equipment required for one volunteer to clear their local beach of fishing litter.

To: £30 helps clear a local beach of dangerous fishing litter.

From: £1,000 could help MCS to carry out 10 underwater surveys to identify areas with vulnerable and rare habitats and wildlife that need protection.

To: £1,000 buys 10 surveys to identify areas that need urgent protection.

While the difference seemed small, removing the charity from the equation clarified the role of the donor and helped improve results.

A bigger gain came after amending the original fundraising proposition from:

MCS has worked hard to identify the solutions which could transform the future for healthy, diverse, and flourishing seas fit for human and sea life alike. Please give what you can to help us.

To: Help protect our seas for future generations.

This clarity is surprisingly easy to achieve by rediscovering one of the oldest superpowers known to fundraising: the art of simple storytelling. It lies at the heart of human social development – when our ancient ancestors gathered together around a campfire to tell each other tales in a conversational, intriguing, and epic way. Alas, there was nothing epic about the story of the 'homelessness coach' featured previously. Worthy yes, but also very dull.

Compare his account with the opening passage for another charity helping the homeless, Merchants Quay Ireland.

...Every day a man named Donal walks through our door.

Silver flecks his hair. Nearer my age – not a young man. Grubby. Battered. Down on his luck.

He is also kind to a fault. Gracious. Gentle. Quiet.

Donal is one of Ireland's hungry. One of Ireland's homeless.

It is hard for him to accept help. But without Merchants Quay he wouldn't eat at all. So Donal always has a 'thanks

very much' for anyone who helps him – whether with a hot meal, a dry pair of socks, or a hot cup of tea.

And Donal sees how our dining room fills now. Once... twice... three times. He doesn't linger, instead he finishes his own meal quickly, to make room for a weary girl years younger...

Most of the people who walk through our doors have nowhere to go. They've been barred from shops and businesses. Degraded. Dehumanised.

Today I write to you about the faces you don't see, to tell you about the ones whose stories you may never read, but whose gratitude for your kindness will be forever etched on their hearts.

The writer has taken us into his world, a world most of us will never see. Within just two sentences he has introduced us to the emotional heart of the appeal – Donal. While he may be grubby (great real-world word), Donal is clearly gracious and kind; we feel both empathy and sympathy for him. From a fundraising point of view, this is crucial because many potential donors reject the homeless as undeserving, perceiving them as a feral, lazy underclass.

We get a sense of how people like Donal are pushed to the margins by businesses, perhaps because they represent an inconvenient truth. And finally, as part of the ask, the writer positions the donor as hero, able to bring some good into this forsaken world through their kindness.

It's a brilliant passage of copy, made all the more poignant for me because it's a shining example of a dying craft – of taking the reader on the journey from ignorance to engagement and giving in under 200 words.

I remember the phrase coined by fundraising guru (and then new boss) David Strickland-Eales, during my first-day induction in 1987, which still holds true today.

'Most people don't give to the brilliance of charities, they give to the agonies of people. We must convince our clients to get out of the way of their own message. If we can do that, we can all watch the money roll in.'

WHO KILLED GENDER MARKETING?

It was billed as the next big thing in direct marketing – gender-specific marketing.

Back in the early 2000s, Target Direct, the agency I had co-founded with the brilliant Stephen Pidgeon and Pauline Lockier, was riding high. A well-regarded good cause specialist employing over 100 people, we worked with most of the UK's top thirty charity brands. We were always looking to innovate and after being inspired by *Men are from Mars, Women are from Venus'* by American writer John Gray, our quest led us into the world of gender marketing.

It raised a question in our minds: if so much of marketing relies on communicating on a one-to-one basis, are we missing a trick by ignoring the sex of the recipient? After developing different gender copy approaches and undertaking qualitative and quantitative research, we found most emphatically that we were.

- Men and women reacted very differently to the style, tone, and language used in communications.

- Both had clear, but different, expectations of the communication context; colour and imagery were more important to women than to men (unless we were talking about cars, in which case the complete reverse was true).

- Women preferred longer copy written in a softer, more conversational style.

- Men were more impatient than women, they needed to get to the point quicker.

These and other indicators gave us the confidence to recommend the approach to clients. In live tests, results for Amnesty and RNIB were encouraging, one for Help the Aged was especially good. We produced two versions of an ophthalmic appeal pack, both featuring a piece of opaque plastic demonstrating the effects of cataracts. The 'female' version contained a three page letter (written in a human centric, emotional and descriptive style) a leaflet, a case study flyer, and a detailed description of life in the India-based project.

The second 'male' version was reduced to a shorter letter (no case studies, and more rational) – the leaflet and detailed project descriptor were also removed. Mailed to men, this shortened pack pulled an astonishing 85% better than the longer 'female' pack. Conversely, this 'male' version mailed to women pulled 15% less than the 'female' pack.

It was a revelation; we had never seen an uplift of that scale achieved through a creative tweak. Highly encouraged, we pushed the idea as a new business recruitment tool for the agency, offering a free video *'Sex for broad-minded clients'*, which described the approach

in more detail. It caused a pleasing stir, generating a lot of new client leads.

Today, gender marketing in the charity sector is no more. So what killed it?

Attitude. A new generation of marketers, raised in a more sensitive culture and anxious to reduce stereotypical gender norms, resisted the notion.

Profusion. Besides males and females, there are now 72 recognised terms for gender identity, including transgender, gender neutral, non-binary, agender, demigender, and pangender.

Cost. Creating bespoke gender versions for every appeal became prohibitive.

I believe there is still room for this sort of targeting in the modern world. Social media's ability to tailor numerous bespoke approaches at minimal cost makes it the perfect channel to resurrect the idea. Producing 72 versions of the same message may appear daunting, but it could be fun trying.

I DIDN'T DO IT, BUT I'M GLAD SOMEONE IN MY AGENCY DID.

I've loved every minute of being a creative, but especially so from the day I became the £1,000-a-day guy. The guy entrusted with the high chair, the final say, the casting vote. The Creative Director.

In that role, I've either personally created or helped shape all the campaigns in this book. But, no matter how hard I tried, it was not always possible to see everything going through a busy agency, especially during activity peaks. So, here is some work which has been created entirely by others. Hugely talented people who have made my job easier and the world a better place.

Christian Aid

This legacy appeal is a great example of the art of storytelling. It told the tale of Territorial Army volunteer Tim Goggs, who was tragically killed while clearing mines in Afghanistan. His commitment to helping others did not end there; before going overseas Tim had made a Will, leaving his house to Christian Aid. This inspirational appeal raised over £7 million in pledges. Kate Woodford at her brilliant best.

CLIC Sargent (*now Young Lives v Cancer*)

Cancer treatment can be frightening for children, especially when a parent cannot be in the room to comfort them. To help, the charity came up with the idea of 'superstring'. The child is given one end of a piece of brightly coloured string which can stretch all the way from the radiotherapy room to a loved one. The parent can pull on the string to make their child feel safer throughout the treatment. A piece of superstring included in the pack added a wonderful tactile dimension to the story. Devised and written by Kate Woodford and Pauline Lockier, this is one of my favourite ever DM packs; it demonstrated how the medium can uniquely bring a story to life. The appeal beat targets by 100%.

Sound Effects Ltd

Ever been driven to distraction by noisy neighbours? One solution is to line your walls with soundproof panelling. Our very own Ian Atkinson was so impressed after buying the product, he put together this door drop for the manufacturer. When the recipient opened it, a small transistor inside played a 10-second clip of rave music. Brilliantly engaging and so effective.

Focus DIY

Another produced by Ian. The leaflet advertising the brand's garden products was impregnated with flower seeds. After reading, it could be planted in a pot to brighten up the home and keep Focus front of mind.

KEEP BRITAIN BEAUTIFUL.
TEAR THIS LEAFLET UP.
AND BURY IT.

FOCUS

Q or not Q.

A or not tonight.

Fed up with the sound of music?

SoundEffectsLtd

Two words
can touch a
thousand
lives

Christian Aid
We believe in life before death

Christian Aid

Dear Sample,

CLIC Sargent

introducing...
Superstring

Dear Mr Sample,

Sometimes, all you need is a piece of string.

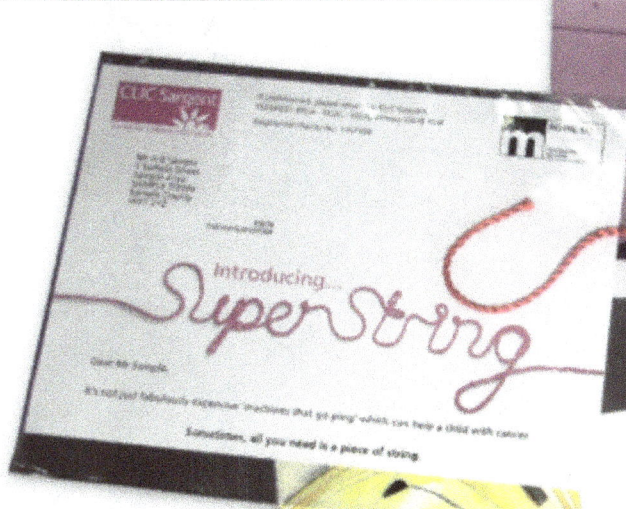

How long
is this piece
of string?

TIMING, BEAUTIFUL TIMING.

Earlier this year, a significant section of my eight-feet high garden wall collapsed, straight into my neighbour's garden. Built in 1874 from pale orange Dumbleton bricks, it finally gave up the ghost on 10th June, 2022. The picture on the previous page shows the aftermath.

Although a financial disaster (the cost of rebuilding the uninsured wall has passed £65,000), if it had fallen five days earlier it would have been a tragedy.

The previous Sunday, when the sun was shining, my neighbour's garden was full of grandparents, parents, and children, all attending our village's Open Garden Weekend. With fifty tons of brick and masonry tumbling on to the pathway next to the wall in a matter of seconds, anyone standing there may well have been killed.

It's a well-worn phrase but it still rings true – timing really is everything. I can bemoan the fact that the wall chose to fall during my ownership of the house, but it could have been immeasurably worse. At the end of the day, a wall fell down, No more, no less.

In marketing, timing remains a hugely influential factor and can be leveraged in several ways to make the difference between a flop and a winner.

1. Reply before date

One of the oldest marketing techniques yet it still remains an effective inertia breaker. The prospect of missing a special offer or crucial timeline is often motivation enough to push someone into responding.

2. Being seasonal

Christmas is normally the most fruitful time of the year, but there are other emotionally-charged, calendar moments that can also be exploited. We conceived a campaign for Prostate Cancer UK to celebrate the role of dads on Father's Day, ten years later, it is still running. For the British Heart Foundation, we created a Valentine's Appeal which also proved very successful.

3. Make your own moment

Create supplementary awareness around your message by engaging in public relations and social media activity. We always encouraged RSPCA to release animal cruelty figures before a big appeal; we utilised similar media tactics for The Salvation Army and the British Legion, to build national sentiment and lend relevance to their large recruitment drives. It helped raise millions more for these two giants of the fundraising arena.

4. Be of the moment

Acting fast and taking advantage of unique media opportunities can dramatically boost response. If your message chimes with the times, it will be far more engaging.

Being aware of events that could amplify your story is one thing, being agile enough to take advantage of them is another. Numerous charities have lost the ability to react quickly because of protracted internal approval procedures. This can have a dramatic effect on results; missing the small moment of fortune offered by a relevant happening or sympathetic news article, can be the difference between making or losing money. I have known appeals triple income simply by getting their timing right.

The following example for The Royal Star and Garter Home shows the merit of being fleet of foot. Having enjoyed considerable success with the military veterans' care charity for many years, we had earned a position of trust with their fundraising director, Mary Concannon. So, when we heard that one of their most famous beneficiaries, the Falklands war veteran Simon Weston, was to feature in a *Radio Times* article, we felt it was too good an opportunity to miss. Our media director had been offered a full page following the article, but there was a catch – we had to get the advertisement to them by that afternoon. We called Mary and she immediately agreed to go for it, despite it costing over £5,000 for the space, a significant amount for the charity.

Dropping everything, we managed to put the creative together and make the deadline. The rush was worth the effort, the ad brought in double the investment and recruited hundreds of new donors.

O WHAT A LUCKY MAN?

It's been nearly 100 years since Alexander Fleming accidentally saved humanity. After returning from a holiday, he noticed a petri dish of bacteria he was testing had been accidentally left uncovered. A specific type of mould called penicillium notatum had fallen into the dish and killed the bacteria, leading to the eventual discovery of the antibiotic which has saved millions of lives. Was this pure luck or simply a happy by-product of his research, something Fleming was sure to discover (sooner or later) anyway?

I subscribe to the theory that you make your own luck in this world. Surely it's no coincidence that the luckiest bastards seem to be proactive, hardworking, conscientious bastards. Equally plainly, there must be good reason Lady Luck rarely visits the lives of the idle, the dreary, or the naysayers?

As for myself, it could be said that I was extremely jammy to have met those who helped me in my career, but that ignores the fact that I put myself in the position to meet these superstars by getting off my backside and going out to look for them.

My real good fortune lay not in possessing some incredible talent, but rather in being given the gifts of curiosity, optimism, ambition, and a strong work ethic. Add to that, being born into a first-world, law-abiding country as a white, middle class, male baby boomer, I feel I've had quite enough blessings for one lifetime. Lady Luck, you owe me nothing.

But if you are listening:

A way to capture (and expel) carbon dioxide from the atmosphere, a cure for dementia and cancer, peace on earth, total gender and wealth equality, lifelong good health for my kids, and a modest Lottery win, would be nice.

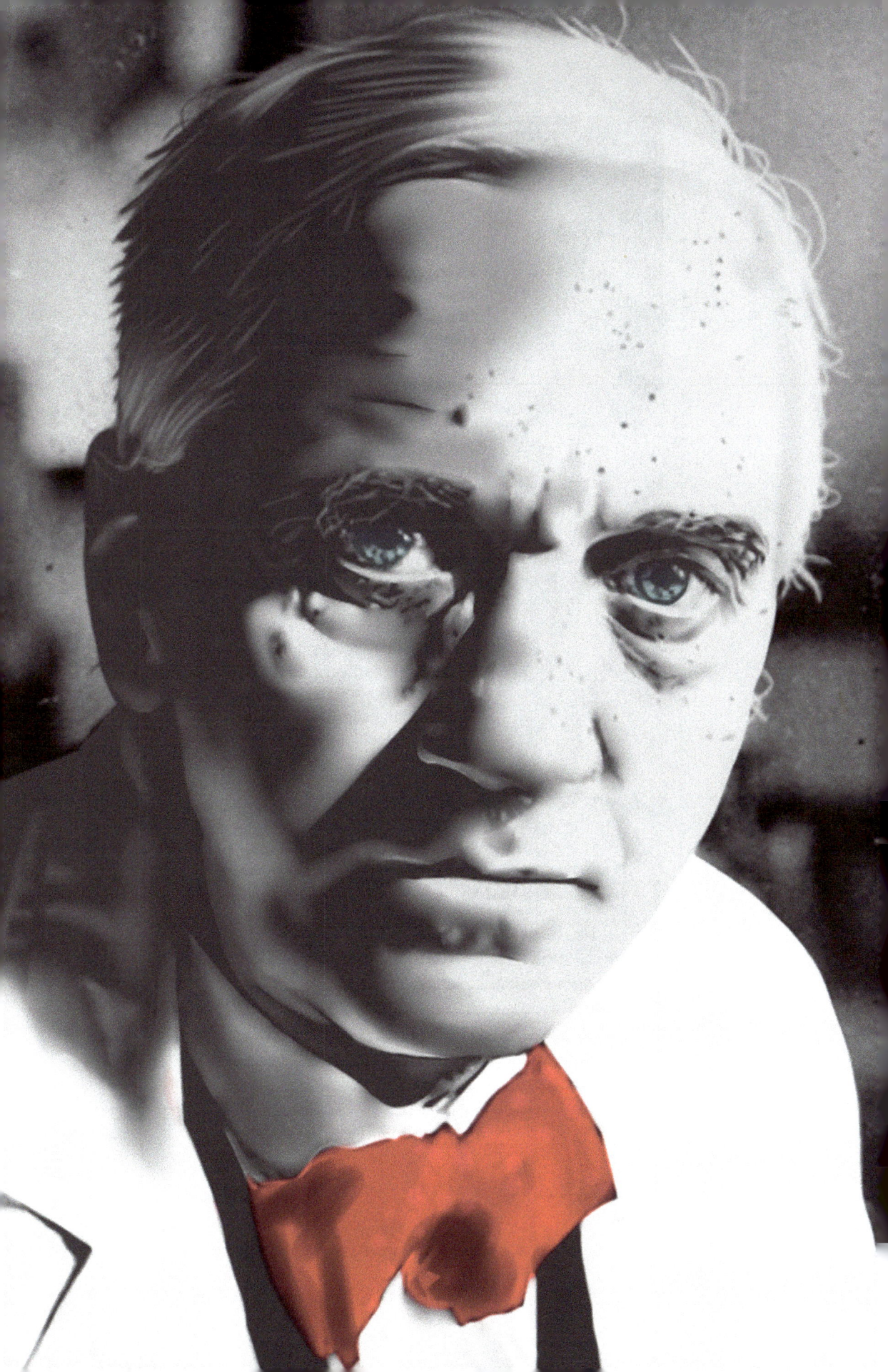

THINKING OF SPONSORING A CHILD?

Sponsoring a child in a poor Third World community is easier than you may think. And the difference it can make to a young life is tremendous.

It could mean your child has the chance to go to school, or to receive proper health care. It may even mean the difference between going hungry and having enough to eat.

PLAN INTERNATIONAL works in 25 countries to make these things possible, not just for one child, but for whole families and communities.

And because you are sponsoring one particular youngster, you'll have the joy of seeing your child growing up – learning, developing and gaining in strength and confidence over the years – through letters, photographs and regular progress reports.

To find out how you can help a child in this very special way, ask for our free Information Pack. Send to PLAN INTERNATIONAL UK, Free-post, 5-6 Underhill Street, London NW1 0YJ. Or phone 071-485 6612.

HERE'S HOW TO FIND OUT MORE

Please send me my free copy of the PLAN INTERNATIONAL Information Pack, and tell me more about sponsorship and how I can help. In particular, I am interested in your work in:

Africa ☐ Asia ☐ Far East ☐ Latin America ☐ Caribbean ☐ Where need is greatest ☐

Name (Mr/Mrs/Miss/Ms)_____

Address_____

_____

_____

Postcode_____ Tel No_____

Send to: PLAN INTERNATIONAL UK,
Freepost, 5-6 Underhill Street, LONDON NW1 0YJ. Or phone 071-485 6612.

Changing the world one child at a time

Charity Registered No 278035

PLAN INTERNATIONAL UK
a World Family

L0213

YOU TALKING TO ME?

Finding your target market. It's the most crucial aspect of any marketing strategy and imperative to boosting engagement and ROI.

It's not rocket science – identifying the group of customers you appeal to most and marketing directly to them will result in a more successful campaign.

Most of the complex analysis required to do this is carried out by left brain thinkers (logical, analytical, linear, factual) rather than a right brainer (creative, artistic, intuitive, emotional) like yours truly. These marketing boffins determine the Goldilocks audience in a reassuringly thorough and precise number of ways. Such as dissecting a competitor's target audience or collecting data from existing customers or determining the similarities that consumers share through Google Analytics and other social media platforms. Or seeking common characteristics such as location, age, gender, interests, and so on.

To me it's bewildering alchemy, but when these data scientists feed their findings into a creative brief, it makes perfect sense. That doesn't mean the targeting task is over – in fact it's only just begun, because invariably the analysis has resulted in your client being dropped into the same media pool as their competitors.

This is where the creative's job of clever differentiation, enticement, and engagement takes over. Happily, one of the best weapons to help us is almost comically simple: the flag.

This involves placing a flagged message at the top of your communication, the first thing your target audience will see. To work best, the flag should anticipate their potential requirements with a direct question or statement. It must tell them unequivocally: 'We understand your wants, needs and desires. This is for you.'

It is the small ad in the lonely hearts column that announces in bold type: **Looking for love?** The opening line spoken by the announcer in the equity release TV commercial: **Got cash locked in your home?** Or the banner at the top of a sponsored magazine article about haemorrhoids: **Suffer painful, embarrassing itching?**

When struggling to achieve the stand out I want, I have always resorted to this technique. It's not a creative cop out but simply pure pragmatism in the cause of improving response. One example using this approach was the first recruitment campaign we produced for Plan International. Despite scores of attempts we never managed to better it.

BOLD TRUMPS BASHFUL, EVERY TIME.

'*Go big or go home.*' I remember those words as if they were spoken yesterday.

It was April 1986 in Knightsbridge, I was sitting in an advertising agency office overlooking the majestic art deco façade of Harrods. The words, delivered by my new creative director, Bill Thompson, were meant as both encouragement and veiled warning.

I had just been hired to establish a new direct response unit within his agency and he wanted to see bold creativity from 'the get go'. As part of his induction, Bill was presenting examples, by way of his personal portfolio, to demonstrate the standard of creativity he wanted to see.

He flicked through multi award-winning work for Commercial Union, the Welsh Development Agency, Ruddles Ales, and Volkswagen, but the one that really caught my eye was a press advertisement for a diet supplement product with the unpromising name of HPD. The layout was conventional, a simple three-column grid with the product shot in the centre. What made this concept so arresting was the headline – HEY, FATSO. READ THIS.

'*How did you get this through?*' I enquired.

Bill leant back in his Pollock Executive Chair and smiled, '*The client challenged us to be bolder, so we did this. He just had to go with it.*'

I remember this story when I'm feeling unsure about pushing boundaries for clients. In today's fractured media landscape with attention so hard to grab, more than ever marketing should be about innovating, and for agencies, being smarter about getting new ideas accepted.

Clients always want their agencies to be more challenging, ingenious, original; they can sack them when they are not perceived as being so. This can be extremely harsh; without prior proof of success, it's difficult to persuade a client to try something new.

When we've shown work that was breaking new ground, often the reaction has been: '*Love the thinking. Have you done it before – and did it work?*'

It can seem an impossible question to answer. At Campfire, we research ideas all the time through online panels; they will prove the strength (or weakness) of concepts and help soothe client anxieties at a relatively low cost.

Along with nervy clients, another block to boldness for agencies can be self-inflicted/self-censoring. It's an easy trap to fall into, especially when you've worked with a client for a few years. It's natural not to want to show ideas which, through previous experience, you think they might reject. While this may seem prudent, in reality this is precisely the moment to push harder to break the mould, otherwise creative solutions become all too predictable.

While working for Practical Action, a brilliantly clever overseas development charity, we had been struggling to get a particular campaign idea accepted. We had been developing it alongside a large stakeholder group; because of conflicting agendas and sensibilities at play, it was proving hard to land a powerful, single minded concept that everyone liked.

Faced with a third attempt to sell a concept they all liked, we were starting to lose our mojo and confidence. After developing a series of fresh approaches at the agency, we put them in order of most to least chance of getting through. Our final approach (and the one I liked best because it was adventurous) was pushed to the back of the presentation. We agreed this would only be shown as a last resort.

During the presentation, we were encouraged to find that they had liked something earlier, so concluded without showing my favoured idea. However, when summarising, the client noticed the concept on the slide show and asked to see it. Immediately as one, the room declared that this was now their favourite. It proved to be one of their most successful ever, winning a prestigious response award.

It was a salutary lesson for all involved in creative endeavours, whether that be book writing, painting, dressmaking, pottery, architecture, or creating marketing – do not censor yourself. Give your creation to your audience, let them decide whether you have produced something brilliant or terrible. Just as we had started to lose the courage of our convictions, happily a stroke of luck reminded us: 'If you don't show it, they can't buy it.'

Finding the courage to be bold is always easier when you have others alongside you striving for the same thing. Campfire was born out of collaboration and the belief that many heads are better than one. When COVID made close teamwork challenging to achieve, we sometimes found ourselves getting a little too conservative – safer. So, when the pandemic had cooled, we got together to reaffirm our commitment to boldness and its importance to our ethos and success.

We vowed to...

Take more risks. Invariably they create opportunities, fame, and fortune.

Be more honest, even if it stings. Push each other to reach higher. The moon is in reach, just ask NASA.

Say no. Particularly to bad briefs and short deadlines. Boldness needs genuinely fresh insights and takes more time to produce.

Say yes. Originality takes positivity, energy, and a can-do attitude.

Be more unpredictable. Hunt for the unexpected, bin the derivative.

Stick to our guns. Steer our course true, do not be deflected by naysayers.

Share our enthusiasm. Present with passion, facts, and persuasion, in equal measure.

Make the first move. Look to innovate, take the initiative.

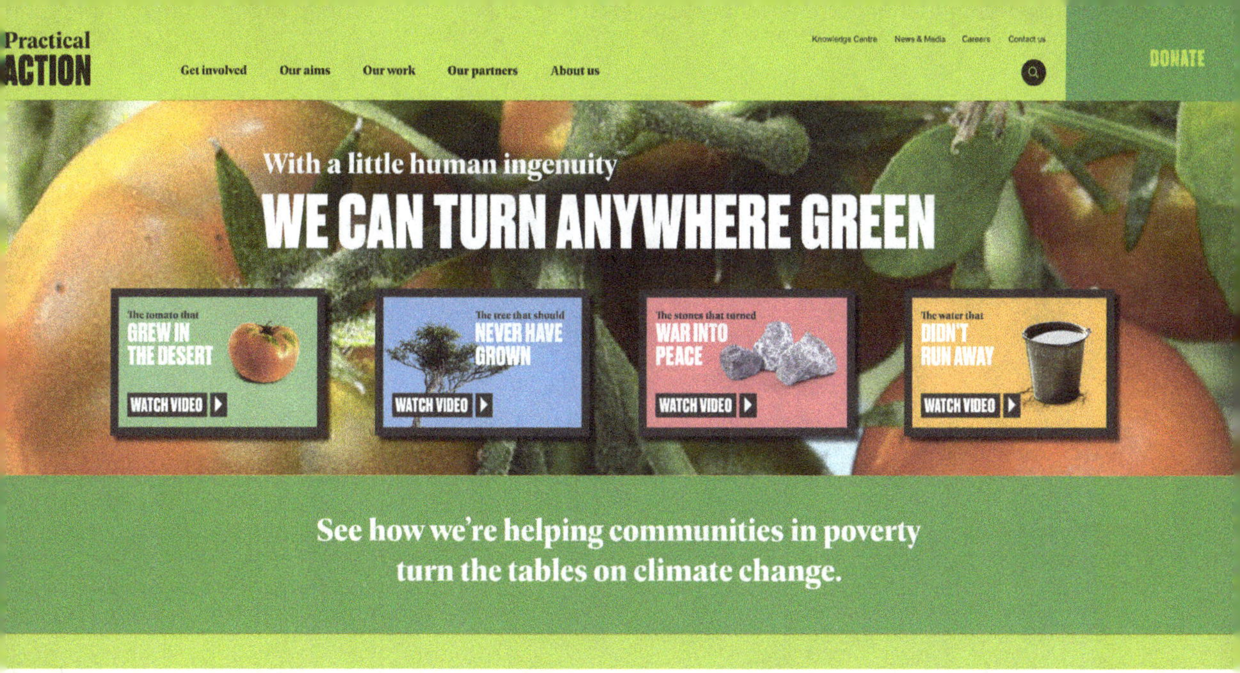

Practical
ACTION
Get involved
Our aims
Our work
Our partners
About us
News & Media
Careers
Contact us
DONATE
With a little human ingenuity
WE CAN TURN ANYWHERE GREEN
The tomato that
GREW IN THE DESERT
WATCH VIDEO
The tree that should
NEVER HAVE GROWN
WATCH VIDEO
The stones that turned
WAR INTO PEACE
WATCH VIDEO
The water that
DIDN'T RUN AWAY
WATCH VIDEO
See how we're helping communities in poverty turn the tables on climate change.

Take pride in our boldness. Celebrate our inquisitiveness, tenacity, and results.

Root out timidity. It will kill our reputation, relegate us to also-rans.

Bring our clients with us. Collaborate at every step, get buy-in early.

So, if bold is often the pre-requisite for successful marketing, why can it be so hard to achieve for agencies and their clients?

The Oxford Dictionary's definition of the word gives clues – *Bold: A person showing a willingness to take risks; confident and courageous.*

It's a truism – we all aspire to be courageous. However, in the real world there are times when being brave is easier than others. It's easy to see why a client may be unwilling to take a gamble when their job may be at risk.

By the same token, playing safe and being me-too can be riskier options. Far too often it is proved that doing the same thing as everyone else means getting lost, not being seen, failure.

We'll always be passionate about pushing ideas that locate the edge of what is acceptable, yet still retain the power to gain attention. We do this partly because it's always more fun, but mainly because usually we get much, MUCH better results.

SO YOU WANT TO START AN AGENCY?

I can hear them next door in the saloon bar. Two ad men. One ad woman. Talking too loud, laughing too long. It's not the alcohol, it's the intoxication of what they're talking about. They're going to start their own agency.

They're pumped about the idea and they've convinced themselves.

They can run an agency better than the old agency schmucks they work for. They want to be the bosses, not the also-rans. These three want their name on the door, a piece of the top table action, a slice of the pie.

Of course, they won't be unique in wanting these things. Last year, not a day went by without a new marketing agency starting up. Over 430 saw the light of day in 2022. That's 5% up on 2021.

Not that it matters to the three amigos in the saloon bar. Because they're not going to establish any old marketing agency, theirs is going to be the best.

They're going to be famous and very rich and those prizes are worth shooting for.

As I listen, I ponder. As someone who has done it myself three times, perhaps I should get out of my seat and offer some insight into what they might need...

A business plan and an understanding bank. They'll probably be giving up well paid jobs and have no immediate income. They'll have to convince someone to lend them money.

A USP. It's always amazed me how many agencies preach about the importance of a unique selling proposition to their clients, but don't have one themselves. With the same incomprehensible bullshit being spoken by so many agencies, it's vital they have a crisp, different and attractive story that will stand out from the pack.

Co-founders with the right stuff. They sound like they get on well enough now but can they trust each other when the going gets tough? Do they share the same vision? Do their skills complement each other? Are they prepared to pull their equal weight? Be paid the same, at least during the formative years? Are they good humoured and hard-working? Are they happy to do the mundane? Like ordering the stationary and the toilet rolls, fixing the light bulbs and chasing clients for money?

Luck. Not just the divine kind because the angels are smiling on them. The sort they'll have to make for themselves by working hard, doing great work and putting themselves in the right places to be noticed. The sort they'll get because they are positive and 'can-do' and the last ones standing.

Great clients. The ones that will believe in them and want to be as famous too. These will be as rare as hen's teeth, they will make their reputation, they must look after them well.

Cash work. The type they'll never win awards for but will pay the bills. This will make up 70% of their turnover and take up 80% of their time.

An understanding spouse or partner. They're going to worry more, which means they'll sleep less, so be crabbier to live with.

A reliable car. To get them to the office, the train, or the inevitable out-of-town client.

Stamina. Stamina. Stamina. The first 18 months will involve long days and hard work. If they've chosen their co-founders well, they will have been fun. Being the new kids on the block is liberating. They'll be winging it, so they'll have the wind in their hair. There will be no rigid internal systems to frustrate them; they haven't had time to write them yet. They'll be reacting fast and furiously. The next 18 months will be tougher. They'll have a reputation to maintain, have to start hiring and firing, start managing, have board meetings. This is the moment the new kids will start gunning for them.

As I continue to listen as they decide on their agency's name, I am a little envious, a touch bittersweet. My start up days working alongside the huge talents of Mike Brown at WAHT, Stephen Pidgeon and Pauline Lockier at Target, and Paul Handley at Campfire, were the most exciting.

Yes, I could go into the saloon bar and distribute some pearls of wisdom but why not let them find it out for themselves, like I did? It worked for this old agency schmuck, it should work for them.

So I sit here warming by the fire, nursing my pint in the snug. Or should that be smug?

VOLUNTEERING. THE PERFECT ANTIDOTE TO IRRELEVANCE.

"Welcome, I am Charles Howard, youngest son of the 5th Earl of Suffolk. A drunken, whoring, gambler."

Standing over six feet, four inches tall, in his burgundy Georgian court costume, high perfumed wig and blanched face, the man presented an imposing figure.

He spoke in the grand manner of a Jane Austen aristocrat and it was hard not to take him very seriously; we were in Blickling Hall after all, the magnificent Jacobean stately home in Norfolk. After driving most of the morning to get here, we were looking forward to immersing ourselves in its history.

Plainly, this formidable apparition hadn't materialised from the 17th Century and wasn't Charles Howard, an Earl in the peerage of England. He was Edward Williamson from the county of Essex, and a member of the National Trust's costumed interpretation group.

For the next few minutes Ed as Charles regaled us with stories of the uniquely scandalous part he played in the history of Blickling. After the performance and out of character, I chatted to Ed and asked him why he did it.

"I took early retirement from the civil service, needed something to occupy my time," he told me in his Essex estuary accent, a mix somewhere between cockney and the pronunciation of newsreaders. *"Always loved amateur dramatics, so this was perfect. Visitors love the history of the place being brought to life. Children can be a little intimidated though."*

He wasn't the only volunteer giving his time that day. There were another six interpreters as well as a dozen guides helping the inquisitive and the lost in different parts of the cavernous house. This story is repeated across all the National Trust's properties, the charity simply couldn't function without Essex Ed and thousands of others like him, prepared to give their time freely to such an important cause. These good souls are so numerous and so crucial to charities, they give the sector its most familiar reference term, The Voluntary Sector.

In 2020-21, 30% of adults in England took part in formal volunteering, approximately 14 million people. The most enthusiastic age group being the over 65s, with 61% volunteering at least once.

When working on 'Poppy People', a volunteer recruitment campaign we created for the British Legion, I met one such incredible individual – 81-year-old Vera Parnaby. Known locally in her native County Durham as 'Mrs Poppy', she had been a collector for the Poppy Appeal since the age of six, raising well in excess of £1m. As well as slogging door-to-door selling poppies herself, Vera also marshalled an army of volunteers to manage collections. Vera's dedication was recognised by Prime Minister Boris Johnson with a special 'Points of Light' award.

I asked Vera why she had dedicated so much of her time to the cause. The initial reason she told me was to honour her father, who had been killed during the Second World War. The reason she had continued for 75 years was because volunteering had given so much to her personally, giving her a sense of community and providing her with lifelong friendships. As importantly, she said with a big smile, *'it has been right good fun.'*

Therein lies the appeal of volunteering for millions of people; giving time can be its own reward. We all fear irrelevance as we grow older, stepping forward to help a good cause can provide renewed purpose and boost self-esteem.

In the main, the voluntary sector works hard to ensure people who offer their time have a positive experience; whether that be as a valued staff member in a busy shop, a well-supported collector on a street corner, or a fully-trained historical reenactor in a home.

Charities take this care of course because they understand how important volunteers are in providing the essential components required for a vibrant sector.

Legacies may provide the lifeblood but volunteers provide the heartbeat.

POPPY PEOPLE WANTED

Just two hours of your time can help keep the Poppy alive in your area.
Please volunteer to collect or organise for the Poppy Appeal this November.

Registered Charity No: 219279

PLEASE GIVE GENEROUSLY

WHAT SHOULD THE NATION EXPECT FROM ITS CHARITIES?

Recently, I was most fascinated to read an article in The Times by Baroness Stowell of Beeston, Chair of the Charity Commission, giving her views on the current state of the third sector. Here's a flavour of what she said...

'The pandemic has exposed how dependent charities are on the public's goodwill.'

'Charities must redouble efforts to respond to the needs of the people they serve.'

'Charities must be clear eyed on where they stand and not indulge in "wishful thinking".'

At a time when the sector is under siege, its blandness is less than instructive. But I can't let one comment go without challenge...

'Charities must do more to keep in step with public expectations.'

I wonder what this means? As with any other sector, charities are well aware that, as an absolute minimum, they need to meet public expectations regarding service levels, quality, honesty, and value for money. Undoubtedly the vast majority do.

On a sector level, using the Charity Commission's own definition – the public expect charities 'to demonstrate good stewardship of funds, to live their values, and demonstrate impact'. Again, in my experience, the vast majority tick all these boxes.

In fact, no other sector I've worked with – automotive, financial, retail, holidays, technology, utilities – knows more about the expectations of its customers than the charity sector.

At Campfire, our charity clients continually ask us to conduct research to help them better understand the needs of donors – from topics they want to hear about, to the frequency of communication they would prefer. It's in a fundraiser's DNA to continually ask what their supporters want and strive to give it to them.

Charities have a hard-wired understanding of donors' expectations to be thanked properly, to feel valued and be continually appraised of the impact of their gift. I would suggest to Baroness Stowell that £3 billion in legacy income annually suggests donor expectations are being met extremely well.

Of course, ambitious causes always aim to *exceed expectations*, like the brilliant Charity: Water with their personal thank you videos. World Vision have always strived to improve a child sponsor's experience and have recently invested in delivering personalised film from a child's community. World Vision has also introduced a new dimension to sponsorship by letting the child choose their sponsor.

But I believe we see the best from charities when they decide to *defy expectations*. Progressive fundraising has always been about understanding motivations to give, and finding new ways to unlock them. To do that well, it helps to have a clear grasp of how humans work.

Recent research in the US has confirmed what we all probably knew, that most people love surprises and actually like having their expectations confounded. The area of the brain which scientists have identified as a pleasure centre, recorded the strongest response to the unexpectedness of a sequence of stimuli. In other words, nothing is as dull for the brain as just simply having your expectations met. Thus, smart charity marketeers understand that sometimes they have to disrupt or be novel to stand out, and there are a wealth of outstanding examples of this.

Save The Children's 'Most Shocking Second A Day' video imagined what it would be like if London experienced a Syrian-like conflict. It shocked viewers and drew hundreds of complaints but has been viewed over 59 million times.

Greenpeace and Iceland's 'Say hello to Rang-tan' film was created to drive interest in the issue of deforestation and the production of palm oil. Banned from broadcast for being too political, it has been viewed 70 million times. Iceland also decided to remove palm oil from its products.

Two other stand-out examples are Care International's raffle, offering people a chance to win a Picasso for $100 and UNICEF's brilliant and successful Paddington's Postcards which we've had the pleasure of taking on to the telly.

Claiming *'charities are not in step with public expectations'* is not just unhelpful, it's untrue. Of course the third sector could do more to demonstrate just how effective it is, but perhaps the Commission should do more to help; after all, its mission is 'to ensure charity can thrive'. I know our great charities are incredibly effective at getting their message across. The sector has been hugely successful at what it does and that enables it to sustain its huge contribution to saving lives, fighting poverty and injustice, protecting the environment and our heritage, and improving the lives of animals. I am also certain the public wants their favourite charities to continue indulging in the 'wishful thinking' it takes to create a better world.

Undoubtedly, charities have to continue to adapt to the times and project their respective causes in ever more creative ways, and evidence suggests that most are rising to the challenge.

Over my years in the fundraising world I have seen enormous changes, but despite the odd revelation and scandal, public expectations of good causes haven't really changed.

Carry on and keep up the good work.

Chosen™
the power to choose in a child's hands

From top:
World Vision,
Save The Children,
Greenpeace.

207

TIME FOR CHRISTMAS CHEER?

So what have charities learnt in 2021? Some uncomfortable home truths.

The public don't need a registered charity to give to a good cause. Captain Sir Tom Moore demonstrated how to raise £33 million with some good publicity and a simple fundraising page.

Fundraising channels are vulnerable. GDPR, the EU's privacy law, has already hit personalised fundraising hard. Social distancing pummelled events, street and door-to-door fundraising, and retail harder still.

With a few exceptions, the sector seems to have faded away. The paltry £750 million package of support offered up by then Chancellor Rishi Sunak suggested even the government believes charities are unimportant.

It's time for the UK's good causes to reassert themselves. What better time to do that than at a moment in the year they have always bossed? Christmas is the fundraising harvest for the sector when supporters are normally more responsive and generous. But of course, 2020 was far from normal. Thus, there are two contradictory factors at play for charities to consider.

Money will be tight. With the economy in recession, people may be more discerning about who and how many appeals they give to. Campfire research has revealed that donors have several 'Christmas causes' they support annually, but there will be pressure to reduce the size of the group this year. So, standing out is more important than ever.

There should be more goodwill around. Millions have burst out of their COVID bubbles and become more aware of the needs of others. We could see an increased desire to display some deep felt humanity and a conscious move away from shallow materialism.

One thing is for certain, after twelve months of high anxiety, people will be more than ready to enjoy the comfort and joy of a blooming good Christmas. Seeing the recent joyous celebrations for the 75th anniversary of VE Day showed that the nation is in the mood to party. The appetite for positivity is never keener than during negative times.

With many charities struggling for cash, it will be tempting for fundraisers to play the shortfall card and plead poverty. I believe they will have more success presenting inspiring messages of hope and positivity.

These are the messages people craved in 2020 and 2021 (clap the brilliant NHS, support the amazing Tom Moore, salute the selfless volunteers, etc.) as they eagerly sought crumbs of comfort amidst the gloom.

The third sector does so much good work yet still remains largely misunderstood and undervalued. This Christmas is the time to show everyone its power and at the same time, impart a healthy slice of much needed good cheer to the nation.

RNIB have experienced record results using uplifting examples of the power of its work at Christmas, particularly for its Talking Books Service. Disability charity Sense has enjoyed success for years with its Sensory Toy appeal; the toy doesn't cost a lot but delivers tangible joy to a deaf-blind child. More than ever, people want solutions, or at least to be given the hope of finding one.

My message to fundraisers and marketers who are starting to think about their own Christmas appeals is, think big, think integrated, and think digital. But also think love and positivity and give people the opportunity to contribute to a brighter world.

And, even more importantly in these extraordinary times, let us take care to show our customers that we are not wholly oblivious to their sufferings by simply bludgeoning them with ours.

TAKE BACK CONTROL

THE ART OF IDIOT PROOFING.

If any marketer needed reminding of the importance of simplicity, they need look no further than the latest offering from the government's former embattled PR man, Dominic Cummings.

This is the marketing maestro who helped seal Brexit with his **'Take back control'** slogan. The pragmatic genius who instructed the nation in the early days of COVID-19 to **'Stay Home. Protect the NHS. Save lives.'** Both calls-to-action were so simple they could almost be described as puerile, but trust me, messages as clear as those are complicated to get to.

Both created the right emotional pitch and imparted a crystal clear objective. Above all, they possessed the most priceless ingredient of great marketing. They were idiot proof.

So, when he revealed his later instructions to the nation: **Stay alert. Control the virus. Save lives**, it seemed like, at the very least, that Cummins had suffered a serious loss of form.

Even a communicator as effective as Boris Johnson struggled to explain the intent.

Apparently, Johnson himself thought the message was confusing when compiling it for broadcast. *'Filming was a total nightmare,'* said an unnamed government source. *'He was stopping and starting, asking to change bits, complaining about the length, saying it was all too complex.'*

You could argue that most right thinking, intelligent people would have easily got the gist, but public health messaging has never been about persuading people with common sense to do something. It has always been about convincing those who need all information spoon fed to them, with no flab, no ambiguity, and absolutely zero scope for misinterpretation of what the bloody hell you are trying to say.

A YouGov survey showed that less than a third of Britons understood what the government's new 'stay alert' coronavirus directive required of them. Inevitably, there would have been some mischief makers amongst those polled; but nevertheless, it's a revelation to know just how 'dumbed down' people need their communications.

Clarity above all else. For a professional marketer, that's valuable to know.

And that's true for any form of communication, such as in films for instance. One of my favourite British actors, Wilfred Hyde-White, best known for his role as Colonel Hugh Pickering in the musical, My Fair Lady understood this well.

He was quoted as saying, *'I went to RADA, and learnt two things. One is: I can't act. The other is – It doesn't matter.'* He, and other actors of the time, including Sir Alec Guinness, Dame Judy Dench, Dame Maggie Smith, and David Niven, shared one underrated quality: you could hear what they said. So many actors today seem to make mumbling an art form, which can make following the plot difficult.

I've made a career in communications and looking back through some of my most successful work – the stuff that produced great results as opposed to winning glitzy awards – I was struck by how simple (i.e., not clever, smart) the propositions were and how plainly they spoke to their intended audiences.

One of the most famous headlines of all and one I wish I could put my name to, was written for Help the Aged's Cataract Appeal: **'Make a blind man see.'** Just five words, but a masterpiece of simplicity and empowerment.

We're lucky in many respects that we didn't have someone in charge of public announcements as reckless as the United States did between 2017 and 2021. Although I'm sure there were still a few people here who contemplated Trump's recommendation of a dose of bleach to quell their COVID anxieties.

The lesson here is as clear as it's always been: if, like Boris Johnson, you feel your message is too complicated, then it probably is. Unlike Boris Johnson, if you do believe that then you should work harder to simplify it.

Because sad to say but true, if you leave any space for misunderstanding, then people will jump right into it.

THE SCULPTOR AND THE FISHERMAN.

Like Doris Day, I love Paris in the springtime. The wonderful architecture, cherry blossom, proper onion soup, proper wine. The season even makes the self-important café waiters momentarily more accommodating. I was fortunate to find myself there last April with my better half and we were determined to see as many of the sites as possible in the time we had; starting with 'the world's most beautiful avenue.'

Exiting from the Metro Champs-Élysées – Clemenceau, we began the gentle climb towards the Arc de Triomphe. In the morning sunshine, this grandest of grand boulevards with its double row of strictly pruned trees, 70 foot wide pavements, high-end stores, restaurants and cafés, it was looking as wonderful as ever.

But while the macro view was stunning, a closer look revealed a familiar problem, the same encountered in most other European cities. Homeless people, scores of them. Sitting beside cash points, sleeping inside dark doorways, lying sprawled under the shade of the trees. Here amongst the five thousand pound handbags and exclusive perfumes, the disparity between the have and have nots seemed obscenely huge. Most of this wretched underclass sat about listlessly, grunting unintelligible requests for money, almost all them ignored by indifferent locals and distracted tourists.

Two of their number tried a different approach. One worked tirelessly on the grey granite pavement creating intricate sand sculptures of animals, the other literally fished for donations with a rod. When we dropped five euros into his bucket he sang his gratitude, a delightful sea shanty delivered in a deep rich Gallic baritone.

The two entrepreneurs were making good money from their enterprises, far more than the other homeless people on the avenue. Both instinctively realising that people wanted some emotional nourishment, a bit of happy before they parted with their money, a transaction. They had looked beyond the idea of 'what can a donor do for me?', both had applied themselves to 'what can I do for my donor?'

The sculptor and the fisherman had understood the value exchange now demanded by many donors. It is a lesson which charities need to take heed of if they are also to flourish.

Two decades worth of data doesn't lie, the old model of simply evoking pity and pricking the conscience is failing, falling to the law of diminishing returns. People don't want to feel worse about the world than they already do.

We don't need to press the guilt button to motivate; offer people the role of

saviour instead and they will be right there with us.

There is more value than ever in showing people how good it feels to be part of something that helps others and themselves. Stand at the finish line at the London Marathon, or sit with poppy sellers counting the money at the end of a day collecting, to see the incredible uplifting effect it can have.

I've heard it said by other marketers that the charity sector is a challenge because it has nothing that its audience actually needs. Rubbish, we have plenty to offer, including one of the most powerful things of all. The power to do something good.

THE IMPORTANCE OF BRANDS IN THE FUNDRAISING FUTURE.

While munching my way through one of my dear Mum's magnificent and mountainous Sunday lunches, I told her about the report I was compiling on the importance of brands to charities. *'That's good, dear,'* she said, *'What's a brand?'*

I explained (in a roundabout way) that it was the embodiment of an organisation's delivery or offer; it's a point of difference between itself and its competitors.

'But charities shouldn't compete, they should work together,' she replied, passing me a bowl overflowing with bread and butter pudding.

'So how do you choose between one charity and another and who to give to?' I replied, mindful not to talk with my mouth full.

'With me,' she said, *'it just depends if I like the look of the person who asked me and whether he or she asked nicely.'*

According to Phyllis Thomas, 80+, middle class, discerning, and representative of a massively important audience, there were no brands. Just polite, or not so polite, looking fundraisers.

Statisticians have labelled my mother a 'Civic', born before the Second World War and brought up in a generation that accepted a moral and civil duty to improve society's ills. Civics have proved a fertile audience for fundraisers, particularly direct marketers. If she is

anyone to go by, brand loyalty means little to them without the age-old courtesies of asking and thanking properly. It's easy to forget in an increasingly professional and sophisticated fundraising environment, that those values still matter.

Brand Clarity, Brand Standout, and even Brand Domination are all phrases beloved of ambitious charities, but to Mrs Thomas the brand experience must feel good.

Where brand values and symbolism really matter even more is with my generation, the Baby Boomers. Those born between 1945 and 1958, and their offspring, have grown up with brand marketing and accept the need for it in providing differentiation and consumer choice. That doesn't make them an easier nut to crack, quite the opposite. They are more cynical, demand more quantitative information, and are not so easily seduced by style and technique. They want facts and to be talked to 'as it really is'.

The continuing success of accessible, accountable appeals, such as Children in Need and Comic Relief, provide proof of this. Their format offers the perfect combination for effective fundraising. Stark need and solutions presented clearly and succinctly. Constant updates on the amount of money raised, all mixed with lively entertainment to keep you watching.

They have become landmark events in the fundraising calendar and almost habitual to give to.

Notably, they are brands that exist and dominate for a very brief time then fade away for the rest of the year, and in the case of Comic Relief, for two years. They utilise a concentrated blitzkrieg marketing approach now adopted by other charities.

Social change will also affect the fundraising future. The breakdown in traditional bonds of society and the family will mean donors will be more transient in behaviour; less inclined to get involved in community or volunteer fundraising.

Future donors will have greater access and demand more control. The next five years will see a convergence of electronic technologies – primarily mobile phones, computers, and televisions. Fuelled by the government's countdown to ending analogue transmissions totally in 2007 and converting solely to digital, domestic televisions of the future will have the potential to become the centre of a home's 'interactive interface' capability.

The Age of Interactive TV is already here. Sky, Telewest, and NTL offer an interactive medium, watched by over 10 million viewers able to buy direct from advertisers.

Our new donors will live longer too. For instance, a recent US health study suggested babies born after 1990 could expect a life span of 130 years – a long time to sustain a loyalty programme and wait for a legacy!

This all means that one of the most valuable assets any organisation can have

in this fragmented interactive future is a strong brand with staying power. If 21st century donors have the technology to give a donation, volunteer, or even make a bequest at the press of a button, they'll give to the charity whose beliefs and values they understand best. It also means they'll be able to access your brand 'experience' quicker too.

Building a 'loving company' was a goal for every major service company in the world during the 1990s; it's an objective the non-profit sector would be wise to follow. Billions have been spent on marketing and staff training to build a common personality and delivery ethic for organisations employing thousands of people. The financial sector is particularly keen on this; they realise their customers have a choice to move or stay and good customer care is vital. I've been with my bank, Barclays, for over thirty years, despite the fact that they're not competitive in terms of products and have one of the highest overdraft fees in the country. But they have a great service ethic, they remember my name, return my calls, and I always have access to senior people. It all adds up to a satisfying 'brand experience'.

Today, 21st century donors will give to the charity whose beliefs and values they understand best.

However, no charity can spend fortunes on total cultural overhauls. But it can examine its most important points of interaction with supporters and ensure they're working well.

These include the vital areas of supporter/care lines and fulfilment services.

Many a gift is lost between 'cup and lip'. For instance, two years ago my mum made a bequest to four charities. One subsequently lost out because, in her words, 'they didn't even say thank you.'

In a recent direct mail fulfilment test conducted with ten different charities who all received a £25 donation, a staggering four didn't even say thank you and two took over three weeks to respond.

All the best brand awareness in the world wouldn't get over that tardy experience.

One of the best 'loving organisations' in the non-profit sector is, unsurprisingly, The Salvation Army. Its core beliefs and values sustain a unique single voice at all points of the charity. In the UK, its fundraising, particularly direct marketing, continues to outperform the sector. But it wasn't always that way. It took a decision three years ago to look at its brand and decided it needed modernising. It invested in television and outdoor advertising to improve awareness of the breadth and modern-day relevance of its work (it is the 2nd largest social services provider after the government) and amplified its core values of Christian beliefs and basic human kindness. Its brand now looks to be in a unique state of rude health.

So if by this point you now accept the need for one, what actually makes a good brand? How do you create and sustain it over time? Who can you learn from

and what are the pitfalls? What are the important areas to concentrate on in moving forward? What's the value of your brand in terms of corporate and commercial opportunities?

I will endeavour to answer these questions and more in two ways.

First, by drawing on my experience of working with over fifty charity brands in the non-profit and commercial sectors; in my capacity as a creative director, I have had the good fortune to have been involved in several brand development 'projects'. Secondly, by talking to the organisations and people who have committed themselves to getting their brand values and delivery right.

Over the next pages I aim to cover:

How to keep your brand fresh and ward off unwanted stains. Brands endure because they change their message to suit the times and act fast when disaster threatens to poison the well. I'll talk to the nimble ones and provide salutary lessons from those who were less proactive.

Superbrands. Investigating the emergence of a Charity Premier League that uses sophisticated multimedia advertising and the move towards mergers of competing brands, I'll demonstrate how some charities achieve brand dominance at a particular time which suits them, for example when they are fundraising.

Changing your brand, the agonies and benefits. How to manage the process

internally and externally. I'll show how to get to the answers quicker and ensure consistency.

Building a 'loving company' has been a goal for commercial organisations, an objective lesson the non-profit sector would be wise to follow.

Selling your brand, finding corporate partners. In a recent Financial Times 'largest ever' survey of global public opinion on the changing role of companies, over half the consumers surveyed cited social responsibility as the most important factor that influenced their opinions. Increasingly, commercial companies are looking for a suitable non-profit to work with. But not all marriages are made in heaven and it's easy to undersell your brand's value.

Brand building on a shoestring. Not everyone has the budget to establish and maintain total brand awareness, but a substantial number of charities punch well above their weight. I'll show how it can be done in ten easy steps.

A brand is a dynamic, ever changing entity, and just like shares, it can go down as well as up. Who would have thought just five years ago that such a rock solid name like Marks & Spencer would now be in such trouble? Or that the pace of change has allowed telecommunications giant Orange, a brand that hardly existed ten years ago, to establish itself and dominate so quickly. There are plenty of brands that do endure, however, and according to advertising guru Jay Chiat they all display an overriding quality –

'comfort'. He argues that it's not about how new a product or service is – it's about how well it resonates with people. And resonate is exactly what a charity's brand should do. Its values should strike a hefty chord, tug furiously at a heartstring, and crucially make you FEEL GOOD about giving. Giving to a good cause means we can do something good with our day. The right packaging or branding will enhance the experience, make it intoxicating even.

Feelgood is the charity's secret weapon. Hugely powerful and underrated, it can overcome tiny advertising and marketing spends. As if by magic, it can make a small press ad, £1 badge box, low budget TV commercial, or humble direct mail piece, shine out like a beacon amongst the clutter.

Sometimes it is very easy to dismiss brand values as an irrelevance to charities, that it isn't the business of non-profit organisations to spend hard won funds on such flights of fancy.

But the fact is that charities own some of the biggest and instantly recognisable brands in the world. As symbols, the British Red Cross's red cross, the Royal British Legion's poppy, and the World Wildlife Fund's pandas are all as recognisable as Coca-Cola in most languages. Non-profit advertising is still among the best and most memorable seen anywhere. Get your brand in shape and the potential for increased sponsorship, merchandising, and fundraising are enormous. Those who are taking their brand proposition and reputation seriously are getting ahead; you only have to witness NSPCC's growth to appreciate that. Its consistent approach to advertising and communication has seen it achieve a critical mass in awareness terms, unprecedented for a charity in the UK. It's thinking big and achieving very big.

Perhaps it's time to make sure your brand offer is in order too, or risk getting left behind in the rush. Watch this space, I'm off to get some more pudding.

Thanks, mum.

STRONG BRANDS NEED BRAVE HEARTS.

Spare a thought for Richard Branson – not a natural impulse I'll agree. But back in autumn last year he must have been suffering, or at least he should have been.

His magical Virgin brand had suffered its first major setback with the rock bottom performance of its train franchise. And in the aftermath of the Hatfield disaster, Railtrack's track repair programme meant that he and the whole industry took another hammering from the media and customers. I know because I was one of the poor sods muttering bad things on overcrowded motorways for weeks on end. So what did Branson do? He did what he always does when one of his ideas is threatened, he made himself personally responsible for fixing it.

He knows that he represents the very essence of his organisation. His youthful, energetic anti-establishment personality lies at the heart of his empire's values and its success.

It worked for him when he took on Lord King and British Airways, exposing along the way some of the underhand tactics employed by the world's favourite airline. His face loomed large at the forefront of Virgin's launch into the financial sector and held centre stage in the recent failed bid for control of the Lottery. In striving to keep your brand fresh and in people's minds, we can learn from Branson in three key ways.

Firstly, why it's important to think of your organisation as not just a good cause, but as a crusade with a defined need (or evil) to overcome, and a goal to achieve. Branson created more than just a set of values and beliefs to follow, he gave everyone at Virgin something to believe in.

Secondly, never underestimate the power and value of publicity. It pays to court the media, who love people with things to say, controversial or otherwise.

Thirdly, when the inevitable crisis looms, decisive action and brave hearts are always needed. Someone has to take responsibility. Branson knows the value of an apology too; it shows honesty and humility – people will forgive a lot when they see that.

When you don't have the luxury of a big marketing budget – as is the case for most non-profits – a good, media-trained spokesperson (which is what Branson is) is worth their weight in gold.

Three excellent 'brand figureheads' that spring to mind, both past and present, are Age Concern's former chief, Sally Greengross, Cancer Research Campaign's Professor, Gordon McVie, and Gavin Grant who trailblazed the RSPCA's cause in the late eighties.

All were and are masters of the soundbite and have earned their respective organisations acres of media coverage at a fraction of the cost of advertising. And they have all reinforced the long held view in marketing and politics that an organisation's beliefs and aims are often best communicated through a single, lucid voice.

Robert Jones, author of the excellent *The Big Idea*, writes *'that today's chief executives hire their own publicists, write books, grant interviews and actively promote their personal philosophies. They do all this because they know that it's the best way to turn their organisation's big idea into something social.'*

No newspaper column on the issues of ageing in the nineties seemed complete without a comment from Greengross. No television news clip on the latest cancer breakthrough was finished without a soundbite from McVie.

Grant in particular was a communication tour-de-force, getting across his case in an utterly compelling manner, regardless of the time or column inches given to him.

In very short order, he made issues such as the abolition of the dog licence and the transportation of livestock major media events. He rubber-stamped one of the

Gavin Grant. A communications tour-de-force.

most memorable non-profit advertising campaigns ever, the infamous pile of dogs.

He changed the perception of the RSPCA brand forever, giving the society a crusade – to stop animal cruelty and punish its perpetrators. Since those days, the RSPCA has continued with a consistently honest (and often brutal) depiction of its work through advertising and in the process given themselves a unique brand positioning.

Of course not every organisation has the benefit of a singular media superstar and has to adopt a different approach. *'The importance of a good spokesperson is essential,'* says Julius Wolff-Ingham, Head of Fundraising and Marketing at The Salvation Army. *'And while most of our media contact is through our External Relations Officer, we also have a team who deal with specific service enquiries.'*

In my research, I talked to most of the biggest UK charities. There seems no doubt that most have got their acts together when it comes to presenting a coherent face to their brand. For some there is only one purpose to the exercise, to be number one in their field. But how important is it? Chris Gardner, Deputy Director of Fundraising and Communications at the Imperial Cancer Research Fund believes it's crucial: *'Building a brand that people want to support is one of our highest priorities'*, he says. *'If you're not the number one player in your subsector, you'll be punished by the charity that is.'*

But should charities spend money to raise money? *'In my experience'*, says Gardner *'healthy competition does raise larger pots of money.'* Last year, Imperial launched its first advertising campaign for many years. Its aims were to raise awareness of the charity and the high incidence of cancer in the UK – a sobering 'one in every three'. According to Gardner, it achieved both aims extremely well and is likely to be continued this year.

Julius Wolff-Ingham has a different approach: *'Our work covers areas such as homelessness, drugs, children and the elderly which are also served by several other large charities. It would be fruitless to try to achieve number one status in all those sub-sectors, so we do little pure brand advertising and concentrate on instilling our values and beliefs through strong, co-ordinated PR fundraising and, in particular, direct marketing.'*

He does not challenge the use of advertising by charities in particular circumstances, but does question its value in the public sector as a whole. *'The government spends tens of millions a year on advertising, but most people would be hard pushed to name any of it. Rather than spending millions competing with each other, I would like to see greater investment in better service provision first, even investigating mergers as a better way forward.'*

Perhaps this is the ultimate modernising view, fewer charities, but bigger ones. More efficient organisations, better managed and administered by the best people in the sector. There are several large charities considering this option, ironically the biggest being a possible merger between Imperial Cancer Research Fund and Cancer Research Campaign. If that happened it would create overnight the biggest non-profit in the country.

But whether you are a huge charity or a small one, the dilemma is often the same. How to get the best value for your brand buck when you have so little of it to spend. *'It's not necessarily about spending big but making sure you spend wisely,'* says Lynne Stockbridge, Head of Communications at RNIB. *'Even as the leading charity for people with sight problems in the UK, we have a relatively small budget. That means we have to concentrate our efforts in short bursts.'* To maximise the effectiveness of her budget, Stockbridge also invests heavily in research. *'Keeping in touch with your audience is essential in maintaining a relevant brand message.*

We conduct focus groups and opinion polls on a regular basis. We are also part of the Future Foundation's Charity Consortium which keeps us on top of what's happening out there.'

Despite her lack of funds, Stockbridge accepts that most charities do have an ace to play in the brand war: *'One major advantage we have over the commercial sector is that our brands are usually underpinned by very strong beliefs and values. Values that companies such as Tesco, Orange, and Nike have to spend millions to try to instil into their customers' own brands and products.'*

One of the best and long-standing exponents of 'concentrated' advertising and cost-effective fundraising is the Royal British Legion with its Poppy Appeal. The multimedia approach is cost-effective but also reaches vital new audiences. But the charity is acutely aware of the changing nature of its supporter base. *'Our image is naturally old, but those with direct experience of us, particularly from the World Wars, are passing away. We must look to a younger generation for support,'* explains Zöe Woods, the Legion's Senior Direct Marketing Manager.

'One of our challenges in the future is to stretch new boundaries while maintaining support from our core audience. The launch of poppy.org was an important step in taking our message to this new frontier.' The website was advertised on all poppy appeal promotional material and featured an interactive game and a poppy screen saver. It also achieved the dizzy heights

of being awarded BBC Radio 2's Steve Wright 'website of the day'. Last year's appeal was hard to miss, but just as it appeared, it was gone.

This year a post-poppy appeal is planned to extend the fundraising window and Woods is clear about the way forward. *'In modernising, we are going back to our roots. The Legion was set up by young people with a vision – to provide unconditional care for all those prepared to serve their country. Returning to those core beliefs will allow us to focus on providing new lifeblood for our brand in the future.'* Most successful organisations were formed on a big idea, and often the first step to new clarity for established charities is rediscovering or refreshing that original idea. Dusted off properly, it is probably just as valid and compelling as it was when it was first conceived.

Some of the stand-out successes in the charity sector in the last ten years – The Salvation Army, the British Heart Foundation, Oxfam, and the NSPCC – have all returned to their roots in some way. They have also been careful about not changing too fast.

'We could modernise quickly and alienate people,' says Woods, *'but we must do it with respect and understanding. There are probably more feelings associated with our brand than any other.'*

This view is shared by John Scourse, Fundraising Director at Guide Dogs: *'Our brand is a national icon and our greatest asset; we have to tread very carefully when marketing it. But if you adopt the discipline that your brand is fixed, you can still do plenty around*

it to make it more lively and modern.' However, Scourse points out that these are uncertain times for all charities, *'Most measures indicate that we are operating in a declining market and therefore have a greater responsibility to show we are spending money wisely.'*

Asked whether a competitive marketing environment for charities is sustainable, he responded with a view that should serve as a warning to the whole sector: *'You only have brand wars when people are essentially selling the same thing. The public will react with due cynicism when they see more and more money being spent on competitive marketing. I sit on research panels and witness the disillusionment first hand, it's a concern.'*

As for modernising your brand, do it, but do it with a purpose, such as to reach a new audience or even to be number one. But treat it with respect, be mindful not to throw away the inspirational idea your brand laid claim to in the first place. It is often said that gaining trust is the best way to somebody's heart and capturing the heart is the quickest way to your supporter's wallet. If this premise is undermined, then the charitable impulse could also be threatened.

'We should always be paranoid about protecting the trust our supporters rest in us,' says Chris Gardner. *'Our income*

base, as with the whole sector, is built on trust; if that gets dented we have serious problems.'

Matters aren't helped by the media's apparent growing interest in the way charities operate, and often it's a dirty area fought with few rules. A senior figure in a leading charity who did not want to be named is very concerned at this new development: *'Let's face it, there is little press control these days; it seems a journalist can print as many inaccuracies as they want as long as there's a juicy exposé to be had. Most charities aren't equipped for that type of assault.'*

Certainly the media seem more willing to adopt an 'expose-first, facts-later' approach and some reporting can, at the very least, seem less than balanced. Anyone who saw Watchdog's Ann Robinson 'interview' the Oxfam spokesman (I use the term loosely because she didn't allow the poor bloke more than five words of reply) on the topic of face-to-face marketing, will agree. *'No charity is safe from the mischievous journalist'*, says Julius Wolff-Ingham. *'All we can do is make sure we are whiter than white, properly audited and well managed.'*

The NSPCC, which has received more media attention than most over the last couple of years with its Full Stop campaign, also came under attack recently for its use of funds, particularly the amount spent on marketing. But in this case the issue was dealt with quickly, as Keith Bradbrook, Head of PR and Media at NSPCC explains:

'In that particular instance it was simply a case of bad journalism, but we still had to act fast. The story actually broke on the radio at 7.00am, but by 9.00am we were slamming the figures and putting our case across. As a result, most of the media had dropped it by early evening.'

NSPCC

Cruelty to children must stop. FULL STOP.

Alongside this willingness to 'have a pop' at charities, Bradbrook also senses a hardening of attitudes towards free editorial coverage. *'Charities have traditionally been big news generators, but now the media are more selective over what they will cover.'*

Whatever the current mood of the media, the message is clear. Run a tight ship and they'll probably leave you alone. But if they turn on you, act as decisively as Richard Branson.

Of course, sometimes mud sticks and it only takes a visit to McSpotlight.com to see how disgruntled customers, employees, and pressure groups, are hurting burger giant McDonalds to appreciate how important it is to ferociously guard the integrity of your brand and its reputation.

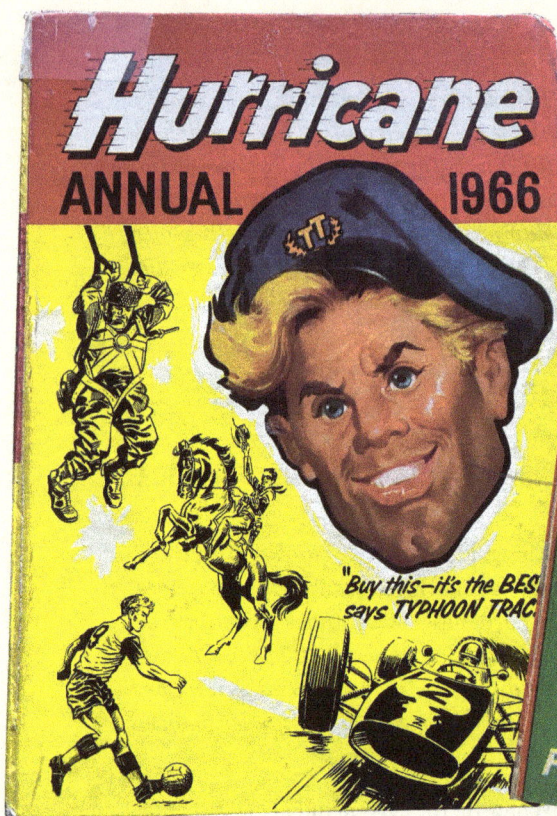

Hurricane ANNUAL 1966

"Buy this—it's the BES! says TYPHOON TRAC

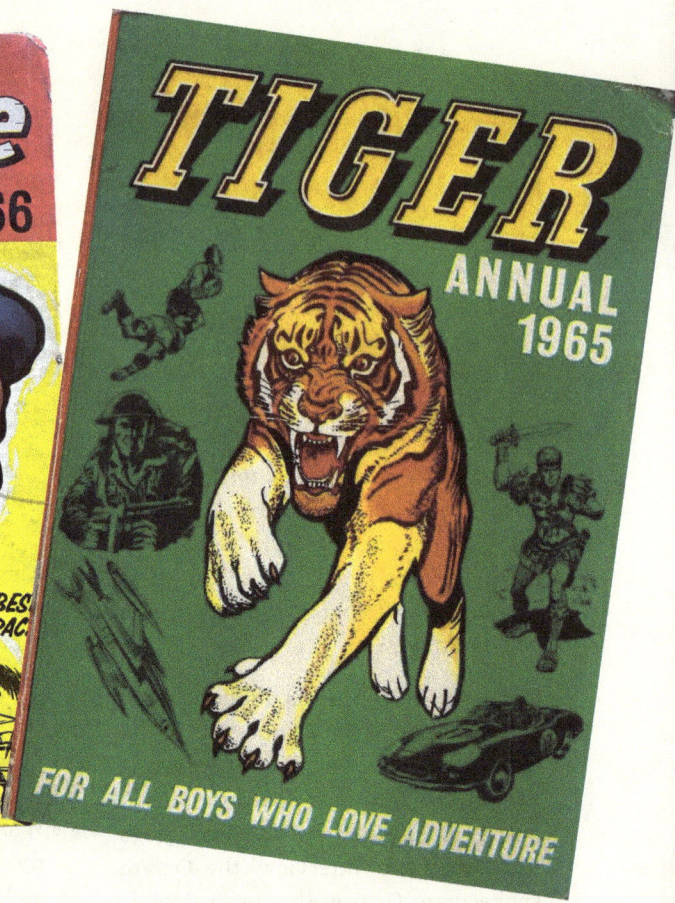

TIGER ANNUAL 1965

FOR ALL BOYS WHO LOVE ADVENTURE

COME TOGETHER, BUILD A STRONGER BRAND.

Life was very simple when I was a lad, it consisted of three things – school, sport, and comics.

My father ran a simple meritocracy too. Doing well at school meant he would drive me around Gloucestershire to play football and cricket. Doing well at those meant pocket money to buy comics. These were huge in the 60s (there was no DVD, satellite TV, or PlayStation back then) and my personal favourite was *Tiger* – the comic 'for all boys who love adventure'.

Tiger boasted a superstar line-up – the eternally young footballer, Roy of the Rovers, the hero of ancient Rome, Olac the Gladiator, and Johnny Cougar, the native American professional wrestler.

It was essential reading when Saturday came; I pored endlessly over every heroic word and incredible last minute escape. But the popularity of comics dwindled in the 70s and many comic titles disappeared or merged. *Tiger* merged with once arch-rival *Hurricane* to become a bigger, better comic. Roy Race and the gang now lined up alongside Typhoon Tracey, Skid Solo, and the Black Avenger. It was a dream team, the best of British comic heroes together and it revived the fortunes of both titles. It became the 'super brand' for all boys who love adventure!

So what lessons can we take from the marriage of two comic titles? Plenty. Much like comics 20 years ago, charities now operate in a similarly oversubscribed, cluttered marketplace and face tough decisions in order to survive. From a brand clarity point of view, the outlook is even worse. From the 185,000 registered charities in the UK today, barely two hundred can afford to engage in anything approaching strategic marketing or brand building. The result – an elite group of super brands and the rest nowhere.

So why not follow the *Tiger and Hurricane* lead and pool the best bits from other causes like yours? After all, it's not the only example of this consolidated-is-best approach. Look how successful the British Lions are in rugby, the European team can now truly compete in golf's Ryder Cup, and even the GB Olympic team is picking up some medals.

That's all very well, I hear you say, for comic titles and sports teams, but the logistics of merging charities is quite different and a potential nightmare. But for one fantasy moment, put aside such mundane considerations as pleasing trustees, moving staff, and protecting your job. Rather, put yourself in another place, the minds of those poor people we call supporters who have to decide to whom they wish to give their money. For the most part, they can't tell one charity from another, one appeal from the next. They simply can't recall who they last gave to or when. Worse still, even so-called 'best donors' can't remember what you do. As a marketeer I've sat through countless research groups and worryingly, the song remains the same.

But really, it's not that surprising. There's just too much information out there, even massive commercial brand spenders struggle to make their message stick. So what chance has an average non-profit got with a minuscule budget? However, let's keep the fantasy moment going. It's clear that these days you have to give it your best shot if you're going to get any quality mind-time with your audience. So our perfect charity would boast a combination of a strong brand offer, clear fundraising proposition, decent marketing budget, extensive regional coverage, and, ideally, no competition.

No competition? That's right, one of the clear advantages of a brand merger is that you join forces with your rivals and eliminate the confusion of choice and competitiveness for the donor.

Accept that first and foremost donors want to support a cause – (cancer research, saving animals, the environment) rather than the charity that happens to serve it. So there would only be one charity serving our cause. In fantasyland, our dream charity is also local and national, big and small. Sounds too much like fantasy?

For two organisations this future isn't make-believe but a clear aim. It is the guiding light of the proposed merger between the UK's leading cancer charities, Imperial Cancer Research Fund and the Cancer Research Campaign. If the proposal goes ahead, it will create the UK's biggest charity with a combined income of nearly £200 million.

But size isn't everything, as Helen Wright, Director of Direct Marketing at Cancer Research Campaign points out, *'One of the biggest challenges that could face us as the new and largest Cancer Research charity in the UK will be our ability not to appear solely as a huge and faceless corporation. We believe that to materially increase our fundraising income, we have to appeal to people at a regional and local level too.'*

If Helen and her team get it right, the creation of this new superpower would seem to possess all the qualities of the perfect charity brand – bigger, better, and near you. We may even see 'new and improved' on their literature. But essentially, all the two charities are doing is re-inventing themselves under a new name which is one of the oldest and easiest tricks in the marketing book and offers a chance to re-launch as something

new for very little investment. When *Tiger and Hurricane* joined together, it was big news for small boys, heralded by an advertising campaign and (joy!) a free gift.

So in fantasyland, who do you merge with? It sounds obvious, but with organisations that can add something to yours. Can your possible partners offer a better regional network, improved corporate links, or a bigger marketing spend?

To thrive, brands need regular exposure and that means lots of opportunities to see (OTS).

So which partners can add to your OTS count? Could it be a charity that enjoys better media relations or possesses a particularly good spokesperson that you'd like on your team.

Put all normal considerations like career and ego aside in choosing your partners; do what you ask donors to do and be truly altruistic and selfless in improving your cause.

There are examples of brand and cause mergers already working well, the best known being the well-established Disasters Emergency Committee, the DEC – a collective of overseas charities which includes the British Red Cross and Help the Aged, that come together in emergencies and fundraise together.

'The public want collective action in times of crisis and to see charities working together,' says Brendan Gormley, the DEC's Chief Executive. *'What you get with our model is strong brand unity*

without losing the power of the individual associate charities. It provides a cost-effective, overarching structure that's convenient and appealing to donors. It is quite literally the Best of British and because of that fact it is often possible to gain free prime time support from both the BBC and ITV.'

To cope with demand, staff from the participating charities are seconded to the fundraising effort during the appeal and Gormley indicates the approach is highly successful.

A fact that hasn't escaped the notice of others. *'A number of countries, including Korea and Canada, are very interested in setting up a similar structure,'* says Gormley. *'One person described it as like having your cake and eating it.'*

Another example of a successful merger involved several AIDS charities, including the Terrence Higgins Trust, a move initially born of necessity. A reduction in statutory funding for AIDS programmes had meant many smaller charities became financially unviable and resulted in Terrence Higgins merging with six regional organisations.

'The initial aim was to reduce overheads,' says Dominic Edwards at Terrence Higgins.

'It meant those charities giving up their names, but it did ensure their survival.' The second merger involved Terrence Higgins and Lighthouse, the second largest AIDS charity in Europe.

'The issue here wasn't so simple, our brands and service were very different,'

BE GOOD IN BED

The Terrence Higgins Trust

For more information about safer sex call our helpline on 071 242 1010.

The Terrence Higgins Trust, a successful merger.

says Edwards. *'We are known best for campaigning, short-term advice and our concentration on the gay epidemic. Lighthouse are better recognised for their Royal patronage and long-term respite care, which has also had the benefit of attracting many influential supporters.'*

In the final analysis, it was decided to reduce costs by streamlining both operations, whereas Cancer Research Campaign merged with Imperial Cancer Research Fund to retain the different strengths of each brand while they continue to fundraise separately.

'We now have a shared executive, fundraising, and marketing department,' says Edwards. *'It seems to be working well, with a collective unity which we believe serves the cause of stopping and preventing AIDS better than ever.'*

Looking down the very latest CAF top 500 fundraising charity listing (which incidentally is for 1998-99) it's easy to pick your own fantasy mergers. There may be 500 different charities but there are very few distinct and different causes.

As the leading cancer care specialists, Marie Curie and Macmillan seem a natural fit.

NSPCC, Barnardo's, and the Children's Society are all strong brands in their own right, but would they be stronger together? Would dogs, cats, horses and hamsters be better served if the RSPCA, Blue Cross, NCDL, and the PDSA joined forces as a fundraising unit?

And surely Greenpeace and Friends of the Earth complement each other perfectly?

Inevitably, most of these established organisations would state they are very successful as they are. Indeed, a multitude of charities serving the same cause often have deep philosophical differences between each other. For these organisations, merger would seem an impossible option.

But let us leave fantasyland for a moment and look at the real world.

There is little doubt that life will get harder for fundraisers over the next 10 years. The traditional charity donor who would willingly give to any cause without question is quite literally dying off. A new audience is emerging, wiser and more demanding. Pressure for change is mounting in the media too and with a new review of the role of the Charity Commission imminent, scrutiny of practice and costs will be tighter than ever.

Is merger the new innovation in the fundraising sector? If so, Imperial and CRC are ahead of the game. The concept of combining strengths and reducing costs seems compelling, and for some charities the issue may be forced on them simply in order to survive. Others can still take the opportunity now to consider the options and build their own dream team.

And others can simply choose to go it alone. Roy of the Rovers did and formed his own comic, even though this no longer exists.

HERO FROM ZERO.

Frustrated by the lack of a marketing budget? Worried sick about your brand clarity? Worry you not (or a little less anyway), in the next 2000 words or so, I'll demonstrate how a little planning and ingenuity can help build you a distinctive brand for next to nothing.

Ladies and gentlemen, I give you 'from a pauper to a millionaire brand in ten inexpensive steps...'

1. Adopt a zero budget mentality.

The first rule of shoestring branding, you will never have enough money to do all that you WANT, so only attempt what you NEED to do. The principle is easier to follow if you only allow yourself a fixed budget or, better still, no budget at all.

Believe me it's possible, the interactive museum @Bristol did just that when in the two years prior to its opening, it wooed and persuaded local business, media, and politicians to lend their support for free. As a result of this strategy, and without spending a penny on advertising, they achieved massive publicity for their launch. It was a great success and last year @Bristol was voted best UK attraction.

2. Look around you, it's free.

It always surprises me how little organisations do this, but observing what the competition is doing, and what opportunities exist, is crucial to developing a brand that stands out amongst the noise. So before you start playing with your brand, gather your competitors' materials together and assess their brand messages to ascertain where a gap might be.

3. What does your name and design say about you?

Borrowing from the famous Ronseal advertising slogan, does it say exactly what it does on the tin? In a cluttered marketing environment, clarity is the number one objective. The ability to communicate your offer quickly (better still, in a nano-second) is vital.

As a brand pauper, you don't enjoy OXFAM and Barnardo's sized budgets that allow them to pump beliefs and values into their brands on a regular basis through television and press advertising. For you, a clear name is worth its weight in gold. If your current name doesn't describe what you do, think of another one that does. In the mid-eighties, Feed the Children launched itself as a disaster relief agency. During the Bosnian and Romanian emergencies, its clear name and niche positioning struck a mighty chord with donors and enabled the organisation to quickly establish itself as a premier player.

Also look carefully at your logo, gather together all examples of it and put it on a big board, letterhead, invoices, business cards, compliment slips, every symbol of your 'business'.

What does your logo say about you? Art is a great shaper of thought and opinion. One way to stick in people's heads is to paint a picture that has clarity and appeal. Rather than employ an expensive designer straight away, there are some excellent and relatively inexpensive books on the power and importance of memorable logos that can help you. I especially recommend the excellent *Corporate Identity* by Wally Olins.

If you do decide to change or modernise your logo, I would still recommend you use a professional designer to create the artwork. Deciding up front what you want your design to convey, can save a great deal of expensive development time. Be persuasive, the designer won't necessarily like it, but you'll get the result you need.

4. Develop an innovative positioning.

Be unconventional. Easier said than done, but if you've followed steps 2 and 3, it may be more apparent where a vacant position might be. There's no point slugging it out with bigger players selling and saying the same thing. Instead, consider a new approach; it might be a completely fresh insight or idea, but a new spin on old issues is equally valid.

It could even mean adopting a brand new specialist position in an established market, such as Breakthrough (breast cancer) and Everyman (male cancers) have done.

Although a heritage is generally considered advantageous, in a fast evolving market new entrants can come without any back story, shaking up the sector with the shock of the new.

Alternatively, a merger with a competitor is another way of creating a new offer, an approach being considered by several large charities. A word of caution – whatever position you adopt, ensure you have the people and determination to deliver it.

There's no point in adopting a controversial or campaigning position if no one is prepared to stand up for it.

5. Be comfortable about who you are. Be consistent.

The key to long lived and loved brands is consistency. This means maintaining a discipline of coherence and delivery over many years, often when it's tempting not to.

A substantial number of long-lived brands have stuck to their original big idea, and mission statement. The great power of brands is to provide certainty – a consistent approach to all communications can provide this. Once you have decided your brand positioning, name, and design, issue a set of guidelines; more importantly, appoint yourself the brand guardian.

As its architect, no one will care as much as you do that these are adhered to.

6. Who are you trying to impress anyway?

Brands like Coca-Cola spend billions of marketing dollars to reach their customers, that's literally everyone on the planet over twelve months old! With your zero budget, you have to be rather more selective.

Decide who your three key audiences are – one will always be your own people, so bear them in mind when you address your brand message and design. Your audience can be as small as you like; some charities define their target audience to be no bigger than a hundred companies and 1,000 high-value donors. Remember, your objective is not to be the biggest brand in the world, but simply the biggest brand to your most important audience.

7. Make friends with the media.

Pound for pound, penny for penny, successful public and media relations are recognised as the most cost-effective marketing method. Therefore, when considering the best way to market your new brand, it's worth taking the time to make some useful contacts in the media business. Journalists and broadcasters need to fill acres of newsprint and hours of airtime with news; they need you. A sympathetic article on your organisation can be worth far more than paid-for advertising. Get in a journalist's phone book. Always make yourself available for comment when they are looking for quotes. Regard the media as a friend rather than an enemy, they can be a huge help in building your profile quickly. If necessary, spend some money (because it'll be well spent) getting media 'savvy'; for instance, the BBC in Bristol runs an excellent one-day media relations course.

8. The lost art of the publicity stunt.

Not everybody's cup of tea, but there is ample evidence that, done properly, they can make a massive impact and give you instant cool factor. Greenpeace has almost turned publicity stunting into an art form. It chooses its targets carefully and the media are invariably there to film it, or if not, Greenpeace supplies the footage itself.

However, effective stunts don't always need such professional PR backup. A brilliant example of how an individual can create a huge impression in the media came some years ago from Katherine Hamnett, the fashion designer and political activist. She was invited to a press reception at 10 Downing Street in honour of successful small businesses. In front of the cameras, she took off her coat to shake hands with the then Prime Minister, Margaret Thatcher, to reveal a T-shirt with the slogan 'Say no to Pershing.' This was a reference to the proposed deployment of US cruise missiles in Europe. The resulting photo became the most used in the world media that year. Of course, not everyone gets that kind of opportunity, but for the price of a T-shirt and some impeccable timing, she certainly made the most of it. A new stunt takes a great deal of creative thinking and planning. Brainstorm ideas with your own people and then show the results to one of the new media friends you've made, they'll soon tell you if it's any good.

9. Get a decent website.

This is an absolute must; the internet provides you with a living, breathing 24 hour interactive brand. This means all interested parties always have access to your organisation. Again, a visit to competitors' sites will help you decide what your site should contain; be sure to crib their best ideas too.

10. Service, service, service.

So you've now got a clear brand, distinctive logo, and a unique positioning; but it will all come to nothing if you fail in the area of supporter services. Big brands may have the marketing money but research shows they are often mistrusted for being faceless, impersonal, and cold. That is the opportunity for the smaller charity. Show complete commitment to your supporters, anticipate their needs, and exceed their expectations. Never forget that they make you what you are and their loyalty is equal to your success. Thank them, love them, need them. Target the people who are important to your organisation and make them feel wanted – always. It's the most important brand value of all and it needn't cost you a penny.

While the Government looks the other way, another 350,000 dogs look like this.

RSPCA

Registration, not extermination.

IT PAYS TO ADVERTISE.

The RSPCA's dog licence advertising campaign. I have never wanted to hate a series of ads more than those. It is April 1989, just a few weeks previously my agency had lost out in a pitch for the £100,000 campaign to highlight the folly of the government's plans to abolish the dog licence and risk more irresponsible ownership. We had been confident of winning. We had produced some great concepts and had run successful advertising the previous year on the same topic. But our client had seen something better from Abbott Mead Vickers and they were given the job. So even before seeing their execution, I was ready to bitch like hell and tear their pathetic and feeble efforts apart mercilessly.

But, of course, the work was brilliant, breathtaking in its visual power and intelligent argument. The client and agency were triumphant and I gladly ate humble pie. From that day to this, the country's leading animal charity and advertising agency have been inseparable. Together they have produced decades' worth of mostly memorable advertising. The agency's planners and creatives have ensured that the RSPCA has remained its sector's brand leader, and the charity seems to understand the ongoing role and importance of advertising in ensuring it remains there. As Nick Daniel, RSPCA's Personal Fundraising Manager explains: *'We use advertising in two ways, firstly to fundraise for our work but also to effect change. We have succeeded in altering the opinions of the general public and key decision-makers in government and industry on several important animal welfare issues.'* Despite the non-profit sector's long held reluctance to invest in advertising, there is growing evidence of a re-appraisal of its merits in brand building and raising profiles. Barnardo's, NSPCC, RNIB, Macmillan, and Christian Aid all believe in maintaining an above the line presence. More than ever, advertising is recognised by a growing band of non-profits as a key element in shaping popular culture and public opinion.

In the USA, the world's greatest marketing culture, public service advertising is huge – in 1990 alone, roughly $2 billion worth of advertising time was devoted to it. As a consequence, some of the most memorable non-profit advertising has been created there. One of my personal favourites in recent times is the campaign for PETA – People for the Ethical Treatment of Animals. The best advertising gets its hooks into you in a nano-second and demands your attention. PETA makes you interested in their cause by going into the laboratories of pain, and putting you in the wretched animals' place. Can an animal feel pain and terror? Of course it can. Just look at the picture; whoever risked their life taking it, their efforts were well worth it. Despite all the advances in electronic communication, the humble, paper-based poster or press advertisement remains the quickest way to tell a story and build a brand. Regular exposure is the lifeblood of all brands; without it, they become stale and eventually

forgotten. Good public relations can deliver spectacular results when the media choose to run your story, but only advertising can deliver to the agenda, timetable, and frequency you need.

Of course, and I've said it before throughout these articles, charities don't have the budgets to run large-scale advertising campaigns. But as we enter the new millennium can they afford not to? Individual charitable giving is in decline, the traditional charity donor is literally dying off. The days of the blind faith giver are drawing to a close. A new generation of the more discerning donor is upon us, a generation that needs convincing that actions like donating £15 and leaving a legacy is rewarding, effective, and even a pleasurable duty.

In short, they need persuading, something which, traditionally, advertising is rather effective at. Charities must recognise their need to educate this new audience to support good causes and acknowledge their future role as agents of social change. It's beginning to happen. A group of major charities have now formed a consortium to promote legacy giving. It is a fantastic idea and should serve the sector as a whole well. I have made my views clear on the dangers of flying solo in a cluttered marketplace. Without distinct brand separation, the smaller players risk getting ignored and eventually failing. Consortiums, partnerships, mergers (whichever is more palatable to the organisation), and with them the prospect of larger marketing budgets, are clearly a way forward for a large number of 'marginal' causes.

The new, media-savvy donor recognises the need for clearer messaging and advertising, even if some charities don't, and some are even prepared to help their favourite cause pay for it. When WDCS – Whale and Dolphin Conservation Society – wanted to shout about the disgraceful actions of some whaling nations at the annual International Whaling Convention, it asked its donors to help it advertise.

It wrote to its best supporters, showing them the actual advertisement it wanted to run and asked for the cash to support this. For a donation of £50, donors would, in return, have their names on the advertisement. The appeal was a big success and two full-page insertions were paid for which produced extra revenue for the campaign. In one advertisement, the charity had found its voice and a new role as a vigorous campaigning organisation. Even better, its donors felt part of the revolution too.

That's the great thing about advertising – a better brand is usually only one good poster or press ad away. If this is true for the individual charity, then the same could be said for the sector as a whole. Without a strong lobbying voice defending and upholding its values, the non-profit sector has failed to shake off its dusty and secretive image. It has a brand problem. 'Where does my money go and how much is spent on administration?' These were questions asked by donors 25 years ago, mostly in idle curiosity. But today's donors are serious about these issues, as are the media.

In the final analysis, there is a fundamental problem with the concept of a charity as a brand. They have few of the qualities of a strong brand. There is generally no 'brand experience' (save the thank-you letter/certificate/newsletter), no money back satisfaction guarantee, no high street presence (save the charity shop, many of which are in serious decline), no product sampling before you buy, and hell, no product either!

The industry of philanthropy needs a publicity makeover aimed at the new breed of donor before the decline in giving becomes really serious. And there's plenty to shout about and get excited over. Individual charities in this country are doing a fantastically effective job fighting child abuse, beating animal cruelty, and eradicating famine. Thousands of disabled people are helped every day. Every minute, hundreds of publicly funded scientists come closer to beating cancer. Our national treasures are safe for generations to come. The list is long and impressive.

Giving to good causes has always been part of the British way of life, but it needs new stimulation to sustain it. This can come from serious investment in 'shouting about it' through promotion and advertising. This will inevitably cost money which could come from two sources. The government is the obvious first source, more precisely the COI (Central Office of Information). As one of the biggest advertisers in the country, with an annual budget of around £70m, it produces campaigns on issues as diverse as drink driving, army recruitment, and teacher training. It is run by highly-skilled marketing professionals who employ the cream of the advertising industry to produce the ideas.

It should be given a serious budget to uplift giving, promoting a positive image of the sector's work.

Serious money means more than the token £1m allocated to the 'Giving Campaign', launched by the government in July to boost charitable donations by £500m through tax breaks introduced in the 2000 budget. The sector has rightly greeted the campaign with scepticism. *'I don't think it's enough to promote the long-term, cultural change that will be necessary to change attitudes towards giving,'* said Stephen Burgess, National Director at the Life Education Centre. That's putting it mildly, it's a daft target and a derisory budget. But it is a start, so let's allocate £5m next year!

The second source of investment comes from the charities themselves who could form a body equivalent to the Ad Council in the USA which coordinates the country's public service announcements. The body's main objective would be to work alongside the COI to promote the sector. Contributions would be received on a sliding scale from the top 500 charities. You think its pie-in-the-sky nonsense? According to Lord Joffe, Chairman of the Giving Campaign, there is huge scope for improving the nation's philanthropy: *'On average we give about half a per cent of our income to charity, while in the US people give 2%.'* Their corporate giving is far higher too, largely because of the more positive image and association the non-profit sector enjoys there. In the future, I believe individual charity brands will only flourish and their income materially grow if the sector itself has a good image; one of honest endeavour, clear accountability, and positive progress.

In fact, positivity is gradually becoming the new currency for fundraisers – donors want to feel good about helping. Tired of relentless, negative images of disasters, disease, and innumerable social horrors, donors are responding better to solutions, happy outcomes, and visions. Visions such as NSPCC's mission to eradicate child abuse in ten years, or Cancer Research Campaign's goal to increase child cancer survival rates.

One study by the Harvard University School found that melodramatic scenes in charity commercials did not have a lasting impact on young people who viewed them. The study suggested that in order to truly effect behavioural changes, ads need to abandon shock-and-scare tactics and begin to incorporate some of the more sophisticated, life-enhancing marketing approaches employed in consumer ads.

However, it is easier to influence buying decisions than to change ingrained behaviour and beliefs. The more realistic objective is that a new advertising campaign for the sector may become part of an open dialogue that gradually shifts public attitude towards a positive view of giving.

As the 21st century turns its back on Christianity and looks to new forms of spiritual fulfilment, helping good causes could even become a new religion. In fact, if I was writing the creative brief for the campaign today my proposition might read 'Happiness is being a charity donor!' (with grateful thanks to the Oregon Donor programme).

If anybody out there thinks this is a good idea, make sure I'm on the pitch list. I have a score to settle with a certain advertising agency on the Marylebone Road.

HOW MUCH WOULD YOU GIVE TO SAVE A BABY WHALE?

In a few days from now at the International Whaling Commission conference in Mexico, the very existence of whales on this planet will be put in jeopardy as the world's whalers, led by Norway and Japan, vote to end the international whaling ban currently in force. This may be the last chance we have to save the world's whales. Please help us stop the whale eaters by giving a donation today.

The harpoon hurtles into her, exploding on impact, flooding her body with pain. There's no escape. She's writhing in agony, but still they go on, cutting and tearing into her flesh, dragging the last breath of life from her.

But it's not over yet. She's still alive, so now they've started electrocuting her, throwing her body into a series of terrifying spasms. Then tiring, they lash her to the side of the boat and leave her hanging. She drowns, slowly, in agony.

They haul her bleeding, butchered body up onto the factory ship and get to work with the knives, hacking and slicing into her soft flesh. Soon they reach her womb. A pale fluid spills out onto the deck, mixing with her blood which lies in pools beneath their feet. But there's something else. They stoop to look. It's a baby, her unborn foetus. They pay it no more attention, tossing it aside and continuing their butchery of the mother she never lived to be.

NORWAY AND JAPAN ARE KILLING OUR WHALES

It's not pretty. It's not nice to talk about. But it's going on and about to get worse if they're not stopped.

Japan and Norway like to think they can do what they like to whales. They've conveniently taken ownership of them when in fact the whales belong to no-one and everyone.

They swim and live in our seas too, not just near Norway and Japan. They pass our shores on their annual migration. They feed and nurture their young within miles of our houses and towns. Some also spend several months in our waters. Minke whales, for example, are a common sight off the Island of Mull and in the Moray Firth in Scotland.

But now the whaling nations want to turn our seas red with their blood.

This coming week - the International Whaling Commission is meeting in Mexico and the two most powerful contenders, Norway and Japan are determined to throw out the current moratorium so they can start whaling again on a massive scale.

If they succeed there's no doubt at all that it will spell the beginning of a new and brutal chapter in the bloody history of whaling.

WE'VE ONLY GOT 5 DAYS TO STOP THEM.

DON'T LET THEM FOOL YOU!

The whalers have powerful arguments to support their bloody trade. They tell you that there are plenty of whales left to hunt.

Not true! Stocks of blue, sei, fin, humpback, sperm and right whales have been virtually wiped off the face of the earth by their relentless hunting. So much so that hunting them has no longer become commercially 'viable', so the whalers have turned their attention to the smaller minke whales, claiming they are in abundance when in fact, the opposite is true.

They don't mind killing pregnant whales either.

Yet another whale that will never grace our seas. Ripped from its mother's womb by the men who want to start the slaughter of whales again on a massive scale.

In fact, they make a point of singling them out for the kill because they are slower and bigger than the rest of the herd. On one Japanese killing trip 330 whales were killed. 163 were females and 124 were carrying young.

They also tell you that the whales don't suffer.

Not true! They do and terribly. They're highly intelligent mammals. They feel pain. They bleed like we do. They suffer stress like we do. They know fear like we do.

When the whalers' arguments fail - and they do on all counts - they tell you that whaling is part of their culture, something they've always done and cannot do without.

Again, blatantly untrue! Whaling is simply the icing on a very lucrative cake. They don't need to go whaling. They do so purely out of ruthless greed to line their own pockets.

SO WHAT CAN WE DO TO STOP THEM?

Don't have any illusions that this is a clean fight. It's not. Japan and Norway are up to every trick in the book. They've got money and power and they use it.

The Whale and Dolphin Conservation Society (WDCS) is determined to stop them - but we urgently need your help.

WHO ARE WDCS?

WDCS is the UK's biggest charity devoted solely to fighting for the protection of the world's whales and dolphins.

Set up in 1987, we expose and confront those responsible for the needless slaughter of whales and dolphins.

We have a proven track record of bringing pressure successfully to bear on Governments of pro-whaling nations to halt the barbaric practice of whaling.

We haven't got lots of money but we have got the force of public opinion behind us and that's a mighty powerful weapon.

You can help us use it to bring down the whalers by adding your voice to our campaign now.

SEND A DONATION TODAY so we can keep up the pressure on the whale killers until they stop their bloody trade.

We've already proved we've got the power to stop them.

In a recent campaign to halt the horrific slaughter of pilot whales for sport in the Faroe Islands, we led the campaign to introduce an international boycott on the sale of Faroese fish.

Now Asda, Safeway, Co-op, Marks and Spencer, Tesco and Sainsbury's have all either stopped stocking Faroese fish or have agreed to label their fish so people can make their own choices.

HIT THE WHALERS WHERE IT HURTS - IN THEIR POCKETS.

You can also help us by:

COMPLETING THE DONATION SLIP BELOW and returning it today. We'll use it to convince those who can't afford to ignore public opinion, to vote for the whales, not for those who want to put whale meat on the dining table.

PLEASE HELP US GET WHAT WE WANT:

An end to the slaughter. An end to the pain. Safer seas for all whales - and those yet to be born.

Once deemed too small to be of commercial interest, the gentle, graceful minke whale has become the target of the whalers' deadly harpoons.

We want a ban on all commercial and scientific whaling. WDCS believe that one whale killed is one too many.

If that's what you want - and you must if you live in this country and care about what happens to our marine heritage - then you must help us today.

ONLY 5 DAYS LEFT TO SAVE OUR WHALES

There's no time to lose! We've only got 5 days to get as many people as possible on our side. Don't let the whalers resume their brutal trade. Speak up for the whales.

Don't let the killers get away with it! Support WDCS today!

Please be as generous as you can and return the coupon below immediately to: WDCS, FREEPOST, (SN863), Bath, BA1 2XF.

Thank you.

Norway has a fleet of vessels ready and waiting to provide food for the world's whale eaters.

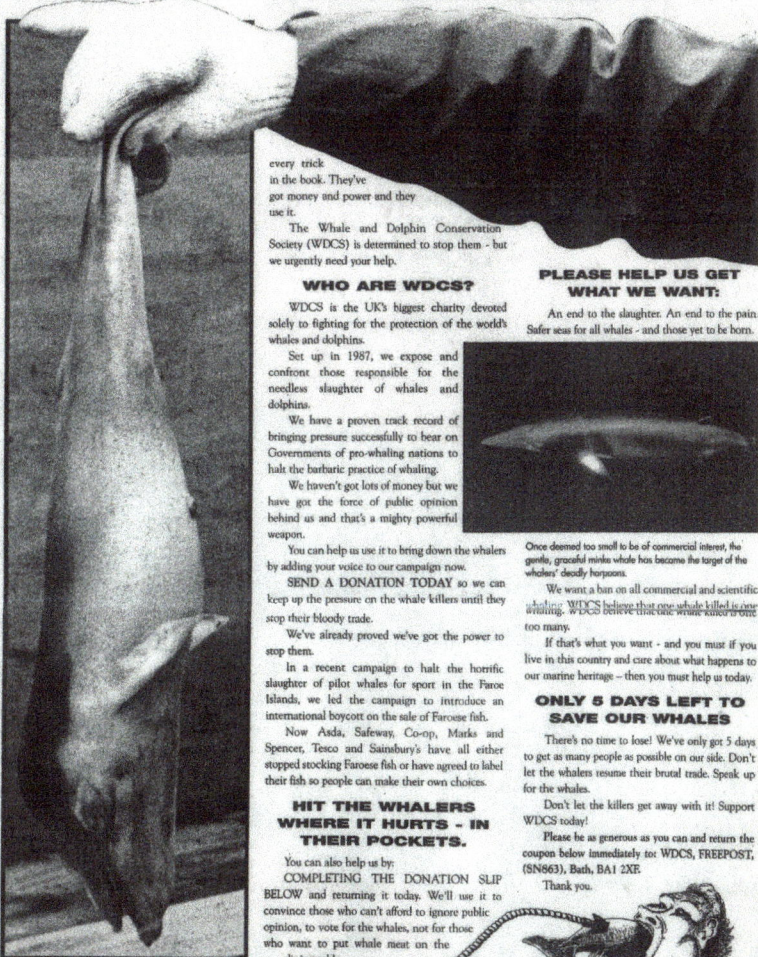

HELP US SAVE OUR WHALES FROM THE WHALE EATERS!

URGENT PLEASE REPLY WITHIN 5 DAYS

YES, I'll help you stop the whale eaters. Use my vote to convince the people with power to vote for the whales, not the whalers.

☐ I vote to keep the IWC moratorium in place.

Mr/Mrs/Ms/Miss (IN CAPITALS) _____

Address: _____

_____ Postcode _____

£250* ☐ £100 ☐ £50 ☐ £25 ☐ £15 ☐ I prefer £ ____ to give

*A gift of £250 is worth £333 through the Gift Aid Scheme

Here is my donation to help you keep the pressure on to make our seas safe for every whale. I enclose a cheque/postal order (payable to WDCS) for: £ ____

Or please debit my Access/Visa/Mastercard* (*delete as appropriate)

Card No: |__|__|__|__|__|__|__|__|__|__|__|__|__|__| Expiry Date: ____/____

Signature: _____

WHALE & DOLPHIN CONSERVATION SOCIETY

Registered Charity No. 1014705.
Company Registration No. 2137421

To make an instant donation phone our Hotline:
0225 334511/482548
Weekdays 8.30 - 5.30pm. Weekends 10.00 - 5.00pm

G1

A HAPPY ENDING?

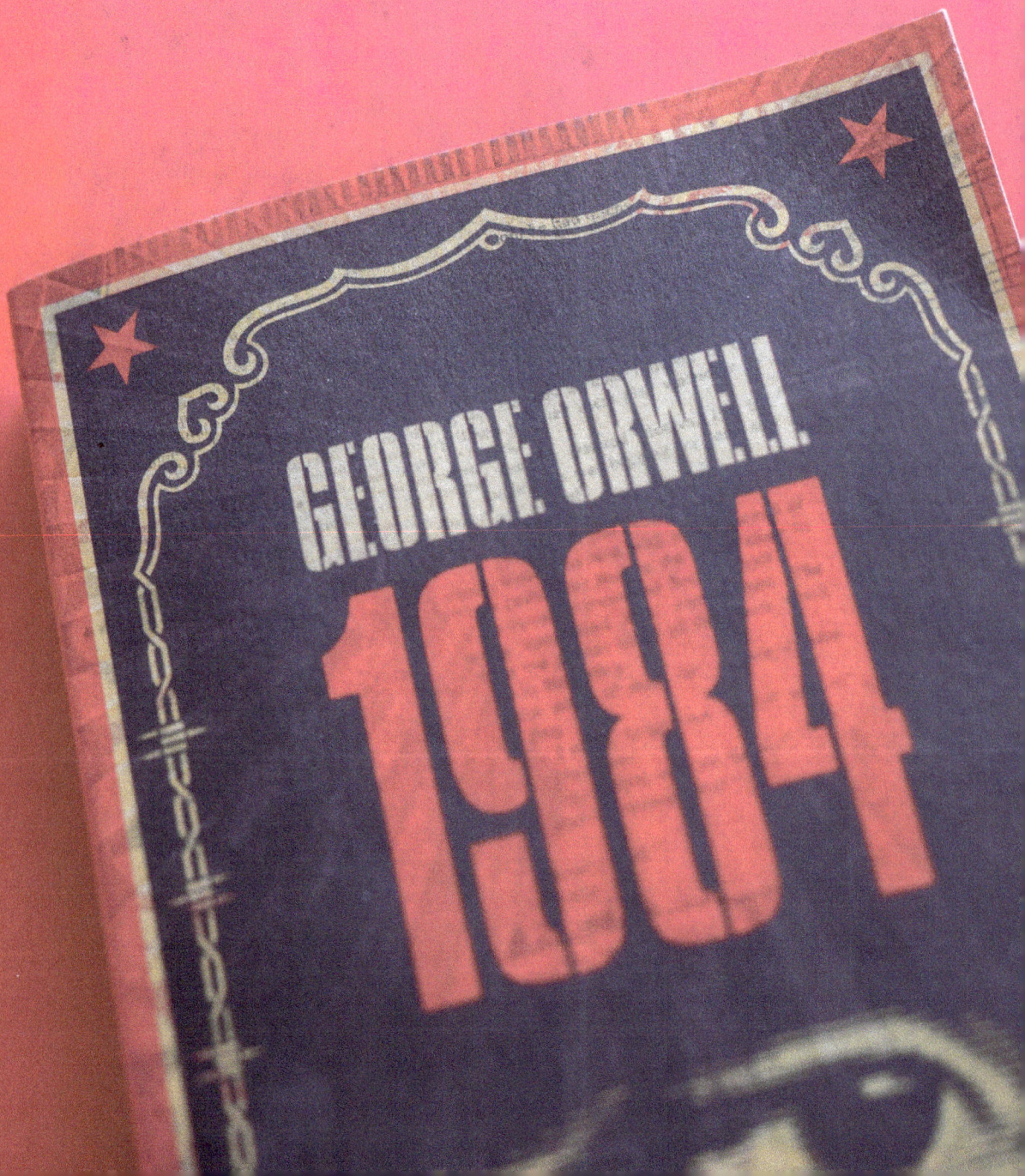

A recent survey to mark World Book Day revealed that we overwhelmingly prefer a novel with a happy ending.

Many who took part were so keen on them, they even suggested reversing stories that ended badly.

They wanted Cathy to marry Heathcliffe in *Wuthering Heights*. Wished Rhett Butler would have 'given a damn' in *Gone with the Wind* and returned to Scarlett O'Hara. Would have loved Winston Smith in *1984* to have overthrown Big Brother and settled down with Julia.

Of course, there is no real surprise behind why we crave a happy ending, they simply make us feel better. They inspire hope that obstacles can be overcome, love can last, and good can triumph over evil.

All fanciful nonsense? Many argue that most humans already live a fantasy life. The French philosopher Simone Weil famously said 'Imagination and fiction make up more than three quarters of our real life.'

Dozens of psychologists contend delusions, dreams and make believe are what make us human.

Clearly there is a rational explanation for this rampant escapism. It helps preserve our mental health. After all, if we thought too hard about the threat of climate change or nuclear annihilation, it would paralyse us.

In a world devoid of hope, what intelligent being would bother to tackle the seemingly insurmountable problems of our age? With no possibility of a happy outcome, what would be the point of striving for one?

And this is where good causes have an important place in the future.

More than ever we need to offer our audience optimism. It's the least our supporters deserve but also crucial if we are to mobilise the support necessary to improve our world.

We must make believers, because they are worth 100 times more than someone with just an interest. Believers uniting behind the vision that we really can beat cancer, can stop dementia, can achieve equality, can end child cruelty, can slow global warming.

Creating happy endings is a noble endeavour. If we can make giving to a good cause feel less about pragmatism and more about wish fulfilment and emotional satisfaction, we'll have a chance.

CREDITS

I have already acknowledged the role certain individuals have played in helping me to strive for better and stay clear of mediocrity. This book would not have been possible without them.

A special thank you to Rusty, Paul, Jules and Pidge. Your belief and friendship sustained me more than you'll know.

I would also like to thank the following superstars:

Jess, my brilliant eldest daughter, for designing this book. Endlessly patient and proactive, you have saved the day on numerous occasions.

Heather, my beautiful better half, for dealing with my mood swings as I grappled with the text.

Patrick, my son, who despite being an engineer with a brain the size of a planet, insists on preserving the child in his dad.

Evie, my youngest, who keeps me grounded and in my place.

Terry Keogh, for being an encouraging friend and for proofreading with such diligence (I hope!), and adding some brilliant design touches.

All those who have put up with me in the peculiarly precious and rarefied world of agency land. You kept me going through the lows and helped me appreciate the highs.

All those clients who took a punt on me and my colleagues.

To all of you I thank you and I love you. It's been a helluva ride.

I would also like to acknowledge the following:

Six Seconds. The emotional intelligence network.

BBC News, 'Got climate anxiety? Here's what scientists can teach us about coping with climate doom'. By Joe Whitwell.

www.ingramcontent.com/pod-product-compliance
Lightning Source LLC
Chambersburg PA
CBHW080527220326
41599CB00032B/6228